Formal Assessment

ELEMENTS OF
Literature
FIFTH COURSE

*Literature of the United States
with Literature of the Americas*

SELECTION TESTS
LITERARY ELEMENTS TESTS
LITERARY PERIOD INTRODUCTION TESTS
LITERARY PERIOD TESTS
THE AMERICAN LANGUAGE TESTS
ANSWER KEY

HOLT, RINEHART AND WINSTON
Harcourt Brace & Company

Austin • New York • Orlando • Atlanta • San Francisco • Boston • Dallas • Toronto • London

Staff Credits

Associate Director: Mescal Evler

Manager of Editorial Operations: Robert R. Hoyt

Managing Editor: Bill Wahlgren

Project Editor: Katie Vignery

Component Editors: Cheryl Christian, Darleen Ramos

Editorial Staff: *Associate Editors,* Kathryn Rogers, Jennifer Southall; *Assistant Managing Editor,* Amanda F. Beard; *Copyediting Manager,* Michael Neibergall; *Senior Copyeditor,* Mary Malone; *Copyeditors,* Joel Bourgeois, Jeffrey T. Holt, Suzi A. Hunn, Jane Kominek, Désirée Reid; *Editorial Coordinators,* Marie H. Price, Robert Littlefield, Mark Holland, Jill O'Neal, Marcus Johnson, Tracy DeMont; *Support Staff,* Pat Stover, Matthew Villalobos; *Word Processors,* Ruth Hooker, Margaret Sanchez, Kelly Keeley, Elizabeth Butler

Permissions: Tamara A. Blanken, Ann B. Farrar

Design: *Art Director, Book Design,* Richard Metzger; *Design Manager, Book & Media Design,* Joe Melomo

Prepress Production: Beth Prevelige, Simira Davis, Sergio Durante

Manufacturing Coordinator: Michael Roche

Printed in the United States of America

ISBN 0-03-052387-7

123456 022 03 02 01 00 99

TABLE OF CONTENTS

AMERICAN ROMANTICISM

COLLECTION 4:
THE TRANSFORMING IMAGINATION

THE AMERICAN RENAISSANCE

COLLECTION 5:
THE LIFE WORTH LIVING

COLLECTION 6:
THE REALMS OF DARKNESS

A NEW AMERICAN POETRY

COLLECTION 7:
THE LARGE HEARTS OF HEROES

COLLECTION 8:
TELL IT SLANT

THE RISE OF REALISM

COLLECTION 9:
SHACKLES

COLLECTION 10:
FROM INNOCENCE TO EXPERIENCE

THE MODERNS

COLLECTION 11:
LOSS AND REDEMPTION

COLLECTION 12:
THE DREAM AND THE REALITY

COLLECTION 13:
No Time for Heroes

Selection Tests

COLLECTION 14:
Shadows of the Past

Selection Tests

COLLECTION 15:
I, Too, Sing America

Selection Tests

COLLECTION 16:
MAKE IT NEW!

AMERICAN DRAMA

COLLECTION 17:
THE BREAKING OF CHARITY

CONTEMPORARY LITERATURE

COLLECTION 18:
THE WAGES OF WAR

COLLECTION 19:
DISCOVERIES AND AWAKENINGS

COLLECTION 20:
FROM GENERATION TO GENERATION

COLLECTION 21:
THE CREATED SELF

The copying masters in the *Formal Assessment* have been organized by literary period, corresponding to the eight literary periods covered in the Pupil's Edition. Within the literary period division, copying masters are organized by selection and other features within the collection. The Answer Key for all tests is located at the end of the booklet.

Literary Period Introduction Tests

An objective, multiple-choice test is provided for each literary period introduction in the Pupil's Edition. These tests cover the key events and concepts presented in each introduction and assess critical reading skills.

Selection Tests

Every major selection in *Elements of Literature, Fifth Course* has an accompanying Selection Test. In addition to an essay question, the Selection Tests include objective questions which assess the following areas:

- Comprehension: tests understanding of the selection

- Reading Skills and Strategies: tests comprehension of the specific reading strategy tied to the selection

- Literary Elements: tests mastery of the key literary elements explained and defined in the context of the selection

- Vocabulary: tests acquisition of vocabulary words for each selection

Based on state-of-the-art assessment practices, the Selection Tests provide you with an accurate tool for evaluating individual performance.

When administering Selection Tests that cover poetry, you may want to allow students to use the textbook since these tests often require students to respond to the precise wording, rhythm, or meter of a particular poem. These tests are marked with an "open book" icon:

The American Language

For each of The American Language features in the Pupil's Edition, a multiple-choice reading test is provided.

Literary Elements Tests

These objective, multiple-choice tests are provided to assess the Elements of Literature features that appear in the Literary Periods in the Pupil's Edition. The tests cover key concepts for each literary element and assess the student's ability to understand literary terms and devices.

Literary Period Tests

Each of these end-of-unit assessments allows students to apply their newly acquired skills to a literary selection not included in the Pupil's Edition. Students are asked to read a brief selection and respond to vocabulary questions, multiple-choice questions, open-ended questions, and an essay question. The literary selection is from the same literary period that students have just studied, and students are challenged to make connections between this selection and selections they have read.

Answer Key

The Answer Key provides answers to objective questions in the *Formal Assessment*. The Answer Key also provides model responses for open-ended items and criteria for evaluating all essay responses.

LITERARY PERIOD INTRODUCTION TEST

Beginnings

On the line provided, write the letter of the *best* answer to each of the following items.
(10 points each)

_____ 1. The first people to migrate to North America were
    a. explorers from Spain
    b. the Norse by way of Iceland and Greenland
    c. Ice Age hunters via the Bering land bridge
    d. English Puritans who traveled across the Atlantic Ocean

_____ 2. The greatest legacy of the French and Spanish explorers was
    a. long-lived political institutions that still exist today
    b. written accounts of the New World in the fifteenth and sixteenth centuries
    c. moral, ethical, and religious convictions that have shaped the American character
    d. inventions that made agriculture more productive

_____ 3. Which of the following statements about the English Puritans is **not** true?
    a. They were Protestants who sought to purify the Church of England and return to a simpler form of worship.
    b. They believed that the clergy and government should act as intermediaries between the individual and God.
    c. Some thought the Church of England was too corrupt to reform and called for complete separation from it.
    d. They wanted to establish a new society patterned after God's word and a self-sustaining, profitable colony.

_____ 4. Because Puritans believed that the arrival of God's grace was demonstrated by saintly behavior,
    a. they thought it was easy to differentiate between the saved and the damned
    b. they could try to earn salvation by giving money to the church
    c. they tried to behave in as exemplary a way as possible
    d. they thought there was no need for rigorous self-examination

_____ 5. The Mayflower Compact paved the way for
    a. a national church
    b. a constitutional democracy
    c. the Salem witch trials
    d. war against the American Indians

_____ 6. Harvard College was founded soon after the first Pilgrims landed
    a. so that scholars could work on a new translation of the Bible
    b. so the children of the "elect" could acquire the skills necessary to govern
    c. to organize and maintain the records of the church in America
    d. to train ministers for the rapidly expanding Colony

_____ 7. Rationalists believed that all people
    a. were sinners in the eyes of God with no hope of redemption
    b. were either saved or damned, according to God's will
    c. could change the course of human events through prayer
    d. could think in an ordered manner, thereby improving their lives

_____ **8.** Cotton Mather is best remembered in the annals of science as the
  a. experimenter who began a public campaign for inoculation against smallpox
  b. smallpox patient who believed himself to be one of the "elect" and refused treatment
  c. minister who said that inoculation against smallpox was unnecessary, since God's will would prevail
  d. devout Puritan who refused to support any smallpox treatment developed by Muslim doctors

_____ **9.** According to the deists, the best form of worship was
  a. deep introspection
  b. creating greater business profits
  c. regular prayer in church
  d. doing good for others

_____ **10.** Which of the following statements *best* describes Benjamin Franklin's *Autobiography*?
  a. It expounds the moral, ethical, and religious tenets of the Puritans.
  b. It describes Franklin's devout religious practices.
  c. It provides the model for the classic American rags-to-riches story.
  d. It shows that the notion of a self-made person is an unrealistic myth.

SELECTION TEST

from **Of Plymouth Plantation**
William Bradford   **Pupil's Edition page 27**

Comprehension *(35 points; 5 points each)*
On the line provided, write the letter of the *best* answer to each of the following items.

_____ **1.** The Pilgrims regard their voyage as
   a. only a spiritual journey
   b. only a physical journey
   c. both a physical and a spiritual journey
   d. neither a physical nor a spiritual journey

_____ **2.** The seamen are astonished by the death of the profane seaman and attribute his demise to
   a. the heavy storms   **c.** his fondness for rum
   b. the will of God   **d.** his carelessness

_____ **3.** The Pilgrims' ship first reaches land in America
   a. at Cape Cod
   b. near the Hudson River
   c. at Boston
   d. at Plymouth Rock

_____ **4.** Bradford describes the American Indians whom the Puritans encounter with
   a. admiration and praise
   b. indifference
   c. a sense of guilt for taking their land
   d. a mixture of disdain, fear, and respect

_____ **5.** At the first Thanksgiving, the Pilgrims are most thankful for
   a. the treaty they have made with the American Indians
   b. the departure of the loathsome sailors
   c. their store of game and corn
   d. the arrival of more people from England

_____ **6.** Which of the following sequences would be a correct chronological outline of the events in "The Starving Time" section?
   a. Half of the Pilgrims became ill and died, the healthy settlers built houses, the diseases spread to the nearby American Indians, the seamen refused to give them beer before the ship sailed away.
   b. The healthy Pilgrims cared for the ill settlers, the seamen took sick and died, the remaining seamen refused to give the Pilgrims beer, the American Indians raided the settlement.
   c. Half of the Pilgrims became ill and died, half of the seamen died, the healthy seamen refused to care for the sick, the healthy Pilgrims took pity on the ill seamen and cared for them.
   d. The seamen refused to give the Pilgrims beer, the illness spread among the seamen, the passengers on the ship refused to care for the ill boatswain, half of the Pilgrims died.

_____ 7. Which of the following is true about the organization of the selection?
    a. The selection is divided into clearly marked excerpts from different chapters of Bradford's original narrative.
    b. Each section consists of short paragraphs with topic sentences.
    c. Bradford uses brief, easy-to-understand sentences.
    d. The selection is not in chronological order.

Literary Element: The Plain Style (*20 points; 10 points each*)
On the line provided, write the letter of the *best* answer to each of the following items.

_____ 8. Why is Bradford's plain style difficult for modern readers to understand?
    a. His syntax and vocabulary have become outdated.
    b. He uses too many comparisons.
    c. He does not write about his own experience.
    d. His writing style is too informal.

_____ 9. Which of the following is typical of plain style?
    a. ornate language
    b. similes and metaphors
    c. straightforward, factual writing
    d. Latin quotations

Vocabulary (*20 points; 2 points each*)
Match the Word to Own on the right to the correct definition. Write the letter of the Word to Own on the line provided.

_____ 10. angry words; curses   **a.** profane
_____ 11. included   **b.** haughty
_____ 12. to soften   **c.** execrations
_____ 13. irreverent   **d.** reproved
_____ 14. some   **e.** consultation
_____ 15. proud; disdainful   **f.** sundry
_____ 16. allies; persons who share a common purpose   **g.** relent
_____ 17. reprimanded   **h.** discourse
_____ 18. meeting to discuss or plan   **i.** confederates
_____ 19. conversation   **j.** comprised

Written Response (*25 points*)

20. On a separate sheet of paper, write one paragraph that describes Bradford's account of the Pilgrims' relationship with the American Indians at Plymouth. Support your ideas with at least two examples from the selection.

SELECTION TEST

from A Narrative of the Captivity
Mary Rowlandson

Pupil's Edition page 39

Comprehension *(25 points; 5 points each)*
On the line provided, write the letter of the *best* answer to each of the following items.

_____ 1. In this selection, Mary Rowlandson's main intention is to
   a. write a bestseller
   b. analyze another culture
   c. arouse hatred toward the Wampanoag
   d. show how her experience revealed God's purpose

_____ 2. The group that captures Rowlandson is forced to keep moving because of its
   a. English pursuers
   b. need for food
   c. treaty with the colonists
   d. religious practices

_____ 3. Which of the following *best* describes Rowlandson's attitude toward her children?
   a. She misses them but believes that it builds character to live separately.
   b. She treats them as if they were adults capable of taking care of themselves.
   c. She cares passionately about them and grieves about being apart from them.
   d. She sternly disapproves of their weeping when she sees them.

_____ 4. Rowlandson primarily draws strength from
   a. her desire to return and tell her story to the Puritans
   b. her belief in God's ultimate purpose
   c. the medicine that a sympathetic woman gives her
   d. her desire to avenge the death of her child

_____ 5. Rowlandson receives food from several members of the tribe in exchange for
   a. cooking
   b. washing clothes
   c. sewing and knitting
   d. gathering firewood

Reading Skills and Strategies: Analyzing Text Structures—Chronological Order
(20 points; 10 points each)
On the line provided, write the letter of the *best* answer to each of the following items.

_____ 6. Which of the following events occurs last in the narrative?
   a. Mary Rowlandson's master leads her to her son.
   b. Mary Rowlandson's child dies.
   c. Mary Rowlandson enters a wigwam.
   d. Mary Rowlandson helps carry an American Indian on a bier.

_____ 7. Which of the following events occurs first?
   a. Mary Rowlandson is reunited with her daughter.
   b. Mary Rowlandson learns to eat bear meat.
   c. Mary Rowlandson cares for her sick baby.
   d. One of the American Indians gives Mary Rowlandson a Bible.

Literary Element: Allusions *(10 points; 5 points each)*
On the line provided, write the letter of the *best* answer to each of the following items.

_____ **8.** Which of the following is an allusion that Rowlandson uses in the narrative?
   a. "Whereupon I earnestly entreated the Lord [to] consider my low estate . . . ."
   b. "Being very faint I asked my mistress to give me one spoonful of the meal . . . ."
   c. "'When thou passeth through the waters I will be with thee . . . .'"
   d. " . . . . it was the night after the Sabbath before all the company was got over."

_____ **9.** Rowlandson uses an allusion to the Biblical story of Jacob to describe
   a. her disgust at cooking bear meat
   b. the trip along the river
   c. her captors' march from the English Army
   d. her grief after her child dies and her daughter Mary is not allowed to visit

Vocabulary *(20 points; 2 points each)*
On the line before each sentence, write the letter of the synonym for each of the italicized Words to Own.

_____ **10.** Mary Rowlandson endured much *affliction*.
   a. austerity   **b.** solitude   **c.** hardship   **d.** suspicion

_____ **11.** She withstood the lure of the *bewitching* pipe.
   a. enticing   **b.** ornate   **c.** compromising   **d.** fragrant

_____ **12.** Some of the horses became *decrepit* over the course of the journey.
   a. ornery   **b.** run-down   **c.** wayward   **d.** hungry

_____ **13.** Rowlandson *entreated* the Lord for relief from her predicament.
   a. asked   **b.** admonished   **c.** harangued   **d.** trusted

_____ **14.** The *melancholy* captive turned to the Bible for relief from her sorrow.
   a. confused   **b.** feverish   **c.** pensive   **d.** sad

_____ **15.** The *plunder* from the battlefield included a Bible.
   a. bound books **b.** ample provisions **c.** seized goods   **d.** retrieved items

_____ **16.** The hungry woman ate the *savory* food with gusto.
   a. edible   **b.** appetizing   **c.** tasteless   **d.** pungent

_____ **17.** The *tedious* journey took its toll on the wounded captors and captives.
   a. ill-advised   **b.** tiring   **c.** tumultuous   **d.** unpredictable

_____ **18.** The journey became even more *wearisome* when no food was available.
   a. fatiguing   **b.** unhealthy   **c.** disconcerting   **d.** treacherous

_____ **19.** The *lamentable* condition of her child filled Rowlandson with anguish.
   a. puzzling   **b.** unfathomable   **c.** ambivalent   **d.** distressing

Written Response *(25 points)*

20. On a separate sheet of paper, write one paragraph describing the link that Mary Rowlandson sees between events during her captivity and the suffering of people in the Bible. Support your ideas with at least two examples from the selection.

SELECTION TEST

from The History of the Dividing Line
William Byrd

Comprehension *(35 points; 7 points each)*
On the line provided, write the letter of the *best* answer to each of the following items.

_____ 1. According to Byrd, which of the following statements about the English settlers at Point Comfort is true?
   a. They frequently married American Indians of the region.
   b. They engaged in power struggles and arguments regarding leadership of the settlement.
   c. They consistently maintained peaceful relations with the local American Indians.
   d. They enjoyed hard work, especially planting and harvesting crops.

_____ 2. When discussing his religion, Bearskin says that he believes in
   a. no god but the spirits of men and women on Earth
   b. three gods of approximately equal rank
   c. two gods representing opposing forces in the universe
   d. one supreme god and several lesser deities

_____ 3. According to Byrd's account, what was the early settlers' main misconception about Virginia?
   a. They believed the natural surroundings would be unspoiled.
   b. They expected provisions to be sent there from England.
   c. They thought they would instantly find wealth there.
   d. They anticipated meeting people from other cultures.

_____ 4. Byrd believes that Bearskin's religion
   a. contributes to the tensions between the American Indians and the colonists
   b. revolves around sophisticated philosophical concepts and ideas
   c. fosters a sense of unity among different American Indian tribes
   d. embodies the positive characteristics of religions based on nature

_____ 5. Byrd argues that the settlers would benefit from marrying American Indians because
   a. the American Indians would be more likely to show the settlers where to find gold
   b. the settlers would no longer be lonely
   c. marriage would keep settlers from returning to England
   d. marriage would ensure the security of the colony and its settlers

Reading Skills and Strategies: Identifying Tone *(10 points)*
On the line provided, write the letter of the *best* answer to each of the following items.

_____ 6. Byrd's language and tone imply that he is
   a. interested in farming
   b. open-minded and realistic
   c. ready to return to England
   d. a biased man

Literary Element: Satire *(10 points; 5 points each)*
On the line provided, write the letter of the *best* answer to each of the following items.

_____ 7. An example of Byrd's use of satire is his description of
   a. Captain Smith frightening off the American Indians
   b. the amount of money the English spent to build their church and tavern
   c. the American Indians' physical appearance
   d. his realization that Bearskin differentiates between good and evil

_____ 8. In his description of the Company of 1606, Byrd ridicules
   a. aristocratic English youths
   b. the British monarchy
   c. the American Indians
   d. Captain John Smith

Vocabulary *(20 points; 2 points each)*
Match the Word to Own on the right to the correct definition. Write the letter of the Word to Own on the line provided.

_____ 9. refused	**a.** procure
_____ 10. outstanding	**b.** allay
_____ 11. respected	**c.** eminent
_____ 12. to obtain	**d.** reprobates
_____ 13. easily offended	**e.** disdained
_____ 14. to relieve	**f.** prudent
_____ 15. people with no sense of decency	**g.** populous
_____ 16. transmitted	**h.** squeamish
_____ 17. crowded	**i.** propagated
_____ 18. cautious	**j.** venerable

Written Response *(25 points)*

19. Which of the following statements do you think supports Byrd's assertion that the English colonists should marry American Indians? On a separate sheet of paper, write the letter of the answer you choose, then write one paragraph defending your choice. There is more than one possible choice. Support your ideas with at least one example from the selection.
   a. The colonists would be able to convert the American Indians to Christianity.
   b. Intermarriage would foster peaceful relations between the two groups.
   c. Intermarriage would put the colonial settlers on equal footing with the French in Canada.
   d. Other: _____
   _____

SELECTION TEST

from The Interesting Narrative of the Life of Olaudah Equiano
Olaudah Equiano   **Pupil's Edition page 57**

Comprehension *(35 points; 5 points each)*
On the line provided, write the letter of the *best* answer to each of the following items.

_____ 1. Equiano is permanently separated from his sister
    a. immediately after they are abducted from their home
    b. on the morning of their third day in captivity
    c. after a brief reunion at the seacoast
    d. moments before Equiano is taken aboard the ship

_____ 2. Which of the following statements about the selection is **not** true?
    a. Equiano's father had many slaves and a large family.
    b. Equiano is adopted into the family of a wealthy widow.
    c. A member of the ship's crew is flogged unmercifully and dies.
    d. Many captives on slave ships die during the voyage across the Atlantic Ocean.

_____ 3. The conditions of the enslaved people in the ship's hold are
    a. cramped but sanitary, with plenty of food
    b. dangerous, because of frequent storms
    c. suffocating and stinking, with minimal food
    d. deadly, because of a tuberculosis epidemic

_____ 4. The destination of the slave ship is
    a. Barbados
    b. Massachusetts
    c. Cuba
    d. Virginia

_____ 5. Which of the following actions by the crew members provides the *best* evidence that many of them are motivated by cruelty as well as profit?
    a. They refuse to let the captives eat fish, which the crew has in abundance.
    b. They refuse to let sick people come up onto the deck.
    c. They keep the enslaved people from knowing their destination.
    d. They force Equiano to look through a quadrant.

_____ 6. Upon arrival in Barbados, Equiano and his fellow passengers are
    a. herded up like cattle and sold at auction
    b. released from confinement and given small farms
    c. reunited with their family members
    d. given money and food and new clothes

_____ 7. While he is in the merchant's custody, Equiano is astonished to see
    a. people in fine uniforms
    b. men riding horses
    c. familiar landmarks from his homeland
    d. flying fishes

Literary Element: Autobiography *(10 points; 5 points each)*
On the line provided, write the letter of the *best* answer to each of the following items.

_____ **8.** In Equiano's account of his childhood before his capture, he writes that he
    a. was unbearably unhappy
    b. was training to become a warrior
    c. had no brothers or sisters
    d. spent little time with his mother

_____ **9.** Which of the following statements is **not** true of the selection from Equiano's autobiography?
    a. Equiano recalls his early years and family life.
    b. Equiano expresses his feelings concerning the immorality of slavery.
    c. Equiano writes vividly of his horrific trip on the slave ship.
    d. Equiano explains in detail his sister's experience as a slave.

Vocabulary *(20 points; 2 points each)*
Match the Word to Own on the right to the correct definition. Write the letter of the Word to Own on the line provided.

_____ **10.** spacious	**a.** assailant
_____ **11.** placed at intervals	**b.** distraction
_____ **12.** discouragement	**c.** alleviate
_____ **13.** gentle	**d.** interspersed
_____ **14.** great amounts of	**e.** commodious
_____ **15.** attacker	**f.** countenances
_____ **16.** mental disturbance or distress	**g.** dejection
_____ **17.** faces	**h.** copious
_____ **18.** careless	**i.** improvident
_____ **19.** to relieve	**j.** moderate

Written Response *(35 points)*

20. On a separate sheet of paper, write one paragraph that compares the treatment Equiano received during his enslavement in Africa with the treatment he received on the slave ship. Make at least two references to details in the selection to support your comparison.

SELECTION TEST

Here Follow Some Verses upon the Burning of Our House, July 10, 1666

Anne Bradstreet   Pupil's Edition page 69

Huswifery

Edward Taylor   Pupil's Edition page 73

Comprehension *(25 points; 5 points each)*
On the line provided, write the letter of the *best* answer to each of the following items.

_____ **1.** In her poem, Bradstreet mostly criticizes herself for
  a. losing her faith in God's goodness
  b. failing to react quickly in an emergency
  c. not taking proper precautions against fire hazards
  d. valuing material possessions too much

_____ **2.** Bradstreet emphasizes both the things she has lost and
  a. the people who escaped in the fire
  b. the new home that neighbors are building for her
  c. her memories of happy occasions in the house
  d. the items she has rescued from the flames

_____ **3.** When Bradstreet writes "I blest His name that gave and took . . . ," she implies that
  a. she is being punished for the sin of vanity
  b. material objects are ultimately God's and not hers
  c. she secretly wants all her possessions to vanish
  d. God will be appeased if she says a prayer to him

_____ **4.** The speaker in "Huswifery" seems to imagine himself or herself as
  a. an instrument that God can shape
  b. a person who has no goals or desires in life
  c. a wagon wheel endlessly turning in place
  d. a favorite child who deserves special treatment

_____ **5.** Which phrase *best* illustrates the speaker's wish in "Huswifery"?
  a. All the speaker's words and actions reflect God's purpose.
  b. God relieves the speaker of his or her boring, day-to-day tasks.
  c. The speaker learns how to prosper from making cloth.
  d. The speaker proves his or her faith by mastering a difficult craft.

Reading Skills and Strategies
On the line provided, write the letter of the *best* answer to each of the following items.

Analyzing Text Structures: Inversion *(20 points; 10 points each)*

_____ **6.** Which of the following quotations is the *best* example of inversion?
  a. "And make thy Holy Spirit, Lord, wind quills . . ."
  b. "Then mine apparel shall display before ye . . ."
  c. "My Conversation make to be thy Reel . . ."
  d. "Then weave the Web thyself. The yarn is fine."

____ 7. What is the most likely reason for Bradstreet's inversion of the lines "In silent night when rest I took / For sorrow near I did not look"?
   a. to establish the poem's structure
   b. to create an end rhyme
   c. to invent an extended metaphor
   d. to insert a simile

Analyzing Text Structures: Extended Metaphors (20 points; 10 points each)

____ 8. Which of the following *best* describes the progression of the extended metaphor in "Huswifery"?
   a. from spun wool to dyed yarn to a woven tapestry
   b. from a spool to a spinning wheel to a reel
   c. from unspun wool to thread to clothing
   d. from a soul to a body to a spirit

____ 9. In "Huswifery," the speaker compares God to a
   a. homemaker making skeins of yarn
   b. teacher instructing a weaver
   c. judge weighing evidence
   d. person building a spinning wheel

Literary Element: The Conceit (10 points; 5 points each)
On the line provided, write the letter of the *best* answer to each of the following items.

____ 10. Which of the following comparisons is an example of a conceit?
   a. The cat's eyes were like emeralds.
   b. The sun blazed like fire.
   c. His hair shone like gold.
   d. Time scurries like a rat.

____ 11. The conceit of Taylor's poem is his comparison of
   a. the speaker to a spinning wheel
   b. God to a spinning wheel
   c. the speaker to God
   d. the speaker to a weaver

Written Response (25 points)

12. Both Bradstreet and Taylor use extended metaphors to illustrate ideas about their Puritan faith. On a separate sheet of paper, describe one of these extended metaphors and explain what the metaphor suggests about the speaker's religious beliefs. Make at least two references to details in the poem to support your ideas.

SELECTION TEST

from Sinners in the Hands of an Angry God
Jonathan Edwards

Pupil's Edition page 78

Comprehension *(35 points; 5 points each)*
On the line provided, write the letter of the *best* answer to each of the following items.

_____ **1.** In his sermon, Edwards mainly taps into his audience's fear of
   a. their minister's wrath
   b. burning forever in a fiery pit
   c. associating with sinners
   d. floods and other natural disasters

_____ **2.** When Edwards refers to the "unconverted persons in this congregation," he chiefly addresses the
   a. men and women who do not believe in God
   b. church visitors who are followers of other religions
   c. parishioners who don't want Edwards as their leader
   d. members who do not accept Christ as their Savior

_____ **3.** Edwards presents God as a being who
   a. wants humans to suffer
   b. continually redefines the universe
   c. is often angry and vengeful
   d. easily forgives repentant sinners

_____ **4.** Edwards builds a sense of urgency and peril by suggesting that
   a. death and damnation may occur at any moment
   b. the church is being persecuted by unholy forces
   c. ministers alone can determine who is to be saved
   d. the end of the world is coming soon

_____ **5.** Edwards contends that the only way people can escape from God's anger is to
   a. obey the Ten Commandments
   b. attend church regularly
   c. experience a "change of heart" and accept God
   d. reform all aspects of their life

_____ **6.** Edwards's purpose in delivering this sermon is to
   a. frighten his listeners so much that they never return to church
   b. jolt his congregation into mending their ways and seeking salvation
   c. give such a memorable speech that his congregation will never forget him
   d. dominate his congregation and maintain his position in the church

_____ **7.** According to Edwards, the only thing that has saved his listeners from hell is God's
   a. hand   **c.** compassion
   b. wrath   **d.** love

Reading Skills and Strategies: Analyzing Literary Language *(10 points)*
On the line provided, write the letter of the *best* answer to each of the following items.

_____ **8.** What does Edwards mean when he says, "The bow of God's wrath is bent, and the arrow made ready on the string . . ."?
    a. God is violent.
    b. God's wrath is misdirected.
    c. God is prepared to demonstrate his anger.
    d. God's anger will cause much pain.

Literary Element: Figures of Speech *(20 points; 10 points each)*
On the line provided, write the letter of the *best* answer to each of the following items.

_____ **9.** Which of the following quotations is the *best* example of a figure of speech?
    a. "However you may have reformed your life"
    b. " . . . your guilt in the meantime is constantly increasing. . . ."
    c. " . . . the mere arbitrary will, and uncovenanted, unobliged forbearance of an incensed God."
    d. " . . . the floods of God's vengeance have been withheld. . . ."

_____ **10.** Edwards makes all of the following comparisons **except** that of
    a. wickedness to the weight of lead
    b. forgiveness to a lightened load
    c. the wrath of God to dammed waters
    d. unsaved people to spiders

Vocabulary *(10 points; 1 point each)*
Match the definition on the left with the Word to Own on the right. Write the letter of the Word to Own on the line provided.

_____ **11.** attributed to a certain cause   **a.** abhors
_____ **12.** all-powerful   **b.** abominable
_____ **13.** scheme; plan   **c.** ascribed
_____ **14.** scorns; hates   **d.** appease
_____ **15.** unimaginable   **e.** constitution
_____ **16.** enraged; angered   **f.** contrivance
_____ **17.** to persuade; force   **g.** inconceivable
_____ **18.** physical condition   **h.** induce
_____ **19.** disgusting; loathsome   **i.** omnipotent
_____ **20.** to calm; satisfy   **j.** provoked

Written Response *(25 points)*

21. On a separate sheet of paper, describe two major ideas Edwards expresses in his sermon. Support your ideas with at least two details from the selection.

SELECTION TEST

from The Autobiography
Benjamin Franklin   **Pupil's Edition page 85**

Comprehension *(45 points; 5 points each)*
On the line provided, write the letter of the *best* answer to each of the following items.

_____ 1. Franklin leaves Boston mainly because he
    a. wants to live a quiet life in the countryside
    b. yearns for the life of a sailor
    c. is engaged to marry Miss Read in Pennsylvania
    d. has left his apprenticeship and needs to find work as a printer

_____ 2. In this selection from his autobiography, Franklin seems most eager to portray his
    a. ability to work steadfastly toward his goals
    b. willingness to break away from convention
    c. deep resentment of people who have wronged him
    d. frugality in financial matters

_____ 3. Franklin considers moral perfection to be
    a. an illusion promoted by ministers and religion
    b. an annoying claim made by hypocrites
    c. a state attainable through study and practice
    d. a pathway to heaven and God's grace

_____ 4. In developing a method for examining virtues, Franklin reveals his
    a. doubt that real goodness can be attained
    b. logical and orderly mind
    c. scorn for traditional philosophy
    d. deeply emotional side

_____ 5. Franklin ranks the virtues according to
    a. how the clergymen of his day ranked them
    b. the popularity of individual virtues among his friends
    c. the idea that the mastery of one virtue facilitates the next
    d. the belief that the most difficult virtues must be developed first

_____ 6. During a squall off Long Island, Franklin saves
    a. a minister who slipped and cut his head
    b. a drunken Dutchman who fell overboard
    c. an innkeeper who had a beautiful daughter
    d. the author of *Pilgrim's Progress*

_____ 7. Franklin relies on which forms of transportation to reach Philadelphia?
    a. ship and horseback
    b. horseback and carriage
    c. coach and walking
    d. ship and walking

_____ 8. Franklin gives telling details about which of the following characters?
   a. his friend Collins, who arranged for his passage to New York
   b. his brother
   c. Dr. Brown, the innkeeper
   d. Mr. Read, his future father-in-law

_____ 9. Franklin's descriptions of himself as a young man
   a. reveal his sense of humor
   b. show that he has always taken himself much too seriously
   c. indicate his lack self-confidence
   d. suggest that he prefers to recall only the good times of his youth

Vocabulary (20 points; 2 points each)

Match the definition on the left with the Word to Own on the right. Write the letter of the Word to Own on the line provided.

_____ 10. correctness   a. abate
_____ 11. difficult   b. arbitrary
_____ 12. careless in speech or action   c. arduous
_____ 13. to declare; claim   d. assert
_____ 14. following   e. eradicate
_____ 15. to eliminate   f. facilitate
_____ 16. based on whim   g. indiscreet
_____ 17. traveling   h. itinerant
_____ 18. to simplify   i. rectitude
_____ 19. to lessen   j. subsequent

Written Response (35 points)

20. Based on what Franklin reveals about his habits and experiences, which of the thirteen virtues do you imagine would be the most difficult for him to master? On a separate sheet of paper, explain your opinion on this subject. Support your ideas with at least two details from the selection.

SELECTION TEST

Speech to the Virginia Convention
Patrick Henry   Pupil's Edition page 101

Comprehension *(20 points; 5 points each)*
On the line provided, write the letter of the *best* answer to each of the following items.

_____ 1. Henry points out a contradiction between British
     a. claims of peaceful intent and their growing military presence in America
     b. settlement of America and maintenance of their government in Britain
     c. interest in the Colonies and neglect of the colonists' needs
     d. democratic tradition and the institution of royalty

_____ 2. Henry recounts several instances in which the colonists sought agreement and acceptable terms with the British. He does this to persuade the delegates that
     a. it is treason to seek peace with the British
     b. the colonists have behaved in a cowardly way
     c. the British army is weak and can be easily defeated
     d. all peaceful options have been tried and have failed

_____ 3. Henry states that the colonists have the advantage over the British of
     a. a more rigorously trained army
     b. a greater number of people
     c. moral correctness and conviction
     d. knowledge of the terrain

_____ 4. Henry advocates immediate action by the colonists because
     a. the British army is preparing to march into Virginia
     b. the king is too far away to order a quick response
     c. the conflict has already begun and the colonists have no other choice but to fight
     d. the colonists will become apathetic with time

Reading Skills and Strategies: Recognizing Modes of Persuasion *(20 points; 10 points each)*
On the line provided, write the letter of the *best* answer to each of the following items.

_____ 5. One mode of persuasion that Henry uses early in his speech is
     a. fiction
     b. flattery
     c. oxymoron
     d. emotional appeal

_____ 6. When Henry declares, "I know of no way of judging of the future but by the past. And judging by the past, I wish to know what there has been in the conduct of the British ministry . . . to justify those hopes with which gentlemen have been pleased to solace themselves . . . " he is using:
     a. parallel structures to clarify his intentions
     b. images that his listeners may not understand
     c. deceptive language to confuse his listeners
     d. logic to engage his listeners' attention

Literary Element: Persuasion *(15 points; 5 points each)*

On the line provided, write the letter of the *best* answer to each of the following items.

____ 7. The main purpose of Patrick Henry's speech is to
    a. convince the delegates that he should be chosen to lead the revolution
    b. describe the history of British colonization in America
    c. seek revenge for personal injuries committed by the British king
    d. persuade his fellow delegates to fight against the British

____ 8. Which of the following is the *best* example of persuasion through an emotional appeal?
    a. "There is no retreat, but in submission and slavery! Our chains are forged!"
    b. "Sir, we have done everything that could be done."
    c. "I know of no way of judging of the future but by the past."
    d. "Mr. President, it is natural to man to indulge in the illusions of hope."

____ 9. Which of the following is the *best* example of persuasion through an appeal to reason?
    a. "Let us not deceive ourselves, sir. These are the implements of war and subjugation; the last arguments to which kings resort."
    b. "They are sent over to bind and rivet upon us those chains which the British ministry have been so long forging."
    c. "An appeal to arms and to the God of Hosts is all that is left us!"
    d. "The war is actually begun! The next gale that sweeps from the north will bring to our ears the clash of resounding arms!"

Vocabulary *(20 points; 2 points each)*

Match the definition on the left with the Word to Own on the right. Write the letter of the Word to Own on the line provided.

____ **10.** opponent		**a.** adversary
____ **11.** warlike		**b.** avert
____ **12.** watchful		**c.** inevitable
____ **13.** to prevent; turn away		**d.** insidious
____ **14.** to comfort		**e.** inviolate
____ **15.** earnest plea		**f.** martial
____ **16.** uncorrupted		**g.** solace
____ **17.** rejected		**h.** spurned
____ **18.** sly; sneaky		**i.** supplication
____ **19.** not avoidable		**j.** vigilant

Written Response *(25 points)*

20. Imagine that you are a newspaper reporter covering Patrick Henry's speech. On a separate sheet of paper, write a lead paragraph for a news story about the speech. Describe the main point Henry makes, two ideas he uses to support it, and the delegates' different reactions to the speech.

SELECTION TEST

from The Crisis, No. 1
Thomas Paine

Pupil's Edition page 107

Comprehension *(25 points; 5 points each)*
On the line provided, write the letter of the *best* answer to each of the following items.

_____ 1. Paine argues that the best way to defeat the British is for
    a. each state to fight independently as the British approach
    b. the states to train their militias in guerrilla tactics
    c. the troops of all the states to join together in the fight
    d. the states to persuade the American Indians to join the revolution

_____ 2. Paine suggests that a state that surrenders its arms to the British would have to
    a. face destruction by the British troops
    b. send its own ambassadors to Britain
    c. suffer the hostility of the other states
    d. create its own government

_____ 3. Paine contends that the Tories are
    a. preparing to leave America to return to Britain
    b. committing treason by spying on their neighbors
    c. enjoying greater wealth than the average American
    d. possibly aiding and encouraging the British army

_____ 4. By comparing the British king to a thief and a housebreaker, Paine suggests that
    a. British soldiers are launching sneak attacks against the colonists
    b. the king is in dire need of money for his treasury
    c. the British are trying to take what is not theirs
    d. Britain has robbed America of its natural resources

_____ 5. In his conclusion, Paine intends to inspire readers by
    a. explaining why General Howe will succeed
    b. describing in detail the battle of Princeton
    c. recounting all of the wrongs the colonists have suffered
    d. pointing out the strengths of the colonial army

Reading Skills and Strategies: Recognizing Modes of Persuasion
(20 points; 10 points each)
On the line provided, write the letter of the *best* answer to each of the following items.

_____ 6. Which of the following anecdotes does Paine use in the selection?
    a. General Gage's attack on Quebec
    b. the innkeeper who reads *Pilgrim's Progress*
    c. the Tory tavern keeper who makes a thoughtless statement before a child
    d. Washington's crossing of the Delaware River

_____ 7. Which mode of persuasion is used in Paine's line, "Tyranny, like hell, is not easily conquered"?
    a. logic   **c.** anecdote
    b. personification   **d.** analogy

Literary Element: Style *(10 points; 5 points each)*
On the line provided, write the letter of the *best* answer to each of the following items.

_____ 8. When Paine writes, "The heart that feels not now, is dead: The blood of his children will curse his cowardice, who shrinks back at a time when a little might have saved the whole," he is using
   a. dramatic imagery
   b. a family-based theme
   c. allusions to emphasize his points
   d. plain, ordinary language to present his thoughts

_____ 9. Which of the following is **not** an example of Paine's use of plain language?
   a. "I thank God that I fear not. I see no real cause for fear."
   b. "My own line of reasoning is to myself as straight and clear as a ray of light."
   c. " . . . I turn with the warm ardor of a friend to those who have nobly stood, and are yet determined to stand the matter out . . . "
   d. "A single successful battle next year will settle the whole."

Vocabulary *(20 points; 2 points each)*
Match the vocabulary word on the left with the Word to Own on the right. Write the letter of the Word to Own on the line provided.

_____ 10. well-articulated, persuasive speech
_____ 11. given up
_____ 12. persistence
_____ 13. comfort
_____ 14. oppression
_____ 15. false claim
_____ 16. divine; perfect
_____ 17. act of violent destruction
_____ 18. irreverent
_____ 19. rule

   a. celestial
   b. consolation
   c. dominion
   d. eloquence
   e. impious
   f. perseverance
   g. pretense
   h. ravage
   i. relinquished
   j. tyranny

Written Response *(25 points)*

20. Read the following lines from Paine's essay.
   " . . . I call not upon a few, but upon all; not on *this* state or *that* state, but on *every* state; up and help us; lay your shoulders to the wheel; better have too much force than too little, when so great an object is at stake."

   On a separate sheet of paper, describe how the quotation reflects one of Paine's themes. Explain what he means by "lay your shoulders to the wheel" and what the "object" is.

SELECTION TEST

from The Autobiography:
The Declaration of Independence

Thomas Jefferson   Pupil's Edition page 115

Comprehension *(25 points; 5 points each)*
On the line provided, write the letter of the *best* answer to each of the following items.

_____ 1. Jefferson states that the king has established tyranny over the colonies. To back up this statement, Jefferson
    a. cites lies that are self-evident
    b. portrays the king as a pawn of greedy British nobles
    c. describes Britain's colonization of other nations
    d. lists several specific actions of the king

_____ 2. Jefferson emphasizes that the colonists
    a. desire a form of self-government
    b. expect guidance from the British Parliament
    c. want to rebel against all formal rules and regulations
    d. need an army to restore law and order

_____ 3. The passage condemning Britain's involvement in the African slave trade was struck out of the original Declaration of Independence because
    a. Jefferson disliked the way the passage was worded
    b. not all the states were involved in the slave trade
    c. two states wanted to continue importing slaves
    d. the passage would have been especially offensive to the British

_____ 4. Jefferson seems especially angered by
    a. the outcome of the French and Indian War
    b. the presence and actions of the British military in the colonies
    c. the king's ambassadors to the colonies
    d. the way in which the British handled the Boston Tea Party

_____ 5. Jefferson believes that the final version of the Declaration of Independence is
    a. perfect because it resolves all existing tensions
    b. worthless because all factions remain at odds
    c. incomplete because of its many omissions
    d. good publicity for his presidential campaign

Reading Skills and Strategies: Identifying the Main Idea *(20 points; 10 points each)*
On the line provided, write the letter of the *best* answer to each of the following items.

_____ 6. Which of the following statements *best* summarizes Jefferson's main idea?
    a. Responsibility should be avoided.
    b. Freedom is a right.
    c. Chaos is always caused by liberty.
    d. Everyone deserves a free press and freedom of religion.

_____ **7.** Jefferson supports one of his main themes by
    a. urging the colonists to take up arms against the British army
    b. making a case against slavery
    c. explaining the reasons for taking action
    d. listing everything that the colonies have done to provoke the British

Literary Element: Parallelism *(10 points; 5 points each)*
On the line provided, write the letter of the *best* answer to each of the following items.

_____ **8.** Which of the following is the *best* example of parallelism?
    a. "A prince whose character is thus marked by every act which may define a tyrant is unfit to be the ruler of a free people."
    b. " . . . we mutually pledge to each other our lives, our fortunes, and our sacred honor."
    c. "Prudence, indeed, will dictate that governments long established should not be changed for light and transient causes. . . ."
    d. "We hold these truths to be self-evident: that all men are created equal. . . ."

_____ **9.** Which of the following statements is **not** true of the parallel structures used by Jefferson?
    a. Similar grammatical structures are used to introduce clauses.
    b. Identical words or phrases are repeated at the beginning of several paragraphs.
    c. The clauses, phrases, or sentences often have similar rhythms.
    d. Clauses and phrases are always linked by conjunctions.

Vocabulary *(20 points; 2 points each)*
Match the vocabulary word on the left with the Word to Own on the right. Write the letter of the Word to Own on the line provided.

_____ **10.** given up responsibility for
_____ **11.** seizure of property by authority
_____ **12.** temporary; passing
_____ **13.** forces
_____ **14.** nobility of spirit
_____ **15.** unbiased; fair
_____ **16.** strong, disapproving criticisms
_____ **17.** to give up
_____ **18.** to agree or accept quietly
_____ **19.** to erase; remove

a. abdicated
b. acquiesce
c. candid
d. censures
e. confiscation
f. constrains
g. expunge
h. magnanimity
i. renounce
j. transient

Written Response *(25 points)*

20. The Continental Congress first approached John Adams to write the Declaration of Independence. Adams declined and recommended Thomas Jefferson because Jefferson was the best writer among all the delegates. On a separate sheet of paper, explain what you think Adams admired in Jefferson's style. Describe at least two ways in which the Declaration displays the hallmarks of good writing.

NAME _____ CLASS _____ DATE _____ SCORE _____

THE AMERICAN LANGUAGE

"Revolutionary" English **Pupil's Edition page 127**

On the line provided, write the letter of the *best* answer to each of the following items.
(10 points each)

_____ 1. Some of the differences that developed between the British and American languages
were caused by
  a. the addition of new words to British English
  b. the increasingly nasal pronunciation of British English
  c. the strong influence of American Indian languages on American English
  d. the physical separation of Britain and America

_____ 2. Changes in language usage occurred
  a. only in America
  b. only in Britain
  c. in both America and Britain
  d. in neither America nor Britain

_____ 3. The word *Americanism* identifies a word or expression that
  a. was adapted from an American Indian language
  b. describes the American lifestyle
  c. is used by the British to describe American attitudes
  d. originated in, or is peculiar to, the United States

_____ 4. Their dislike of Americanisms showed that some British purists
  a. believed the English language had reached perfection in the eighteenth century and
     should not be changed
  b. believed a new American literature could supplant British literature as the authority
     for usage
  c. were concerned that these phrases would contribute to political unrest
  d. were intimidated by the improvements made to British English

_____ 5. Many Americans and Britons feared that
  a. their languages eventually would change so much that the two peoples would be
     unable to understand each other
  b. language differences would cause economic problems in America
  c. language differences would undermine the political power of both nations
  d. American English would corrupt British English

_____ 6. In eighteenth- and nineteenth-century America, the conflict between language purists
and advocates of linguistic change
  a. was strictly a linguistic matter
  b. became embroiled with politics
  c. led to the founding of an academy to regulate usage
  d. became an issue in international trade

_____ 7. Advocates of Federal English were convinced that
  a. Americans should imitate British English
  b. Americans should establish Latin as their official written language
  c. American English could become a pure and independent language
  d. American and British English should be united

Elements of Literature *Formal Assessment* **23**

____ **8.** The greatest virtue of American English, according to its advocates, was its
  a. precise usage
  b. natural pronunciation
  c. logical spelling
  d. democratic character

____ **9.** The most radical proposal regarding the language to be spoken in America suggested the
  a. creation of an American dialect
  b. adoption of Federal English
  c. establishment of a completely new language
  d. rejection of British authority in language

____ **10.** An American who spoke in favor of the natural evolution of American English was
  a. Thomas Jefferson
  b. John Adams
  c. John Witherspoon
  d. Basil Hall

LITERARY ELEMENTS TEST

The Plain Style
The Conceit

Pupil's Edition page 35

Pupil's Edition page 74

The Plain Style
On the line provided, write the letter of the *best* answer to each of the following items.
(80 points; 16 points each)

_____ 1. The Puritans favored the plain style because
    a. it mirrored their style of worship
    b. they did not know any Latin
    c. it allowed them to use figurative language
    d. they had little formal training

_____ 2. The writing of the Puritans was greatly influenced by
    a. John Donne's prose
    b. the Geneva Bible
    c. the *Odyssey*
    d. *Pilgrim's Progress*

_____ 3. The plain style includes all of the following **except**
    a. simple sentences
    b. everyday language
    c. classical allusions
    d. direct statements

_____ 4. The plain style reflected the split between the Puritans and the
    a. Irish
    b. American Indians
    c. Whigs
    d. Anglicans

_____ 5. Bradford's writing is an example of the plain style because it is
    a. laden with figurative language
    b. ornate and fashionable
    c. direct and simple
    d. filled with comic relief

The Conceit
On the line provided, write the letter of the *best* answer to each of the following items
(20 points; 10 points each)

_____ 6. A conceit is
    a. a metrical unit of poetry
    b. a startling figure of speech
    c. a conventional, stock phrase
    d. the use of language to evoke forced rhyme

_____ **7.** Conceits are used to
   a. stretch the reader's imagination, creating a surprising connection
   b. make ordinary comparisons
   c. show clever connections between humans and nature
   d. record important memories so that they will not be forgotten

LITERARY PERIOD TEST

Beginnings

Applying Skills

This test asks you to use the language skills and strategies you have learned. Before you begin reading, take a minute to remember what you know about identifying tone and main idea and about the plain style. Read the essay carefully. It is a famous tribute to America by a widely traveled French writer named Michel-Guillaume Jean de Crèvecoeur. He confirms the hopes of people disillusioned and burdened by history. After you read the passage, answer the questions that follow.

from "What Is an American?"
Letters from an American Farmer
by Michel-Guillaume Jean de Crèvecoeur

I wish I could be acquainted with the feelings and thoughts which must agitate the heart and present themselves to the mind of an enlightened Englishman when he first lands on this continent. He must greatly rejoice that he lived at a time to see this fair country discovered and settled; he must necessarily feel a share of national pride when he views the chain of settlements which embellishes these extended shores. When he says to himself, this is the work of my countrymen, who, when convulsed by factions, afflicted by a variety of miseries and wants, restless and impatient, took refuge here. They brought along with them their national genius, to which they principally owe what liberty they enjoy and what substance they possess. Here he sees the industry of his native country displayed in a new manner, and traces in their works the embryos of all the arts, sciences, and ingenuity which flourish in Europe. Here he beholds fair cities, substantial villages, extensive fields, an immense country filled with decent houses, good roads, orchards, meadows, and bridges, where a hundred years ago all was wild, woody, and uncultivated!

What a train of pleasing ideas this fair spectacle must suggest! It is a prospect which must inspire a good citizen with the most heartfelt pleasure. The difficulty consists in the manner of viewing so extensive a scene. He is arrived on a new continent; a modern society offers itself to his contemplation, different from what he had hitherto seen. It is not composed, as in Europe, of great lords who possess everything, and of a herd of people who have nothing. Here are no aristocratical families, no courts, no kings, no bishops, no ecclesiastical dominion, no invisible power giving to a few a very visible one, no great manufacturers employing thousands, no great refinements of luxury. The rich and the poor are not so far removed from each other as they are in Europe.

Some few towns excepted, we are all tillers of the earth, from Nova Scotia to West Florida. We are a people of cultivators, scattered over an immense territory, communicating with each other by means of good roads and navigable rivers, united by the silken bands of mild government, all respecting the laws without dreading their power, because they are underlined equitable. We are all animated with the spirit of industry, which is underlined unfettered and unrestrained, because each person works for himself. If he travels through our rural districts, he views not the hostile castle and the haughty mansion, contrasted with the clay-built hut and miserable cabin, where cattle and men help to keep each other warm, and dwell in meanness, smoke, and indigence. A pleasing uniformity of decent competence appears throughout our habitations. The meanest of our log houses is a dry and comfortable habitation.

Lawyer or merchant are the fairest titles our towns afford; that of a farmer is the only underlined appellation of the rural inhabitants of our country. It must take some time before he can reconcile himself to our dictionary, which is but short in words of dignity and names of honor. There, on a Sunday, he sees a congregation of respectable farmers and their wives, all clad in neat homespun, well mounted, or riding their own humble wagons. There is not among them an esquire, saving the unlettered magistrate. There he sees a parson as simple as his flock, a farmer who does not riot on the labor of others. We have no princes for whom we toil, starve, and bleed; we are the most perfect society now existing in the world. Here man is free as he ought to be; nor is this pleasing equality so transitory as many others are. Many ages will not see the shores of our great lakes replenished with inland nations, nor the unknown bounds of North America entirely peopled. Who can tell how far it extends? Who can tell the millions of men whom it will feed and contain? For no European foot has as yet traveled half the extent of this mighty continent!

Vocabulary Skills: New Words in Context (20 points; 5 points each)
Each of the following underlined words has also been underlined in the selection. Re-read those passages and use context clues to help you select an answer. On the line provided, write the letter of the word or phrase that *best* completes each sentence.

_____ 1. People who are "convulsed by factions" are
  a. violently agitated
  b. denied upward mobility
  c. given extra responsibility
  d. ignored as troublemakers

_____ 2. Equitable laws may be considered
  a. misleading
  b. heartfelt
  c. just and impartial
  d. cruel

_____ 3. An unfettered spirit of industry is
  a. devious
  b. not restricted
  c. imaginary
  d. unworthy of serious attention

_____ 4. A person's appellation is his or her
  a. reputation
  b. political organization
  c. name or title
  d. equipment or gear

Vocabulary

When a Dictionary Can Help (20 points; 5 points each)
On the line provided, write the letter of the *best* answer to each of the following items.

_____ 5. Words that we no longer use or that have changed meaning over time are called
  a. redundancies
  b. archaisms
  c. antonyms
  d. anomalies

_____ 6. To look up words not in current use it is best to consult
  a. an unabridged dictionary
  b. a student dictionary
  c. a dictionary of slang
  d. a Latin dictionary

_____ 7. When a familiar word in a work by an early American author does not make sense it may be because
  a. the meaning was not widely accepted
  b. the early writers felt free to use words without regard to meaning
  c. the word was not yet defined at the time of the writing
  d. the meaning of the word has changed or a meaning has gone out of use

_____ 8. An unabridged dictionary will give
  a. only definitions which are no longer current
  b. complete lists of definitions
  c. only the most common definitions
  d. the same number of definitions found in other dictionaries

Comprehension (25 points; 5 points each)
On the line provided, write the letter of the *best* answer to each of the following items.

_____ 9. Crèvecoeur believes an English person arriving in North America would probably feel
  a. envy   **c.** hostility
  b. pride   **d.** anger

_____ 10. The "national genius" that Crèvecoeur believes the Americans inherited from the British lies in their
  a. artistic taste   **c.** industriousness
  b. literary ability   **d.** sense of humor

_____ 11. According to Crèvecoeur, most people in America during this period
  a. were wealthy landowners   **c.** traveled constantly
  b. experienced abject poverty   **d.** lived modestly and comfortably

_____ 12. Crèvecoeur describes the North American continent as
  a. wildly beautiful and rugged   **c.** crowded and overpopulated
  b. vast and unexplored   **d.** artistically inspiring

_____ 13. According to Crèvecoeur, an important difference between Europe and North America is that the latter lacks
  a. humble farmers   **c.** lawyers or merchants
  b. aristocratic families   **d.** religious leaders

Reading Skills and Strategies
Identifying Tone (10 points)

14. A writer's tone may be either subjective or objective. Decide which of these two words best describes the tone of "What Is an American?" On a separate sheet of paper, state whether the writer's tone is objective or subjective. Then, list three phrases from the text that indicate this tone and explain briefly why the phrase indicates a subjective or objective tone.

Identifying the Main Idea (10 points)

15. From the following options, choose the one you think best states the main idea of the essay. On the lines provided, write the letter of the answer you choose, and briefly defend your choice with supporting details from the essay.
  a. North America is a land of equality.
  b. North America is a land of danger.
  c. North America is a land of great manufacturers.
  d. North America is a land of luxury.

Literary Element: The Plain Style (15 points)

16. Crèvecoeur writes in a style very different from the plain style of the Puritans. The everyday language and avoidance of imagery and figures of speech which the Puritans preferred is replaced in this selection with language that is more literary and ornamental. On a separate sheet of paper, write two paragraphs in which you describe elements of Crèvecoeur's style which are different from plain style writing. Use at least two examples from the excerpt to support your ideas.

LITERARY PERIOD INTRODUCTION TEST

American Romanticism

Pupil's Edition page 138

On the line provided, write the letter of the *best* answer to each of the following items.
(10 points each)

_____ **1.** Which sentence states an opinion held by American Romantic writers?
    a. Cities are centers of corruption and ugliness.
    b. European literature has no traditions worth considering.
    c. Westward expansion is exploitative and dangerous.
    d. Ordinary readers do not appreciate Romantic ideals.

_____ **2.** American Romantic writers rejected rationalism because they believed that
    a. logical thought was not possible
    b. scientific thinking had not yet been well developed
    c. scientific reasoning discouraged intuition and spontaneity
    d. the rationalist tradition had produced no worthwhile writers

_____ **3.** Through Gothic novels, Romantic writers explored
    a. the reasons for the decay of European society
    b. mysteries linked to the subconscious mind
    c. the civilization of the Goths
    d. lessons to be drawn from traditional religions

_____ **4.** The journey in American Romantic literature can *best* be characterized as
    a. leaving civilization and entering the world of nature
    b. escaping duty in order to do what one pleases
    c. rejecting traditional poetry and inventing new forms
    d. abandoning all intellectual pursuits for a frontier life

_____ **5.** American Romantic writers believed that poetry was
    a. a good form for describing momentous historical events
    b. an art that had been ignored by European writers
    c. an effective way to bring about social change
    d. the greatest witness to the power of imagination

_____ **6.** Unlike European Romantic novelists, American Romantic novelists were particularly inspired by
    a. exotic settings and supernatural events
    b. childlike qualities, such as innocence and virtue
    c. wilderness and the westward expansion
    d. the idea of a quest for higher truths

_____ **7.** As literary models, American Romantic poets used
    a. ideas in the novels of American Romantics
    b. the experimental forms being created by young poets
    c. the rhythms and rhyme schemes of folk songs
    d. poems by established European Romantics

_____ **8.** The typical American Romantic hero was
    a. interested in the future and in the growth of industry
    b. deeply intuitive and ruled by superior principles
    c. determined to conquer and subdue the natural world
    d. sophisticated and knowledgeable about worldly matters

_____ **9.** The American Fireside Poets are best known for their
    a. comfortable subjects appealing to families
    b. hotheaded, passionate ideas and messages
    c. disdain for American subjects and settings
    d. humorous approach to important issues

_____ **10.** Whittier threw a volume of Walt Whitman's poetry into the fire because
    a. he didn't appreciate the innovations in Whitman's work
    b. he was jealous of Whitman's talent and success
    c. Whitman's poetry was a throwback to the thinking of the rationalists
    d. Whitman had made fun of the Fireside Poets

SELECTION TEST

Rip Van Winkle
Washington Irving   Pupil's Edition page 153

Comprehension *(20 points; 5 points each)*
On the line provided, write the letter of the *best* answer to each of the following items.

_____ 1. The theme of "Rip Van Winkle" involves a wish coming true. Which phrase below most accurately reflects the wish?
   a. to be free of both British and Dutch rule
   b. to stay young forever
   c. to find new friendships
   d. to escape domination and enjoy life

_____ 2. The most momentous historical event that takes place during Rip's long sleep is
   a. the death of his wife   **c.** the secession of New York
   b. Hendrick Hudson's arrival   **d.** the American Revolution

_____ 3. Rip Van Winkle is a stereotypical American Romantic hero in that he
   a. discovers great truths through intuition
   b. finds solace and comfort in the wilderness
   c. has profound insights into the limits of science
   d. meets supernatural beings in the forest

_____ 4. In the end, most of the inhabitants of Rip's village
   a. doubt his truthfulness
   b. believe, enjoy, and retell his tale
   c. consider him deluded
   d. ignore his story

Reading Skills and Strategies: Drawing Inferences and Making Predictions
(20 points; 10 points each)
On the line provided, write the letter of the *best* answer to each of the following items.

_____ 5. What is the first detail that allows the reader to infer that Rip has slept a long time?
   a. He can't find the amphitheater.
   b. He does not recognize people as he approaches the village.
   c. His gun is old and rusty.
   d. The children make fun of his gray beard.

_____ 6. The description of Diedrich Knickerbocker's research techniques enables the reader to predict that
   a. an ordinary tale will be told
   b. he is an ordinary man
   c. a historical essay will follow
   d. an unusual story will follow

Literary Element: Setting *(10 points; 5 points each)*
On the line provided, write the letter of the *best* answer to each of the following items.

_____ 7. From Irving's descriptions of the Kaatskill Mountains, the reader can conclude that he found this setting to be
    a. spooky and dangerous   **c.** majestic and wondrous
    b. humorous and unreal   **d.** spoiled and degraded

_____ 8. In his descriptions of Rip's hometown, Irving shows how a place and its people can change as a result of
    a. independence and commerce
    b. neglect and indifference
    c. the disappearance of one of its residents
    d. the destruction of the natural environment

Vocabulary *(20 points; 2 points each)*
Match the definition on the left with the Word to Own on the right. Write the letter of the Word to Own on the line provided.

_____ 9. likable; agreeable
_____ 10. painstaking
_____ 11. honest and careful
_____ 12. accuracy
_____ 13. repeated
_____ 14. quiet; calm
_____ 15. emphatically
_____ 16. submissive; overly obedient
_____ 17. capable of being shaped
_____ 18. inactive period

    a. fidelity
    b. malleable
    c. scrupulous
    d. vehemently
    e. amiable
    f. conscientious
    g. torpor
    h. obsequious
    i. reiterated
    j. placid

Written Response *(30 points)*

19. Everyone in unpleasant or oppressive circumstances longs for escape. Some of the things from which people wish to escape include dangerous political situations, painful relationships, and economic hardship. "Rip Van Winkle" is a classic story of wish fulfillment, in that Rip manages to escape from many different things. From what do you think Rip escapes? What makes this wish fulfillment theme appealing or unappealing? On a separate sheet of paper, respond to these questions in a paragraph. Support your ideas with at least two incidents from "Rip Van Winkle."

SELECTION TEST

Thanatopsis
William Cullen Bryant

Pupil's Edition page 170

Comprehension *(50 points; 10 points each)*
On the line provided, write the letter of the *best* answer to each of the following items.

____ 1. In "Thanatopsis," nature urges the poet to find comfort in the
    a. fact that he is young and death is far off
    b. knowledge that death joins us with all others
    c. promise of resurrection after death
    d. idea that he will be famous after he dies

____ 2. Which statement *best* summarizes the cycle described in "Thanatopsis"?
    a. The dead are replaced by the living, who, in turn, die.
    b. The natural world is destructive.
    c. We move from cheerfulness to sorrow and back again.
    d. Nature speaks to us gently, then harshly.

____ 3. "Thanatopsis" strongly suggests that human beings are
    a. the highest form of living things
    b. doomed to live in dread of death
    c. an ongoing part of the earth itself
    d. incapable of improving their lives

____ 4. Which facet of "Thanatopsis" makes it a good example of Romantic poetry?
    a. The natural environment has provoked deep emotions and insights in the speaker.
    b. The poem is written in unrhymed lines and focuses on the supernatural.
    c. The poet is absorbed in thoughts of dying.
    d. The poet applies logic and rational thinking to human concerns about life and death.

____ 5. All of the following words describe the tone of "Thanatopsis" **except**
    a. gloomy   **c.** hostile
    b. celebratory   **d.** accepting and reassuring

Reading Skills and Strategies: Reading Inverted Sentences *(10 points)*
On the line provided, write the letter of the *best* answer to the following item.

____ 6. Which of the following quotations is the *best* example of an inverted sentence?
    a. "The oak / Shall send his roots abroad"
    b. " . . . the dead reign there alone"
    c. "All that breathe / Will share thy destiny"
    d. "and thee / The all-beholding sun shall see no more"

Written Response *(40 points)*

7. In "Thanatopsis," Bryant expresses his views on both the process of life and the nature of individual lives. On a separate sheet of paper, describe Bryant's views on the latter, and analyze how his use of language inversion, sound effects, and rhythm communicates those views. Make at least two references to the poem to support your ideas.

SELECTION TEST

The Tide Rises, the Tide Falls
The Cross of Snow
Henry Wadsworth Longfellow

Pupil's Edition page 176
Pupil's Edition page 178

Comprehension *(70 points; 10 points each)*
On the line provided, write the letter of the *best* answer to each of the following items.

_____ 1. In "The Tide Rises, the Tide Falls," the rising and falling of the tide suggests
   a. waves of despair
   b. the passage of time
   c. the unpredictability of nature
   d. the end of summer

_____ 2. The principal message conveyed in "The Tide Rises, the Tide Falls" is that
   a. humans have little control over their fate
   b. life is short
   c. the sea is dangerous
   d. people bustle about, but nature moves slowly

_____ 3. The repeated last line of each stanza in "The Tide Rises, the Tide Falls" is meant to convey
   a. the traveler's footsteps
   b. the unceasing motion of the tide
   c. the dawn following each night
   d. the unchanging call of the curlew

_____ 4. What can we conclude about the female subject of "The Cross of Snow"?
   a. She is one of the few childhood friends of the speaker.
   b. She is a lonely person who lives in isolation from society.
   c. She is remembered fondly and deeply missed by the speaker.
   d. She is very spiritual and in touch with the ways of nature.

_____ 5. In "The Cross of Snow," the images of a halo, fire, and sunlight contrast with the
   a. image of a snowy, sun-capped mountain
   b. face of the speaker's dead wife
   c. image of a sunless mountain ravine
   d. recollection of a happy marriage

_____ 6. In "The Cross of Snow," the cross that the speaker wears is
   a. his guilt about the accident that killed his wife
   b. a medallion that his wife gave to him
   c. an emotional pain that has never been wiped out
   d. his memento of a trip he took with his family

_____ 7. What is surprising or unexpected about the image of the cross of snow in Longfellow's poem?
   a. Unlike real snow, it becomes dirty.
   b. It exists only in the speaker's mind.
   c. It refers to a sense of religious conviction.
   d. It persists through time.

Literary Element: Meter and Sonnet *(10 points; 5 points each)*
On the line provided, write the letter of the *best* answer to each of the following items.

_____ **8.** Longfellow uses an iambic meter for "The Tide Rises, the Tide Falls" to
       a. create a singsong effect
       b. mirror the ebbing and rising tide
       c. avoid a predictable rhythm
       d. express his feelings about death

_____ **9.** "The Cross of Snow" is an example of
       a. a couplet
       b. an Italian sonnet
       c. a Shakespearean sonnet
       d. free verse

Written Response *(20 points; 10 points each)*

10. Choose what you believe is the *strongest* response to the following question. There is more than one possible answer. Then, briefly defend your answer on the lines provided. Use at least two examples from the two poems to support your ideas. *(15 points)*

Longfellow's imagery serves the following purpose(s):
a. to balance positive aspects of the human condition with negative ones
b. to express the speaker's reactions to personal experiences
c. to call attention to the inevitable sadness in life
d. to point out what can be learned from a study of nature

_____

_____

_____

_____

_____

_____

_____

_____

_____

_____

11. Judging from your reading of these two poems, how would you describe Longfellow's attitude toward life? Do you find him optimistic or pessimistic? On a separate sheet of paper, explain your point of view in one paragraph. Support your interpretation with at least two references from the poems.

SELECTION TEST

from Snow-Bound: A Winter Idyll
John Greenleaf Whittier

Pupil's Edition page 182

Comprehension *(50 points; 10 points each)*
On the line provided, write the letter of the *best* answer to each of the following items.

_____ 1. Most of the imagery in "Snow-Bound" contrasts
    a. the bitterness of winter with the softness of spring
    b. a winter scene outdoors with a home scene indoors
    c. relying on oneself with cooperating with others
    d. the virtues of farming with the dangers of the city

_____ 2. A major reason for the popularity of "Snow-Bound," both in its day and in the present, is its
    a. vivid portrait of a Romantic hero
    b. autobiographical sketch of a famous man
    c. picture of people from different backgrounds living in harmony
    d. description of people challenged by natural forces

_____ 3. The children described in the poem react to the storm by
    a. noting the changes   **c.** playing cards
    b. reading books   **d.** staying in bed

_____ 4. The speaker mentions an intense isolation. What makes this isolation a positive experience?
    a. The speaker has learned a great deal about himself during the storm.
    b. The emergency has helped the family to settle old quarrels.
    c. A storm-battered visitor has arrived to entertain the family.
    d. The snow-bound family has risen to the challenge with merriment and enterprise.

_____ 5. All of the following items are characteristics of an idyll **except**
    a. a description of the country   **c.** an idealized scene
    b. an emotional conflict   **d.** an intimate, comforting tone

Reading Skills and Strategies: Recognizing Allusions *(10 points)*
On the line provided, write the letter of the *best* answer to the following item.

_____ 6. Which of the following lines includes a literary allusion?
    a. "We had read / Of rare Aladdin's wondrous cave"
    b. "The well curb had a Chinese roof"
    c. ". . . the clothesline posts / Looked in like tall and sheeted ghosts"
    d. ". . . seemed to tell / Of Pisa's leaning miracle"

Written Response *(40 points)*

7. Whittier uses imagery to describe how two environments are transformed. On a separate sheet of paper, describe the transformations and explain how Whittier uses images to convey a sense of amazement toward these changed situations. Support your ideas with at least two references to images from the poem.

SELECTION TEST

The Chambered Nautilus
Old Ironsides
Oliver Wendell Holmes

Pupil's Edition page 188

Pupil's Edition page 190

Comprehension *(60 points; 10 points each)*
On the line provided, write the letter of the *best* answer to each of the following items.

_____ **1.** In "The Chambered Nautilus," the speaker implies that if he hadn't meditated on the nautilus, his life might have resembled
    a. a series of endless corridors leading nowhere
    b. a person who drowns in the sea
    c. the noise from an ancient sea god's horn
    d. the ever-changing and restless sea

_____ **2.** The speaker finds the chambered nautilus remarkable because it is
    a. a rare shell seldom found on beaches
    b. broken and abandoned by its tenant
    c. evidence of how a living thing develops
    d. able to move through the water like a boat

_____ **3.** In "The Chambered Nautilus," what does the speaker seem to wish for himself?
    a. an opportunity to live his life over again
    b. a carefree life by the seashore
    c. a fame that will endure long after his death
    d. a spirit that eventually will break free

_____ **4.** The opening line in "Old Ironsides" is ironic because the speaker really wants to
    a. preserve the ship's past glory
    b. use the ship as scrap metal
    c. sink the ship
    d. write a poem about the ship's beauty and construction

_____ **5.** In "Old Ironsides," the harpies symbolize
    a. land birds attacking seabirds
    b. scavengers destroying something noble
    c. a story from Norse mythology
    d. the defeat of the British in 1812

_____ **6.** When it was published, the poem "Old Ironsides" served a purpose similar to that of a
    a. newspaper editorial
    b. strikers' picket line
    c. birthday celebration
    d. sympathy note

Literary Element: Extended Metaphor *(10 points; 5 points each)*
On the line provided, write the letter of the *best* answer to each of the following items.

_____ **7.** In "The Chambered Nautilus," the poet develops an extended metaphor comparing the empty shell to
   a. the lack of meaning in his own life
   b. a body that once housed a soul
   c. a new building that will soon be occupied
   d. an estate that has been recently robbed

_____ **8.** In "Old Ironsides," the words *she* and *her* help to develop the metaphor comparing the ship to
   a. a valiant human being who has served gallantly in a war
   b. an old woman who has outlived her children
   c. a human being who has traveled throughout the world
   d. a mermaid who wants to return to the sea

Written Response *(30 points; 15 points each)*

9. Choose the option that *best* completes the following statement. (There is more than one possible answer.) On the lines provided, write the letter of the answer you choose and briefly defend your choice. Use at least one example from each poem to support your ideas.

The most striking similarity between "Old Ironsides" and "The Chambered Nautilus" is the
   a. poet's attempt to influence the reader's attitude
   b. use of oceangoing "vessels" as subjects
   c. tone of respect for the past
   d. statement of the poet's spiritual beliefs

_____

_____

_____

_____

_____

_____

_____

_____

_____

_____

10. On a separate sheet of paper, write a one-paragraph essay discussing how Holmes's two poems reflect the characteristics of American Romanticism. Support your ideas with at least two details from the poems.

THE AMERICAN LANGUAGE

"Noah's Ark": Webster's Dictionary

On the line provided, write the letter of the *best* answer to each of the following items.
(10 points each)

_____ **1.** In England, the ultimate linguistic authority traditionally rested with
   a. everyday usage
   b. the king
   c. Noah Webster
   d. dictionaries

_____ **2.** Determining matters of linguistic usage by common agreement is
   a. impossible in any society
   b. possible only where the social structure is fluid
   c. possible only in a relatively stable social structure
   d. possible under all conditions

_____ **3.** In the late eighteenth century, English schools introduced into their curriculum the study of
   a. English grammar
   b. Latin grammar
   c. Greek grammar
   d. German grammar

_____ **4.** After the Revolution, a major impediment to establishing American linguistic independence was the fact that
   a. Americans were proud of their diversity
   b. there were no schools in the colonies
   c. most Americans could not read or write
   d. the only available grammar textbooks came from England

_____ **5.** Until the eighteenth century, the spelling of American English
   a. was regulated by an academy
   b. followed flexible rules
   c. copied British rules
   d. was influenced by Samuel Johnson's *Dictionary of the English Language*

_____ **6.** Noah Webster believed that accurate and uniform American spelling would promote
   a. clearer writing
   b. greater conformity with British English
   c. uniform American speech
   d. better language skills in the United States

_____ **7.** Webster's first dictionary reveals that he
   a. appreciated fashionable and urban ways
   b. was radical in matters of spelling and pronunciation
   c. was strict in matters of grammar and usage
   d. had had extensive training as a linguist

_____ **8.** Webster's *A Compendious Dictionary of the English Language* included frequent inaccuracies in
    a. pronunciation
    b. word histories
    c. usage
    d. grammar

_____ **9.** Webster's influence is evident today in our adoption of
    a. British spelling conventions
    b. his word histories
    c. some of his recommendations for spelling and pronunciation
    d. all of his recommended pronunciations

_____ **10.** Webster's *American Dictionary* was
    a. the first dictionary to include Americanisms
    b. criticized for its brevity
    c. praised by Samuel Johnson
    d. carefully researched by a team of scholars

LITERARY ELEMENTS TEST

The Sonnet

On the line provided, write the letter of the *best* answer to each of the following items.
(10 points each)

____ 1. All of the following elements are characteristic of a sonnet **except**
  a. introduction of the subject in the first few lines
  b. fourteen lines
  c. free verse
  d. iambic pentameter

____ 2. In a typical sonnet, the meter can be described as
  a. a trio of syllables in which an unstressed syllable follows two stressed syllables
  b. one-syllable words that have an *abba* rhyme scheme
  c. a pair of syllables in which a stressed syllable follows an unstressed syllable
  d. six dactylic feet followed by four trochaic feet

____ 3. What is another name for the Petrarchan sonnet?
  a. the Italian sonnet
  b. the Elizabethan sonnet
  c. the English sonnet
  d. the Octavian sonnet

____ 4. The Elizabethan sonnet consists of
  a. one octave and one sestet
  b. three quatrains and a couplet
  c. two tercets and one cinquain
  d. one sestet and four couplets

____ 5. Which of the following is the rhyme scheme of a Petrarchan sonnet?
  a. *abba, cddc, abba, cddc, eeff*
  b. *abab, cdcd, efef, gg*
  c. *abba, cdcd, abba, efef, ffgg*
  d. *abba, abba, cde, cde*

____ 6. Which of the following symbols is indicative of an iamb?
  a. ˘ ´ ´ ´ ˘
  b. ˘ ´
  c. ´ ˘ ˘
  d. ˘ ´ ˘ ´

____ 7. Which of the following writers was one of the earliest masters of the sonnet?
  a. Elizabeth Barrett Browning
  b. John Keats
  c. William Shakespeare
  d. Robert Lowell

_____ **8.** Which of the following is the rhyme scheme of an Elizabethan sonnet?
    a. *abba, abba, cde, cde*
    b. *abba, cdcd, abba, efef, ffgg*
    c. *abba, cddc, abba, cddc, eeff*
    d. *abab, cdcd, efef, gg*

_____ **9.** The Elizabethan sonnet is also called the
    a. Donne sonnet
    b. Miltonian sonnet
    c. Shakespearean sonnet
    d. British sonnet

_____ **10.** The last group of lines in a sonnet usually
    a. has different meter than the rest of the poem
    b. comments on the subject of the poem
    c. rhymes with the first two lines of the poem
    d. introduces a new subject

LITERARY PERIOD TEST

American Romanticism

Applying Skills

This test asks you to apply what you know about using context clues, drawing inferences, and analyzing setting. Read the following poem. Then, answer the questions that follow.

Inscription for the Entrance to a Wood
by William Cullen Bryant

Stranger, if thou hast learned a truth which needs
No school of long experience, that the world
Is full of guilt and misery, and hast seen
Enough of all its sorrows, crimes, and cares
5   To tire thee of it, enter this wild wood
And view the haunts of Nature. The calm shade
Shall bring a kindred calm, and the sweet breeze
That makes the green leaves dance, shall <u>waft</u> a balm
To thy sick heart. Thou wilt find nothing here
10   Of all that pained thee in the haunts of men,
And made thee loathe thy life. The primal curse
Fell, it is true, upon the unsinning earth,
But not in vengeance. God hath yoked to guilt
Her pale tormentor, misery. Hence, these shades
15   Are still the abodes of gladness; the thick roof
Of green and stirring branches is alive
And musical with birds, that sing and sport
In <u>wantonness</u> of spirit; while below
The squirrel, with raised paws and form erect,
20   Chirps merrily. Throngs of insects in the shade
Try their thin wings and dance in the warm beam
That waked them into life. Even the green trees
Partake the deep contentment; as they bend
To the soft winds, the sun from the blue sky
25   Looks in and sheds a blessing on the scene.
Scarce less the cleft-born wildflower seems to enjoy
Existence, than the wingèd plunderer
That sucks its sweet. The mossy rocks themselves,
And the old and ponderous trunks of <u>prostrate</u> trees
30   That lead from knoll to knoll a causey rude
Or bridge the sunken brook, and their dark roots,
With all their earth upon them, twisting high,
Breathe fixed tranquility. The rivulet
Sends forth glad sounds, and tripping o'er its bed
35   Of pebbly sands, or leaping down the rocks,
Seems, with continuous laughter, to rejoice
In its own being. Softly tread the <u>marge</u>,
Lest from her midway perch thou scare the wren
That dips her bill in water. The cool wind,
40   That stirs the stream in play, shall come to thee,
Like one that loves thee nor will let thee pass
Ungreeted, and shall give its light embrace.

Vocabulary Skills: New Words in Context *(20 points; 5 points each)*
Each of the italicized words below has also been underlined in the selection. Re-read those passages and use context clues to help you determine the meaning of each word. In the space provided, mark each true statement *T* and each false statement *F.*

_____ **1.** *Waft* refers to a species of tree.

_____ **2.** Birds that sing in *wantonness* of spirit are defending territory.

_____ **3.** *Prostrate* describes trees that have collapsed under the burden of age or weight.

_____ **4.** A person who treads the *marge* walks along the edge.

Vocabulary

Using Context Clues *(20 points; 5 points each)*
For each phrase below, use context clues to determine the meaning of the underlined word. Write the letter of the meaning of the underlined word.

_____ **5.** ". . . shall waft a <u>balm</u> / To thy sick heart."
    a. ointment   **c.** hope
    b. wind   **d.** calm

_____ **6.** ". . . lead from knoll to knoll a <u>causey</u> rude / Or bridge the sunken brook"
    a. bridge   **c.** road
    b. grassy   **d.** forest

_____ **7.** ". . . Of all that pained thee in the haunts of men, / And made thee <u>loathe</u> thy life."
    a. hate   **c.** protect
    b. change   **d.** cherish

_____ **8.** "Hence, these shades / Are still the <u>abodes</u> of gladness; the thick roof / Of green and stirring branches . . ."
    a. forests   **c.** gifts
    b. nests   **d.** homes

Comprehension *(25 points; 5 points each)*
On the line provided, write the letter of the *best* answer to each of the following items.

_____ **9.** "Inscription for the Entrance to a Wood" focuses primarily on
    a. the premature death of heroes   **c.** ambition as the highest human goal
    b. the comfort of nature   **d.** guilt as the cause of human misery

_____ **10.** At the end of the poem, the stranger is welcomed into the world of nature through
    a. religious teachings   **c.** reason
    b. riddles   **d.** love

_____ **11.** The poem portrays various elements of nature as
    a. living in a fragile state of coexistence with each other
    b. part of a cyclical pattern of life and death
    c. rejoicing in the comfort of their existence
    d. constantly battling the human world in order to survive

____ **12.** The insects in the poem are described as
    a. a marginal part of the natural world
    b. the lowest form of living beings
    c. annoying but hard-working creatures
    d. reflections of sublime beauty and grace

____ **13.** The speaker suggests that human beings should approach nature
    a. with fear and caution   **c.** with a rational mind
    b. with total abandon   **d.** with openness and optimism

Reading Skills and Strategies: Drawing Inferences: *(20 points; 10 points each)*

____ **14.** What does Bryant imply about the effect of a walk in the woods? From the following options, choose the one you think is the best response to this question. On a separate sheet of paper, write the letter of the answer you choose, and briefly defend your choice. Use at least one example from the selection to support your ideas.
    a. He implies that it will awaken a person to the pleasures of physical exercise.
    b. He implies that it will bring forgiveness for sins.
    c. He implies that it will prepare a person for death.
    d. He implies that it will ease the pain of living in the world.

15. On a separate sheet of paper, write a brief paragraph in which you discuss whether the following statement can be inferred from the poem. Use examples and details from "Inscription for the Entrance to a Wood" to make an argument for or against this statement. Be sure to support your opinion with at least one example from the poem.

Nature is a better companion in suffering than another person would be.

Literary Element: Setting *(15 points)*

16. Bryant paints a positive picture of the setting by describing it in admiring and reverential tones. In the left-hand side of the following chart are listed three details of setting used by Bryant that could have a negative feel to them if used in a different context. In the middle column, write a word that is associated with this detail in the poem and that expresses the positive tone that the speaker gives to his experience with nature. In the right-hand column, make a few notes about the negative feeling this detail could have in another context. A sample answer is provided.

Detail	Positive Association in Poem	Possible Negative Association
shade (l. 6)	"calm"	shadowy, unknown, threatening
"throngs of insects" (l. 20)		
roots of uprooted trees (ll. 31–32)		
wind (l. 39)		

LITERARY PERIOD INTRODUCTION TEST

The American Renaissance
A Literary Coming of Age

Pupil's Edition page 206

On the line provided, write the letter of the *best* answer to each of the following items.
(10 points each)

_____ 1. The first flowering of a uniquely American literature, sometimes referred to as the American Renaissance, was directly influenced by
    a. intellectual and social ferment in New England
    b. an American version of an old philosophy called Aphorism
    c. the inspiration and lectures of Nathaniel Hawthorne
    d. the politics of the European Renaissance

_____ 2. Nathaniel Hawthorne and Herman Melville both
    a. had published books of lyric poetry
    b. were ex-seamen with little education
    c. explored the dark side of human existence in their work
    d. doubted that America would produce writers as good as Shakespeare

_____ 3. The philosophy embraced by Ralph Waldo Emerson's Transcendentalists had its roots in all of the following **except**
    a. Puritan thought exemplified by William Bradford, Anne Bradstreet, and Jonathan Edwards
    b. nineteenth-century Romantic thought exemplified by William Cullen Bryant
    c. Classical Greek idealistic thought exemplified by Plato
    d. eighteenth-century rational thought exemplified by Benjamin Franklin

_____ 4. In the Transcendentalist view of the world,
    a. everything is a reflection of the Divine Soul
    b. humanity's task is to conquer and tame the natural world
    c. people must struggle against the evil side of their nature
    d. human perfectibility is not an achievable goal

_____ 5. The Lyceum movement was an expression of New England's interest in
    a. the philosophy of Immanuel Kant
    b. self-improvement and intellectual inquiry
    c. the dark side of human nature
    d. eighteenth-century religious revivals

_____ 6. Which of the following statements about Ralph Waldo Emerson is true?
    a. He wrote a novel about sin and hypocrisy in Puritan New England.
    b. He traveled around the country giving sermons.
    c. He helped inspire numerous reform movements.
    d. He criticized a utopian group called "The Transcendental Club."

_____ 7. Utopian communities were founded with the intention of
    a. teaching philosophy to Romantic poets
    b. abolishing the institution of slavery
    c. funding the Lyceum movement
    d. creating a more perfect society

____ **8.** Reform movements during the first half of the nineteenth century included campaigns for
   a. building more factories
   b. improving public education
   c. improving living conditions for slaves
   d. limiting women's rights

____ **9.** The source of Emerson's optimism was
   a. his belief that we can directly find a benevolent God in nature
   b. the popularity of European writers in America
   c. the success of the Dark Romantic writers
   d. his belief that everyone would soon live in a utopian community

____ **10.** Both the Dark Romantics and the Transcendentalists
   a. saw signs and symbols in human events
   b. saw culture as a constant reminder of spiritual goodness
   c. valued logic and reason over intuition
   d. had an optimistic world view

SELECTION TEST

from **Nature**
Ralph Waldo Emerson   **Pupil's Edition page 218**

Comprehension *(50 points; 10 points each)*
On the line provided, write the letter of the *best* answer to each of the following items.

_____ 1. Which of the following statements describes Emerson's attitude toward society?
   a. He believes that society always does good.
   b. He values nature highly and has some contempt for society.
   c. He thinks that societies are becoming increasingly civilized.
   d. He hopes that nature will someday destroy all societies.

_____ 2. According to Emerson, the person who can truly see nature is like a child because he or she
   a. no longer needs to rely upon either reason or faith
   b. perceives nature as being a kind of toy
   c. is free of the burden of thought
   d. sees with the heart as well as with the eye

_____ 3. With which of the following statements would Emerson be most likely to agree?
   a. Human beings should attempt systematically to learn everything there is to know about nature and solve all its mysteries.
   b. The creations of human society, such as laws and cities, are as wondrous as the works of nature.
   c. Nature brings a sense of joy to the observer at all times, even to someone who is grieving.
   d. All elements of nature make a unified impression on those whose minds are open.

_____ 4. The third paragraph of the excerpt ends with this sentence: "This is the best part of these men's farms, yet to this their warranty deeds give no title." In the context of the paragraph, this sentence means
   a. the most valuable quality of the land is something that cannot be owned
   b. the deeds to the majority of the farms do not list the owners' names
   c. the work the farm owners perform does not entitle them to ownership of the land
   d. poets should be given deeds to the land, because only they can understand its worth

_____ 5. Emerson's purpose in this essay is to
   a. express his disappointment with the society of his time
   b. explain and analyze the workings of natural phenomena
   c. describe a profound way of seeing nature
   d. persuade sinners to turn to nature and seek forgiveness from God

Literary Element: Imagery *(10 points; 5 points each)*
On the line provided, write the letter of the *best* answer to each of the following items.

____ 6. Which of the following quotations from the selection does **not** contain an example of sensory imagery?
   a. "The sun illuminates only the eye of the man, but shines into the eye and the heart of the child."
   b. "The stars awaken a certain reverence, because though always present, they are always inaccessible. . . . "
   c. "Standing on the bare ground—my head bathed by the blithe air, and uplifted into infinite space—all mean egotism vanishes."
   d. " . . . the same scene which yesterday breathed perfume and glittered as for the frolic of the nymphs . . . "

____ 7. Imagery can be described as
   a. syllogisms
   b. aphorisms
   c. word pictures
   d. sensory naturalism

Vocabulary *(20 points; 2 points each)*
Match the definition on the left with the Word to Own on the right. Write the letter of the Word to Own on the line provided.

____ 8. outer layer of snake's skin		**a.** admonishing
____ 9. hidden		**b.** integrate
____ 10. recurring yearly		**c.** occult
____ 11. carefree		**d.** blithe
____ 12. without a doubt		**e.** slough
____ 13. many different		**f.** perpetual
____ 14. to unify		**g.** perennial
____ 15. that which inspires awe		**h.** indubitably
____ 16. mildly warning		**i.** sublime
____ 17. constant and unchanging		**j.** manifold

Written Response *(20 points)*

18. On a separate sheet of paper, write a paragraph explaining how the following quotation from *Nature* represents Emerson's ideas about society and nature.

"To go into solitude, a man needs to retire as much from his chamber as from society."

SELECTION TEST

from Self-Reliance
Ralph Waldo Emerson   **Pupil's Edition page 224**

Comprehension *(20 points; 5 points each)*
On the line provided, write the letter of the *best* answer to each of the following items.

_____ 1. Which of the following *best* states one of Emerson's philosophies?
    a. Be true to yourself.
    b. Misery loves company.
    c. Keep your head in the clouds.
    d. Turnabout is fair play.

_____ 2. When Emerson says we are "ashamed of that divine idea which each of us represents," which of the following *best* describes what he means by "that divine idea"?
    a. a wonderful and exciting plan of action
    b. an image of the world
    c. God, as we imagine him
    d. each person's uniqueness, as conceived by God

_____ 3. Emerson states that the most sacred aspect of a person is the
    a. work that person accomplishes
    b. integrity of an individual's mind
    c. person's courage to be a nonconformist
    d. shadow that an individual casts on the world

_____ 4. According to Emerson, the "hobgoblin of little minds" is
    a. society
    b. cowardice
    c. conspiracy
    d. consistency

Reading Skills and Strategies: Understanding Figures of Speech *(20 points; 10 points each)*
On the line provided, write the letter of the *best* explanation for each of the figures of speech from "Self-Reliance" that is quoted below.

_____ 5. "Trust thyself: Every heart vibrates to that iron string."
    a. If you trust yourself, you will come up against a steel wall.
    b. Trust yourself, and you will be strong.
    c. If you trust yourself, you will be broken as easily as a string.
    d. Trust yourself, and you will become a musician.

_____ 6. "Speak what you think now in hard words, and tomorrow speak what tomorrow thinks in hard words again . . ."
    a. It is difficult to speak eloquently and correctly.
    b. Telling the truth is dangerous, so don't do it.
    c. Say what's on your mind in the strongest way you can.
    d. Say what you want regardless of whether you have thought about it.

Literary Element: Figures of Speech *(20 points; 10 points each)*
On the line provided, write the letter of the *best* answer to each of the following items.

_____ **7.** Figures of speech are
   a. different ways in which people speak to one another
   b. figurative and usually use internal rhyme
   c. imaginative and are intended to appeal only to our visual sense
   d. comparative and are not intended to be taken literally

_____ **8.** In the following metaphor, " . . . no kernel of nourishing corn can come to him but through his toil bestowed on that plot of ground which is given to him to till . . . ," which of the following *best* describes what "that plot of ground" represents?
   a. the duties an individual performs
   b. the results of an individual's actions
   c. the circumstances an individual is born into
   d. an individual's daily food

Vocabulary *(20 points; 2 points each)*
Match the definition on the left with the Word to Own on the right. Write the letter of the Word to Own on the line provided.

_____ **9.** secret plot with a harmful or illegal purpose   **a.** proportionate

_____ **10.** surpassing; excelling   **b.** predominating

_____ **11.** belief   **c.** manifest

_____ **12.** having influence   **d.** transcendent

_____ **13.** balanced   **e.** conspiracy

_____ **14.** revealed   **f.** benefactors

_____ **15.** honesty; sound moral principles   **g.** conviction

_____ **16.** clear; plain   **h.** integrity

_____ **17.** intense dislike   **i.** imparted

_____ **18.** people who help others   **j.** aversion

Written Response *(20 points)*

19. On a separate sheet of paper, state the theme of Emerson's essay in one sentence. Then read the following quotation from "Self-Reliance." Does this quotation contradict or agree with your statement of the theme? Provide at least two examples from the selection to support your answer.

"Accept the place the divine Providence has found for you; the society of your contemporaries, the connection of events. Great men have always done so and confided themselves childlike to the genius of their age. . . ."

SELECTION TEST

from Walden, or Life in the Woods
Henry David Thoreau   **Pupil's Edition page 232**

Comprehension *(25 points; 5 points each)*
On the line provided, write the letter of the *best* answer to each of the following items.

_____ **1.** Which of the following activities *best* illustrates Thoreau's doctrine of simplicity?
  a. building his own house
  b. hosting social gatherings for his neighbors
  c. writing books about plants in the forest
  d. keeping a journal and doing research about animals he encounters

_____ **2.** Which of the following is the *best* interpretation of what Thoreau means when he
says, " . . . we do like cowbirds and cuckoos, which lay their eggs in nests which
other birds have built, and cheer no traveler . . . "?
  a. People who try to trick others into doing their work feel guilty.
  b. People who hire others to provide for their basic needs are left unfulfilled.
  c. People who are dishonest are unhappy.
  d. People who are cheerful are usually hard workers.

_____ **3.** With which of the following statements would Thoreau agree?
  a. Most people's lives are too simple.
  b. The chief purpose of everyone's life should be to glorify God.
  c. Most people forfeit their lives by doing what society tells them to do.
  d. People need to learn to compromise in order to get along.

_____ **4.** What reason does Thoreau give for wanting to live at Walden?
  a. He wants to withdraw from life because he is depressed.
  b. He dislikes people and wants to get away from them.
  c. He wants to prove that he does not need other people.
  d. He wants to live life more fully.

_____ **5.** What reason does Thoreau give for finally leaving Walden?
  a. He wishes to move on to other experiences.
  b. He does not find what he is seeking there.
  c. He becomes tired of working so hard for the essentials of life.
  d. He is lonely and misses the company of other people.

Reading Skills and Strategies *(30 points; 10 points each)*
On the line provided, write the letter of the *best* answer to each of the following items.

Drawing Inferences: Generalizations

_____ **6.** Which of the following generalizations *best* summarizes Thoreau's opinion about life?
  a. Solitude is tedious and boring.
  b. Intelligent men need many friends.
  c. A simple life is a happy life.
  d. The mind can only be stimulated by reading.

_____ **7.** Thoreau believes that all of the following are important in life except
    a. details   **c.** appreciation of nature
    b. physical labor   **d.** experience

Unlocking Meaning in Metaphors

_____ **8.** Which statement is the *best* paraphrase of the following metaphor?
"We do not ride on the railroad; it rides upon us."
    a. People are primitive and need technology to succeed.
    b. Life is uncertain; therefore, we must toil to make ends meet.
    c. People are controlled by what they create rather than controlling their creations.
    d. In order to communicate with nature, we must become self-reliant.

Literary Element: First-Person Point of View *(10 points)*

_____ **9.** Which of the following is the *best* interpretation of Thoreau's statement, "In most books
the *I*, or first person, is omitted; in this it will be retained. . . . I am confined to this
theme by the narrowness of my experience"?
    a. Most authors forget to address their readers' interests.
    b. Most authors explain their feelings in their works.
    c. Most authors forget to write about themselves, the most important subject.
    d. Authors' thoughts and feelings inform everything they write.

Vocabulary *(20 points; 2 points each)*
Match the definition on the left with the Word to Own on the right. Write the letter of the Word to
Own on the line provided.

_____ **10.** without stopping	**a.**	pertinent
_____ **11.** impenetrable; resistant	**b.**	effete
_____ **12.** not earthly; spiritual	**c.**	encumbrance
_____ **13.** unnecessary	**d.**	incessantly
_____ **14.** contempt; ridicule	**e.**	impervious
_____ **15.** sterile; unproductive	**f.**	derision
_____ **16.** to the point; applying to the situation	**g.**	temporal
_____ **17.** burden; hindrance	**h.**	tumultuous
_____ **18.** worldly	**i.**	superfluous
_____ **19.** turbulent; stormy	**j.**	ethereal

Written Response *(15 points)*

20. In the section "Where I Lived, and What I Lived For," Thoreau states the following main idea:
"I did not wish to live what was not life . . ." On a separate sheet of paper, explain what he
meant, and support your answer with three specific examples of what Thoreau meant by
"not life."

SELECTION TEST

from Resistance to Civil Government
Henry David Thoreau
Pupil's Edition page 248

Comprehension *(30 points; 6 points each)*
On the line provided, write the letter of the *best* answer to each of the following items.

_____ 1. Thoreau's major purpose in this essay is to persuade people to
    a. rebel against an unjust war
    b. follow their individual consciences
    c. call for immediate end to the government
    d. devote themselves to the eradication of wrongs

_____ 2. In Thoreau's view, the practical reason the majority rules in a democracy is that
    a. this system satisfies most people
    b. the majority opinion is always the just opinion
    c. the majority opinion is more likely to be just
    d. the majority has more physical power on its side

_____ 3. Thoreau's hope for the democracy of his time was that it
    a. was one step along the route to a more perfect state
    b. would disappear as people ceased to vote
    c. would progress from an absolute to a limited monarchy
    d. would abolish poll taxes for all time

_____ 4. Which of the following *best* describes Thoreau's attitude toward government after he was jailed?
    a. He was appalled that he was punished.
    b. He was angry about losing his freedom.
    c. He lost all respect for the government and pitied it.
    d. He worried that he would lose his voting privileges.

_____ 5. Which of the following statements is **not** an opinion?
    a. The ideal individual should respect other people's individuality.
    b. Thoreau objected to the government's support of slavery.
    c. Governments should be equally just to all people.
    d. Thoreau was unreasonable about refusing to pay a tax to the state.

Reading Skills and Strategies: Determining the Precise Meanings of Words *(10 points)*
On the line provided, write the letter of the *best* answer to each of the following items.

_____ 6. What meaning does the word *novel* have in the following sentence?
    "The night in prison was novel and interesting enough."
    a. a new law or decree
    b. a long fictional story
    c. a modernistic setting
    d. an unfamiliar experience

Literary Element: Paradox *(20 points; 10 points each)*
On the line provided, write the letter of the *best* answer to each of the following items.

_____ 7. Which of the following quotations from this selection is an example of paradox?
  a. "What is once well done is done forever."
  b. "*It* does not keep the country free. *It* does not settle the West."
  c. "That government is best which governs not at all."
  d. "I think that we should be men first, and subjects afterward."

_____ 8. Which of the following statements *best* summarizes what Thoreau might have thought about paradoxes?
  a. Contradictory statements never reveal the truth.
  b. Life is complex, so complicated similes should be used to tell the truth about it.
  c. Truths can be revealed by examining contradictions.
  d. The truth can always be revealed by using descriptive details.

Vocabulary *(20 points; 2 points each)*
Match the definition on the left with the Word to Own on the right. Write the letter of the Word to Own on the line provided.

_____ 9. inborn
_____ 10. hindrance; blockage
_____ 11. revolt; rebellion
_____ 12. corrupted; misdirected
_____ 13. impulsive
_____ 14. generations to come
_____ 15. efficient; productive
_____ 16. eagerness; promptness in responding
_____ 17. sorry for doing wrong
_____ 18. means to an end; convenience

a. expedient
b. insurrection
c. perverted
d. penitent
e. posterity
f. effectual
g. alacrity
h. obstruction
i. inherent
j. impetuous

Written Response *(20 points)*

19. On a separate sheet of paper, summarize this selection by creating a list of five major points. As the first item on the list, describe Thoreau's purpose in writing the essay. The following four items in the list should summarize major points or incidents from the selection.

SELECTION TEST

The Fall of the House of Usher
Edgar Allan Poe   Pupil's Edition page 262

Comprehension *(30 points; 5 points each)*
On the line provided, write the letter of the *best* answer to each of the following items.

_____ 1. The narrator's first impression of the House of Usher is of a building that
     a. promises the exciting adventure he longs for
     b. somehow stands in spite of obvious decay
     c. brings back bitter memories of his youth
     d. reminds him of pleasant times at school

_____ 2. Roderick Usher seems to be suffering mainly from
     a. a nervous disorder that affects his sensory reactions
     b. an inability to handle his household responsibilities
     c. poverty, resulting from poor business management
     d. guilt over the bad feelings between him and Madeline

_____ 3. Madeline's eventual fate is foreshadowed by
     a. her dislike of intrusions by visitors
     b. a disease that engenders a temporary, deathlike state
     c. a letter she has sent to the narrator
     d. a nightmare that reveals where she will eventually be buried

_____ 4. Which of the following statements *best* describes what happens to the narrator before
     he finally leaves the house?
     a. He grows in his awareness of the problems of aristocratic families.
     b. He heroically resolves to rescue Roderick from his fate.
     c. He is finally able to distinguish between reality and fantasy.
     d. He becomes enmeshed in the gloom of his surroundings.

_____ 5. From the behavior of the narrator, the reader can infer that the narrator is
     a. being held prisoner
     b. worried about what might happen in the house
     c. in control of both Usher's and Madeline's minds
     d. an avid reader of Gothic poetry

_____ 6. The character of the narrator might be described as all of the following **except**
     a. snobbish   **c.** kindly
     b. imaginative   **d.** terror-stricken

Reading Skills and Strategies: Sensing Connotations *(10 points; 2 points each)*
For each of the following words, classify each word as having either a positive or negative connotation. Write *P* for positive and *N* for negative.

_____ 7. insufferable   _____ 10. vivacious

_____ 8. luminous   _____ 11. pestilent

_____ 9. dilapidated

Literary Elements

On the line provided, write the letter of the *best* answer to each of the following items.

Atmosphere *(10 points; 5 points each)*

_____ **12.** Just before the narrator begins reading the *Mad Trist* of Sir Launcelot Canning, the clouds are described as moving furiously into each other from all directions without ever leaving the immediate vicinity of the mansion. This description contributes to the atmosphere in the story of
    a. abnormality and menace   **c.** festivity and action
    b. loss and melancholy   **d.** contemplation and introspection

_____ **13.** Both Roderick Usher and the narrator mention that the atmosphere surrounding the mansion seems unconnected to the atmosphere of the outside world. This detail both adds to the feeling of gloom and acts as a symbol of
    a. the fact that the mansion is not real
    b. the fact that Roderick Usher is mentally losing contact with the outside world
    c. the fact that there is no way to escape from the mansion
    d. the fact that Madeline has altered reality by casting a spell over the mansion

Poe's Symbols *(5 points)*

_____ **14.** The fungi covering the mansion symbolizes
    a. premature death   **c.** an unidentified evil
    b. violent battles   **d.** healthy growth

Vocabulary *(20 points; 2 points each)*

Match the definition on the left with the Word to Own on the right. Write the letter of the Word to Own on the line provided.

_____ **15.** pale   **a.** demeanor

_____ **16.** behavior; conduct   **b.** equivocal

_____ **17.** likeness   **c.** morbid

_____ **18.** abundant   **d.** pallid

_____ **19.** having more than one meaning   **e.** palpable

_____ **20.** state of mental dullness   **f.** prodigious

_____ **21.** obvious; perceivable   **g.** profuse

_____ **22.** diseased; unhealthy   **h.** similitude

_____ **23.** short stay   **i.** sojourn

_____ **24.** of great size and power   **j.** stupor

Written Response *(25 points)*

25. Whatever the gruesome furnishings of our nightmares, we may—strangely enough—choose to inhabit them for a while. The narrator of "The Fall of the House of Usher" remains for quite some time in the nightmarish atmosphere of the Ushers' home, in spite of the fact that he is gravely troubled. On a separate sheet of paper, suggest at least two reasons to explain why the narrator stays at the house. Support your ideas with at least two details from the story.

SELECTION TEST

The Raven
Edgar Allan Poe

Pupil's Edition page 282

Comprehension *(35 points; 5 points each)*
On the line provided, write the letter of the *best* answer to each of the following items.

_____ 1. The speaker can *best* be described as a
   a. lonely, elderly man longing for visitors
   b. magician conjuring up evil spirits
   c. melancholy person trying to forget a tragedy
   d. poet seeking inspiration for a new work

_____ 2. When the narrator opens the door of his chamber and peers out, he half expects to find
   a. a Greek god come to life in the form of a bird
   b. a host of angels
   c. the image of his own death
   d. the deceased woman with whom he has been in love

_____ 3. At first encounter, the Raven
   a. frightens the speaker
   b. repulses the speaker
   c. angers the speaker
   d. amuses the speaker

_____ 4. When the Raven first says "Nevermore," the speaker takes this to be
   a. a prophecy
   b. the bird's name
   c. a message from Lenore
   d. the words of an evil spirit

_____ 5. The narrator guesses that the Raven says the single word "Nevermore" because
   a. his former master was an unhappy person
   b. he has been listening to the mourning of the narrator for Lenore
   c. he was originally kept as a pet by Lenore
   d. he has been taught this word by an enemy determined to torture the narrator

_____ 6. Near the end of the poem the speaker asks the Raven two questions to which the bird
   answers "Nevermore." These questions concern
   a. what will happen after death
   b. the success of the speaker's literary works
   c. Lenore's love for the speaker
   d. the bird's purpose in visiting the speaker

_____ 7. We can infer from the ending of the poem that
   a. the speaker will soon die
   b. the speaker will be reunited with Lenore
   c. the speaker will never escape his despair
   d. the speaker will make his sorrow the subject of a great poem

**Reading Skills and Strategies: Analyzing the Melodies of Language and
Hearing Sound Effects** *(20 points; 10 points each)*
On the line provided, write the letter of the *best* answer to each of the following items.

_____ 8. In which lines below are the underlined words an example of alliteration?
   a. "'Leave no black plume as a <u>token</u> of that lie thy soul hath <u>spoken!</u> / Leave my
      loneliness <u>unbroken!</u>—quit the bust above my door!'"
   b. "<u>Back</u> into the chamber <u>turning</u>, all my soul within me <u>burning</u>, / Soon again I heard
      a <u>tapping</u> somewhat louder than before."
   c. "What this <u>grim, ungainly, ghastly, gaunt,</u> and ominous bird of yore / Meant in croaking
      'Nevermore.'"
   d. "'On this home by Horror haunted—tell me truly, I <u>implore</u>— / Is there—*is* there
      <u>balm in Gilead</u>?—<u>tell me</u>—tell me, I implore!'"

_____ 9. Which word in the following passage is an example of onomatopoeia?
   "While I nodded, nearly napping, suddenly there came a tapping, / As of someone gently
   rapping, rapping at my chamber door—"
   a. tapping
   b. nodded
   c. napping
   d. suddenly

Literary Element: Sound Effects *(20 points; 10 points each)*
On the line provided, write the letter of the *best* answer to each of the following items.

_____ 10. Which of the following lines does **not** have internal rhyme?
   a. "And each separate dying ember wrought its ghost upon the floor."
   b. "Then this ebony bird beguiling my sad fancy into smiling"
   c. "Startled at the stillness broken by reply so aptly spoken"
   d. "'Surely,' said I, 'surely that is something at my window lattice'"

_____ 11. Which of the following rhyme schemes represents the end rhymes in this poem?
   a. *ababab*
   b. *abcbcd*
   c. *abcbbb*
   d. *abcdcc*

Written Response *(25 points)*

12. Edgar Allan Poe writes that the speaker in "The Raven" is driven by "a thirst for self-torture"
   (see Pupil's Edition page 287). On a separate sheet of paper, discuss the extent to which the
   speaker brings his suffering on himself and the extent to which it is caused by the bird and
   outward events. Support your ideas with at least two details from the poem.

SELECTION TEST

The Minister's Black Veil
Nathaniel Hawthorne

Pupil's Edition page 298

Comprehension *(30 points; 5 points each)*
On the line provided, write the letter of the *best* answer to each of the following items.

_____ 1. Mr. Hooper's sudden adoption of a black veil makes his congregation uneasy because
  a. they think he means to do them harm
  b. they can think of no explanation for his action
  c. it immediately reminds them of his sinfulness
  d. they believe he has had a terrible accident

_____ 2. After the end of services on the first Sunday that Mr. Hooper wears the black veil
  a. no one wants to walk beside Mr. Hooper or invite him to dinner
  b. the parishioners quickly adjust to Mr. Hooper's changed appearance
  c. two of the younger children start to laugh at the strange sight of Mr. Hooper in his veil
  d. Mr. Hooper goes directly home rather than greeting the parishioners in front of the church

_____ 3. After permanently adopting the black veil, Mr. Hooper
  a. ignores his responsibilities as a minister
  b. frequently weeps and flies into rages
  c. accuses his congregation of terrible sins
  d. tends his congregation with his usual care

_____ 4. The only individuals who readily call for Mr. Hooper are
  a. little children
  b. the family of a young woman who has died
  c. people who are facing imminent death
  d. the family of Hooper's fiancée, Elizabeth

_____ 5. When, at the funeral of a young woman, Mr. Hooper says that all people must be prepared for the moment when the veils will be removed from their faces,
  a. the corpse is heard to make a muffled affirmation
  b. the parishioners finally understand the significance of the veil
  c. no one fully understands what he means
  d. he astonishes the mourners by removing his own veil

_____ 6. "The Minister's Black Veil" is a parable mainly because
  a. the characters and setting in the story are fictitious
  b. it is based on a famous story from the Bible
  c. moral themes in the story are crucially important
  d. the lesson of the story is plainly stated at the end

Reading Skills and Strategies *(20 points; 10 points each)*
On the line provided, write the letter of the *best* answer to each of the following items.

Drawing Inferences

_____ 7. From Elizabeth's talk with Mr. Hooper, the reader can infer that
  a. Mr. Hooper is doomed to be lonely
  b. Mr. Hooper wants to end the relationship
  c. Elizabeth understands why Mr. Hooper wears the veil
  d. Elizabeth rejects Mr. Hooper only because she worries about a scandal

Understanding Archaisms

_____ **8.** Which of the following lines from "The Minister's Black Veil" contains an archaism?
a. "But many were made to quake ere they departed!"
b. "Do not desert me, though this veil must be between us here on earth."
c. "The cause of so much amazement may appear sufficiently slight."
d. "That mysterious emblem was never once withdrawn."

Literary Element: Symbol *(10 points; 5 points each)*
On the line provided, write the letter of the *best* answer to each of the following items.

18 _____ **9.** According to Mr. Hooper, the veil is a symbol of the way in which all people
a. are reluctant to see the world clearly
b. hide their innermost selves
c. are constantly aware of death's approach
d. try to alter their physical appearance

_____ **10.** Mr. Hooper chooses to look physically different from other people. This symbolic act is meant to
a. reveal how he is more sinful than other people
b. protect him from other people's sin
c. highlight his role as an agent of holiness
d. represent him as a prisoner of a condition shared by all people

Vocabulary *(20 points; 2 points each)*
Match the definition on the left with the Word to Own on the right. Write the letter of the Word to Own on the line provided.

_____ **11.** wickedness
_____ **12.** strong dislike
_____ **13.** determined
_____ **14.** wise; keenly perceptive
_____ **15.** signify
_____ **16.** conspicuous
_____ **17.** outward appearance
_____ **18.** thinking deeply or seriously
_____ **19.** something hidden or concealed
_____ **20.** believability

a. antipathy
b. iniquity
c. obscurity
d. ostentatious
e. pensively
f. plausibility
g. portend
h. resolute
i. sagacious
j. semblance

Written Response *(20 points)*

21. Hawthorne could have made the main character in this story a banker, a teacher, a shop-keeper, or a person with any other vocation. On a separate sheet of paper, discuss how the meaning of the story is affected by Hawthorne's decision to make the main character a minister. Support your opinion with at least two incidents from the story.

SELECTION TEST

The Quarter-Deck
Herman Melville   Pupil's Edition page 313

Comprehension *(30 points; 5 points each)*
On the line provided, write the letter of the *best* answer to each of the following items.

____ **1.** Ahab's quarter-deck speech engenders in most of the sailors
    a. a distrust of their captain
    b. enthusiasm for finding the white whale
    c. happy memories of previous whaling trips
    d. a demand for extra pay

____ **2.** Captain Ahab's ceremony on deck
    a. resembles a religious communion
    b. resembles a common maritime ritual
    c. represents an appeal to the spirit of Moby-Dick
    d. represents concern for the crew's spiritual welfare

____ **3.** Ahab nails the gold piece to the mast because
    a. he wants it to act as a good luck token
    b. he wants the men to remember the reward for sighting the whale
    c. he wants it to help him keep the objective of his quest clear in his own mind
    d. he wants to make a display of his vast wealth

____ **4.** Starbuck raises an objection to the pursuit of Moby-Dick because
    a. he is concerned that Moby-Dick will kill Ahab
    b. he fears that winter storms will endanger their return home
    c. he believes that whales should be protected rather than slaughtered
    d. he doesn't think the whale's oil will bring much money

____ **5.** When Ahab talks of the importance of breaking through pasteboard masks he is referring to the value of
    a. living action   **b.** visible objects   **c.** shared purpose   **d.** symbols

____ **6.** The three harpooners take part in Ahab's ceremony by
    a. drinking liquor from their harpoon sockets
    b. holding their harpoons over Ahab as he prays
    c. cutting the flesh of their forearms
    d. beating on their harpoons in a parody of native chanting

Reading Skills and Strategies: Drawing Inferences about Character
(20 points; 10 points each)
On the line provided, write the letter of the *best* answer to each of the following items.

____ **7.** From the clues in this passage, we can infer that Ahab's search for Moby-Dick is motivated by his desire to
    a. kill the most valuable of whales
    b. prove that he is a competent hunter
    c. obtain revenge for the loss of his leg
    d. obtain a large profit in whale oil

_____ 8. The descriptions of Starbuck enable readers to infer that he is
   a. reluctant to take risks
   b. devoted to the hunt
   c. uncertain and lacks commitment
   d. a rational thinker

Literary Element: Characterization *(10 points; 5 points each)*
On the line provided, write the letter of the *best* answer to each of the following items.

_____ 9. Which of the following details do **not** contribute to our understanding of Ahab's character?
   a. He allows himself to be seen walking on the deck during the day.
   b. He does not take note of Starbuck's request for God's help.
   c. He is able to excite the sailors with simple questions about pursuing a whale.
   d. He is not concerned about the financial success of the expedition.

_____ 10. When Starbuck murmurs, "God keep me!—keep us all!" Starbuck reveals his
   a. agreement with Ahab's goals
   b. regret at choosing the life of a sailor
   c. plans to encourage a shipboard mutiny
   d. horror at Ahab's apparent madness

Vocabulary *(20 points; 4 points each)*
On the line before each sentence, write the Word to Own that correctly completes each sentence.

imprecations   inscrutable   tacit   volition   rejoinder

_____ 11. After the leader asks the group to follow, he waits for their _____.

_____ 12. The villain's evil is beyond our understanding because his motives are _____.

_____ 13. Although we have never actually said anything to one another about it, we have a _____ agreement.

_____ 14. He fails, not from inadequate talent, but from a lack of _____ .

_____ 15. The prisoner leaves the courtroom amid the _____ of the angry crowd.

Written Response *(20 points)*

16. Ahab is a leader who manages to convert many followers to his cause. On a separate sheet of paper, describe at least three personal characteristics that enable Ahab to draw others into his single-minded quest. Discuss which of these characteristics are qualities of a leader who deserves devotion and loyalty. Use examples from the selection to support your ideas.

SELECTION TEST

from Moby-Dick
Herman Melville   Pupil's Edition page 313

Comprehension *(35 points; 5 points each)*
On the line provided, write the letter of the *best* answer to each of the following items.

_____ 1. Moby-Dick has become a legend among whalers because he is rumored to
    a. change shapes
    b. appear simultaneously in different oceans
    c. breathe out a poisonous vapor
    d. lead lost and damaged ships to safety

_____ 2. In his calamitous first encounter with Moby-Dick, Ahab
    a. uses his willpower to drive the whale away
    b. attacks the whale with a knife
    c. flees in fear from the whale's attack
    d. experiences a religious conversion

_____ 3. For some time after his tragic accident, Ahab manages to
    a. hide his vengeful obsession under a veneer of sanity
    b. openly share his feelings about his mishap
    c. avoid subsequent duties as a whaling captain
    d. transfer his anger with Moby-Dick to other whales

_____ 4. Which of the following is **not** one of the characteristics for which Moby-Dick is known?
    a. his evil intelligence
    b. his unusual song
    c. his great size
    d. his misshapen lower jaw

_____ 5. Which of the following statements is true of Ahab's madness?
    a. Madness can lead to an increase in compassion.
    b. Madness can make a person more powerful.
    c. Madness can unexpectedly disappear.
    d. Madness can lead a person to confusion and loss of focus.

_____ 6. In Ahab's mind, Moby-Dick represents
    a. the difficulties faced by all people who go to sea
    b. a creature of the natural world that is awe inspiring
    c. a creature with virtues Ahab wishes to acquire
    d. all evil that has ever opposed humankind

_____ 7. The ship can be read as a symbol because
    a. it is referred to time and again within each chapter
    b. it has a central place in our imagination as we read the story
    c. ships have always been symbols throughout much of literary history
    d. it has a meaning in itself and can also stand for something more than itself

Reading Skills and Strategies: Drawing Inferences about Character
(20 points; 10 points each)
On the line provided, write the letter of the *best* answer to each of the following items.

_____ 8. The reader can infer that Ahab is intelligent in that he seems
    a. to have a clear plan for revenge
    b. contemptuous of the whale
    c. to have adapted to his ivory leg
    d. to love the ocean

_____ 9. From what we, as readers, know about the narrator's participation in the whaling expedition, we can infer that the narrator's character is marked by
    a. irrationality
    b. reflectiveness
    c. violence
    d. optimism

Vocabulary *(20 points; 4 points each)*
Match the definiton on the left with the Word to Own on the right. Write the letter of the Word to Own on the line provided.

_____ 10. scholarly; well informed

_____ 11. fierce cruelty

_____ 12. disabled

_____ 13. unexpected sight or ghostlike figure that appears suddenly

_____ 14. everywhere at the same time

a. apparition

b. erudite

c. ferocity

d. incapacitated

e. ubiquitous

Written Response *(25 points)*

15. Power and truth often seem to stand in opposition to each other; what is powerful is usually too simplistic to be true and what is true is usually too ambiguous and complicated to be powerful. On a separate sheet of paper, discuss the ways in which Ahab acquires power over the crew. Consider whether any part of his power comes at the expense of seeing the truth. Use examples from the selection to support your ideas.

LITERARY ELEMENTS TEST

Poe's Symbols

On the line provided, write the letter of the *best* answer to each of the following items.
(10 points each)

_____ **1.** Symbols usually are connected to a story's
　　　　　a. theme
　　　　　b. length
　　　　　c. climax
　　　　　d. resolution

_____ **2.** All of the following can be symbols **except**
　　　　　a. an object
　　　　　b. a person
　　　　　c. a place
　　　　　d. a rhyme scheme

_____ **3.** The storm at the end of "The Fall of the House of Usher" symbolizes many things,
　　　　　including the
　　　　　a. narrator's anxiety
　　　　　b. house's deadly indifference
　　　　　c. bleak surrounding landscape
　　　　　d. hero's deep depression

_____ **4.** In general, symbols are
　　　　　a. recognizable only by the writer
　　　　　b. meaningless objects
　　　　　c. literary devices meant to confuse readers
　　　　　d. culturally agreed upon

_____ **5.** Which of the following is **not** true of symbols?
　　　　　a. A symbol is identified with something that is very different from it.
　　　　　b. A symbol is given little emphasis by the writer.
　　　　　c. The symbol and the thing identified with it share a similar quality.
　　　　　d. While a symbol suggests a wider meaning, it also represents itself.

_____ **6.** The "dull, dark, and soundless" autumn day described in the first paragraph of "The Fall of
　　　　　the House of Usher" symbolizes
　　　　　a. boredom
　　　　　b. blindness
　　　　　c. death
　　　　　d. deafness

_____ **7.** In "The Fall of the House of Usher," the deterioration of Roderick's mind is symbolized by his interest in
  a. dirges and painting
  b. dreams and music
  c. raptors and his sister's coffin
  d. statues and poetry

_____ **8.** In "The Fall of the House of Usher," Launcelot's escape from the dragon may symbolize
  a. Roderick's release from madness
  b. Madeline's falling on her brother
  c. Roderick's overcoming his fears
  d. the narrator's escape from the mansion

_____ **9.** In "The Raven," the raven may symbolize
  a. pain
  b. Lenore
  c. anger
  d. hope

_____ **10.** In "The Raven," Pallas represents
  a. beauty
  b. sadness
  c. wisdom
  d. death

LITERARY PERIOD TEST

The American Renaissance: A Literary Coming of Age

Applying Skills

This test asks you to use the language skills and strategies you have learned. Before you begin reading, take a minute to remember what you have learned about etymologies, drawing inferences, and point of view. Read the following letter that Herman Melville wrote to Nathaniel Hawthorne. Then, answer the questions that follow the letter.

June, 1851

My Dear Hawthorne—

 I should have been rumbling down to you in my pine-board chariot a long time ago, were it not that for some weeks past I have been more busy than you can well imagine,—out of doors,—building and patching and tinkering away in all directions. Besides, I had my crops to get in,—corn and potatoes (I hope to show you some famous ones by and by),—and many other things to attend to, all accumulating upon this one particular season. I work myself; and at night my bodily sensations are akin to those I have so often felt before, when a hired man, doing my day's work from sun to sun. But I mean to continue visiting you until you tell me that my visits are both supererogatory and <u>superfluous</u>. With no son of man do I stand upon any etiquette or ceremony, except the Christian ones of charity and honesty. . . .

 I began by saying that the reason I have not been to Lenox is this,—in the evening I feel completely done up, as the phrase is, and incapable of the long jolting to get to your house and back. In a week or so, I go to New York, to bury myself in a third-story room, and work and slave on my "Whale" [the original title of *Moby-Dick*] while it is driving through the press. *That* is the only way I can finish it now,—I am so pulled hither and thither by circumstances. The calm, the coolness, the silent grass-growing mood in which a man *ought* always to compose,—that, I fear, can seldom be mine. Dollars damn me; and the malicious Devil is forever grinning in upon me, holding the door ajar. My dear Sir, a <u>presentiment</u> is on me,—I shall at last be worn out and perish, like an old nutmeg-grater, grated to pieces by the constant <u>attrition</u> of the wood, that is, the nutmeg. What I feel most moved to write, that is banned,—it will not pay. Yet, altogether, write the *other* way I cannot. So the product is a final hash, and all my books are botches. I'm rather sore, perhaps, in this letter; but see my hand! four blisters on this palm, made by hoes and hammers within the last few days. It is a rainy morning; so I am indoors, and all work suspended. I feel cheerfully disposed, and therefore I write a little bluely. . . . If ever, my dear Hawthorne, in the eternal times that are to come, you and I shall sit down in Paradise, in some little shady corner by ourselves; and if we shall by any means be able to smuggle a basket of champagne there . . . and if we shall then cross our celestial legs in the celestial grass that is forever tropical, and strike our glasses and our heads together, till both musically ring in concert,—then, O my dear fellow-mortal, how shall we pleasantly discourse of all the things <u>manifold</u> which now so distress us,—when all the earth shall be but a reminiscence, yea, its final <u>dissolution</u> an antiquity. Then shall songs be composed as when wars are over: humorous, comic songs,— "Oh, when I lived in that queer little hole called the world," or, "Oh, when I toiled and sweated below," or, "Oh, when I knocked and was knocked in the fight"—yes, let us look forward to such things. Let us swear that, though now we sweat, yet it is because of the dry heat which is indispensable to the nourishment of the vine which is to bear the grapes that are to give us the champagne hereafter.

 But I was talking about the "Whale." As the fishermen say, "he's in his flurry" when I left him some three weeks ago. I'm going to take him by his jaw, however, before long, and finish him up in some fashion or other. What's the use of elaborating what, in its very essence, is so short-lived as a modern book? Though I wrote the Gospels in this century, I should die in the gutter.—I talk all about myself, and this is selfishness and egotism. Granted. But how help it? I am writing to you; I know little about you, but something about myself. So I write about myself,—at least to you. . . .

—H. Melville

Vocabulary Skills: New Words in Context *(20 points; 4 points each)*
Each of the following underlined words has also been underlined in the selection. Use context clues in the selection to help you determine each word's meaning. Then, on the line provided, write the letter of the word or phrase that *best* completes each sentence.

_____ **1.** A visit is <u>superfluous</u> if it is
    a. beyond what is required   **b.** welcome and pleasing   **c.** emotional

_____ **2.** A <u>presentiment</u> is a
    a. ceremonial gift   **b.** fearful anticipation   **c.** happy recollection

_____ **3.** <u>Attrition</u> of an object occurs when the object is
    a. connected to a crime   **c.** worn away by friction
    b. lost because of carelessness

_____ **4.** Things or circumstances are <u>manifold</u> when they are
    a. of many, varied kinds   **b.** obvious to all beholders   **c.** designed to mislead

_____ **5.** In the selection, the <u>dissolution</u> of earth refers to the earth's
    a. cruel indifference   **b.** basic evil   **c.** final extinction

---

Vocabulary

Tracing the Origins of Words *(20 points; 5 points each)*
Use the Latin words and definitions which follow to complete the chart below. In the middle column, write the Latin words, listed above the chart, which you think are related to each of the English words. In the right-hand column, write the meaning from the choices given below the chart.

currere = to run   *dis* = apart   *in* = not   *malus* = bad
pensare = to weigh   *rogare* = to ask   *super* = above

English Word	Latin Words of Origin	Meaning from List Below
6. supererogatory		
7. malicious		
8. discourse		
9. indispensable		

    a. doing "above" what is asked
    b. marked by such "weight" that it cannot be set aside
    c. marked by the desire to cause harm
    d. speaking on various subjects by "running" from one to the next

Comprehension *(20 points; 5 points each)*
On the line provided, write the letter of the *best* answer to each of the following items.

_____ **10.** Melville's main excuse for not visiting Hawthorne recently is that he
    a. has been working on his book **c.** has been occupied with farm and household work
    b. is envious of Hawthorne   **d.** is convinced that he has a fatal illness

_____ **11.** Melville is discouraged about writing because
    a. he is at a loss for a subject   **c.** his publisher has refused to read his manuscript
    b. his past mistakes torment him **d.** he cannot sell what he would like to write

_____ **12.** Melville feels that the best environment for a writer is
    a. the excitement of a big city   **c.** a lively, partylike atmosphere
    b. a workshop with other writers **d.** an atmosphere of peace and calm

_____ **13.** In speaking of the "Whale," Melville says, "What's the use of elaborating what, in its very essence, is so short-lived as a modern book?" From a contemporary perspective, what is ironic about Melville's comment?
    a. Melville spent a great deal of time writing his book.
    b. The book has become a long-lived classic.
    c. Much popular fiction is soon forgotten.
    d. *Moby-Dick* is an extremely long and complex book.

Reading Skills and Strategies: Drawing Inferences *(20 points; 10 points each)*

_____ **14.** What sort of friendship does Melville have with Hawthorne? From the following options, choose the one you think is the best response to this question. On a separate piece of paper, write the letter of the answer you choose, and briefly defend your choice. Use at least two examples from the letter to support your ideas.
    a. He enjoys writing letters to Hawthorne, but does not have time for a real friendship.
    b. Although he is cordial to Hawthorne, there is an underlying jealousy which colors everything about their relationship.
    c. He is close enough to Hawthorne to be completely honest with him.
    d. He needs Hawthorne to give him encouragement and financial support and therefore must maintain the friendship at any cost.

15. Melville makes several comments about his writing in this letter. What do the following comments imply about his attitude toward his work? On a separate piece of paper, explain what inferences you can draw from each passage. Remember to look at the context of the passage as you consider the implications.
    a. "So the product is a final hash, and all my books are botches."
    b. "I'm going to take him by his jaw, however, before long, and finish him up in some fashion or other."
    c. "Though I wrote the Gospels in this century, I should die in the gutter."

Literary Element: Point of View *(20 points)*

16. Since this is an actual letter, it is written in first person. However, even though the letter is personal, it contains ideas about outdoor labor, authorship, and eternity which are of general interest. On a separate sheet of paper, write a brief paragraph in which you agree or disagree with the following statement. Use at least two examples from the letter to support your ideas.

The ideas expressed in this letter are powerful because they were written in first-person point of view to a specific audience.

LITERARY PERIOD INTRODUCTION TEST

A New American Poetry
Whitman and Dickinson

Pupil's Edition page 342

On the line provided, write the letter of the *best* answer to each of the following items.
(10 points each)

_____ 1. An important similarity between Whitman and Dickinson is their
a. willingness to break away from literary conventions
b. need to support themselves by selling their works
c. obscurity during their lifetimes
d. rejection by their intended audience

_____ 2. Dickinson's poems flowed from her
a. rich internal life and close observation of nature
b. passionate embrace of democratic ideals
c. admiration and emulation of great narrative poetry
d. frustration over the constraints imposed on women

_____ 3. From the beginning, Whitman expected his poetry to be
a. praised by established American poets
b. carried like a message into the future
c. published and admired in Europe
d. unappreciated by the average reader

_____ 4. Dickinson did not achieve fame during her lifetime because
a. she hid her poetry from her family and friends
b. most of her friends discouraged her from becoming a poet
c. she believed poetry should never be published
d. most of her poetry was not published until after her death

_____ 5. Whitman's feelings about his own poems are *best* revealed by his
a. refusal to publish them until they had been approved by writers he admired
b. dissatisfaction with their wording and his constant efforts to revise them
c. belief that they were important enough to publish at his own expense
d. pursuit of other occupations, while regarding his poetry as a part-time activity

_____ 6. Whitman's style and technique are based on cadence, which is the
a. regular rhythm used in old ballads and epic poems
b. iambic pentameter used by William Shakespeare
c. use of exact rhymes and alliteration
d. rhythm and long sweeps of sound used by great speakers

_____ 7. Dickinson's poetry is noted for its emphasis on
a. purely emotional appeals to the reader
b. precise wording and unique poetic forms
c. ideas that readers can quickly and easily understand
d. thoughts that are acceptable in polite society

____ **8.** Whitman developed a free-verse style, which is
    a. the praise of democratic government and ideals
    b. poetry without predictable end rhyme or meter
    c. an attempt to state old ideas in a new way
    d. verse that uses new techniques from Europe

____ **9.** To highlight the ideas in her poems, Dickinson
    a. abandons all attempt at rhyme or metaphor
    b. uses the technique of cataloging
    c. uses carefully measured rhymes and meters
    d. makes references to classical philosophers

____ **10.** Which of the following statements *best* describes the influence of Dickinson and Whitman on later poets?
    a. Their development of vastly different but equally important personal styles has inspired generations of poets.
    b. Their poetry has appealed more to European than to American poets.
    c. They both wrote for themselves alone, without worrying about form or structure.
    d. Their poetry emphasizes that the only true purpose of writing is to move people to political action.

SELECTION TEST

I Hear America Singing
from **Song of Myself, 10, 33, and 52**
A Sight in Camp in the Daybreak Gray and Dim
Walt Whitman

Pupil's Edition pages 351–366

Comprehension *(30 points; 5 points each)*
On the line provided, write the letter of the *best* answer to each of the following items.

_____ 1. Which of the following is **not** true of the workers described in "I Hear America Singing"?
   a. They are singing one song that belongs to everyone.
   b. They seem happy in their various jobs.
   c. They each sing in a unique way.
   d. They are described as enjoying themselves outside of work.

_____ 2. In "Song of Myself," Number 10, the speaker describes the marriage of a trapper to an American Indian girl. In this section the speaker's position is *best* described as
   a. an interpreter who explains why this event is important
   b. an uninvolved spectator who has an attitude of neutrality
   c. a participant who focuses more on his feelings than on the event itself
   d. an observer who gives hints about his reactions through the selection of details

_____ 3. "Song of Myself," Number 33, presents heroes who
   a. are well-known by name to most Americans
   b. have fought in wars to secure democracy and freedom
   c. represent the valiant deeds of ordinary people
   d. find inspiration through poetry

_____ 4. When the speaker in "Song of Myself," Number 33, writes that agonies are a change of clothing, he means
   a. that every day brings both good and bad experiences
   b. that the speaker can take on the agonies of others like putting on clothes
   c. that the speaker wants to occasionally suffer so that the moments of joy will be more significant
   d. that agony is only a superficial emotion that does not affect the heart

_____ 5. In "A Sight in Camp in the Daybreak Gray and Dim," Whitman stresses the
   a. fierceness of the soldiers in opposing armies
   b. reasons behind the war between North and South
   c. hardships he endured as a nurse during the war
   d. connections between all individual people affected by the war

_____ 6. What aspect of the three soldiers' deaths is emphasized in the last stanza of "A Sight in Camp in the Daybreak Gray and Dim"?
   a. sacrifice   **c.** meaninglessness
   b. mutilation   **d.** beauty

Reading Skills and Strategies
On the line provided, write the letter of the *best* answer to each of the following items.

Summarizing a Text *(10 points)*

_____ 7. In "Song of Myself," Number 10, the poem ends with an image of a gun leaning against the wall in the corner. This detail, when read in the context of the rest of the poem, seems to indicate that the speaker
   a. feels threatened by the runaway
   b. is cautious in spite of apparent goodwill
   c. will give the gun to the runaway slave
   d. trusts the runaway

Comparing Themes Across Texts *(10 points)*

_____ 8. What theme is evident in the Whitman poems that you have read?
   a. There is some common thread that runs among all people.
   b. People should delight in their thoughts and spirit.
   c. Once people have died, they are forgotten.
   d. The natural world is becoming corrupt.

Literary Elements: Catalog and Free Verse *(20 points; 5 points each)*
On the line provided, write the letter of the *best* answer to each of the following items.

_____ 9. "I Hear America Singing" is a catalog because it
   a. lists related categories of people and events
   b. invites readers to choose items from a list
   c. organizes details about the tools needed in different trades
   d. appears in a volume describing the habits of Americans

_____ 10. How could you demonstrate the cadence of Whitman's poetry?
   a. Read the poetry aloud to show how your voice rhythmically rises and falls.
   b. Point out how its images convey meaning.
   c. Explain the theme of kinship that underlies each line.
   d. Show how each line has end rhyme.

_____ 11. Which of the following passages from "Song of Myself," Number 33, is the *best* example of assonance?
   a. "I clutch the rails of the fence, my gore dribs . . ."
   b. "Agonies are one of my changes of garments . . ."
   c. "Death chasing it up and down the storm . . ."
   d. "How the silent old-faced infants and the lifted sick . . ."

_____ 12. Which of the following images from "A Sight in Camp in the Daybreak Gray and Dim" is **not** a visual image?
   a. "in the daybreak gray and dim"   **c.** "flesh all sunken about the eyes"
   b. "in the cool fresh air"   **d.** "ample brownish woolen blanket"

Written Response *(30 points)*

13. In "Song of Myself," Number 33, Whitman says that he understands people by imaginatively participating in their experiences. On a separate sheet of paper, discuss how Whitman's poetry encourages readers to empathetically become participants in the experiences and images described. Use details from at least two poems to support your ideas.

SELECTION TEST

OPEN
BOOK

Poetry of Emily Dickinson

Pupil's Edition pages 374–396

Comprehension *(45 points; 5 points each)*
On the line provided, write the letter of the *best* answer to each of the following items.

_____ 1. In "Heart! We will forget him!" and "I died for Beauty—but was scarce," Dickinson shows her gift for
  a. using poetry to solve the major problems of life
  b. setting up a dialogue between contrasting impulses
  c. incorporating formal religious beliefs into poems
  d. describing the deathbed agonies of a loved one

_____ 2. In "If you were coming in the Fall," Dickinson writes "I'd toss it yonder, like a Rind." In this passage the "it" refers to the speaker's
  a. love   **c.** talent
  b. life   **d.** fame

_____ 3. In "The Soul selects her own Society," what metaphor is used to talk about the soul?
  a. The soul is like a woman in a house.
  b. The soul is like a kneeling empress.
  c. The soul is like a stone monument.
  d. The soul is like a door that is shut.

_____ 4. In "Some keep the Sabbath going to Church," Dickinson writes that the bobolink is the choir member in her church. This is a use of
  a. irony   **c.** slant rhyme
  b. metaphor   **d.** paradox

_____ 5. What is making the speaker metaphorically inebriated in "I taste a liquor never brewed"?
  a. books of poetry
  b. summer days
  c. thoughts of love
  d. spiritual meditation

_____ 6. In "Much Madness is divinest Sense," Dickinson writes that madness is sense. This type of statement is called a
  a. paradox   **c.** pun
  b. metaphor   **d.** slant rhyme

_____ 7. The predominant theme of "Apparently with no surprise" is *best* stated as
  a. all happiness will end in tragedy
  b. God has no control over evil
  c. death is a natural part of God's plan
  d. the sun is indifferent to God's will

_____ 8. Many people consider Dickinson to have been a hermit because
  a. she did not tolerate ideas that were different from hers
  b. her poetry harshly criticizes society, especially urban life
  c. she lived a secluded life in a small town
  d. her poems show a lack of awareness of reality

_____ 9. Dickinson's particular contribution to poetry can *best* be described as exemplifying how to
   a. share ideas with a wide audience
   b. stress thoughts instead of feelings
   c. edit work to make it verbose
   d. express ideas in original ways

Reading Skills and Strategies: Summarizing a Text *(12 points; 6 points each)*
On the line provided, write the letter of the *best* answer to each of the following items.

_____ 10. In "Because I could not stop for death," the speaker
   a. does not take time to mourn a relative's death
   b. resists dying
   c. accompanies Death to a tomb
   d. observes Death taking a friend

_____ 11. The speaker of "Success is counted sweetest" asserts that
   a. people who win a battle really enjoy the spoils of war
   b. only poets understand the meaning of success
   c. the people who succeed are the ones who count success sweetest
   d. those who do not succeed best understand the meaning of success

Literary Element: Slant Rhyme *(18 points; 6 points each)*
On the line provided, write the letter of the *best* answer to each of the following items.

_____ 12. Which of the following pairs of words is **not** a slant rhyme?
   a. Gate / Mat
   b. today / victory
   c. firm / room
   d. scarce / lain

_____ 13. Dickinson's use of slant rhyme indicates her
   a. desire to use language that will make readers notice the words
   b. preference for words that sound best even if they don't make sense
   c. unfamiliarity with the standard conventions of poetry due to her reclusiveness
   d. ability to find words whose sounds echo the meanings

_____ 14. Slant rhyme achieves some of the same effects as Dickinson's occasional choice of formal words (such as *interposed* in "I heard a Fly buzz—when I died"). What is the effect common to both of these techniques?
   a. They remind us of earlier traditions in poetry that Dickinson draws upon.
   b. They allow us to ignore the specific words and concentrate on the general meaning.
   c. They remind us of Dickinson's solitude.
   d. They awaken our attention by seeming slightly out of harmony.

Written Response *(25 points)*

15. Both "Heart! We will forget him!" and "If you were coming in the Fall" concern love. On a separate sheet of paper, write a paragraph describing what you think Dickinson is saying about love. Use details from both poems to support your ideas.

THE AMERICAN LANGUAGE

A Period of Vocabulary Growth

Pupil's Edition page 398

On the line provided, write the letter of the *best* answer to each of the following items.
(10 points each)

_____ 1. One characteristic of the language of the backwoods was its
   a. use of precise syntax
   b. use of exaggerated slang and exuberant bragging
   c. closeness to British English
   d. blending of English and American Indian languages

_____ 2. The Crockett almanacs are notable because they
   a. damaged Davy Crockett's political career
   b. set a new standard for American language
   c. brought backwoods language into Eastern homes
   d. supplied vital information about Tennessee

_____ 3. In the first half of the nineteenth century, Americans called for an independent literature
      that would
   a. capture the distinctive American landscape and culture
   b. deal with the great themes of world literature
   c. copy the style and themes of English literature
   d. set a standard for national American usage

_____ 4. Both Mark Twain and Walt Whitman made use of
   a. the King's English
   b. standard literary American language
   c. the language of American cities
   d. American vernacular

_____ 5. From the political campaigns of the nineteenth century, we have inherited
   a. widespread use of the stump style
   b. colorful words and phrases coined by politicians
   c. the use of exaggerated language
   d. the tradition of long, rambling speeches

_____ 6. Newspapers flourished in the late 1830s because
   a. improved printing methods made them cheap and profitable
   b. they were vastly improved in quality
   c. more and more people knew how to read
   d. the American population had increased greatly

_____ 7. In the late 1830s, newspapers tried to attract readers by
   a. providing comprehensive news coverage
   b. including contests and puzzles
   c. offering special subscription rates
   d. using colorful language

____ **8.** The language used in newspapers often involved the
   a. use of alliteration and assonance
   b. invention of whimsical abbreviations
   c. invention of adjectives and adverbs
   d. use of complex sentences

____ **9.** The immigrant group that had the greatest effect on the American language during the mid-nineteenth century was
   a. Irish
   b. British
   c. German
   d. Polish

____ **10.** The language that provided the greatest number of loanwords to the American language in the nineteenth century was
   a. German
   b. Spanish
   c. Polish
   d. Russian

LITERARY ELEMENTS TEST

Free Verse
Slant Rhyme

Pupil's Edition page 355
Pupil's Edition page 380

On the line provided, write the letter of the *best* answer to each of the following items.
(10 points each)

_____ 1. All of the following elements are characteristic of free verse **except**
    a. rhyme
    b. imagery
    c. alliteration
    d. parallel structure

_____ 2. Cadence is the
    a. use of regular rhyme schemes to emphasize theme
    b. flow of words that have a rhythmic rise and fall in sound
    c. rhyming of two or more words at the end of a line
    d. fixed pattern of unaccented and accented syllables

_____ 3. Which of the following quotations from "I Hear America Singing" contains the *best* example of assonance?
    a. ". . . what belongs to him or her . . . "
    b. "The wood-cutter's song . . . "
    c. ". . . strong melodious songs . . . "
    d. ". . . the party of young fellows . . . "

_____ 4. Parallel structure is the repetition of all of the following **except**
    a. rhythms
    b. sentences
    c. words
    d. clauses

_____ 5. All of the following are unusual elements of Walt Whitman's free verse **except**
    a. foreign terms
    b. invented words
    c. satirical commentary
    d. American slang

_____ 6. Instead of exact rhyme, Emily Dickinson sometimes uses
    a. free verse
    b. slant rhyme
    c. couplets
    d. quatrains

_____ 7. Which of the following word pairs from Dickinson's poems contains the *best* example of slant rhyme?
    a. Drawers / fuse
    b. pausing / nation
    c. today / Victory
    d. length / between

_____ **8.** All of the following are alternative terms for slant rhyme **except**
    a. approximate rhyme
    b. lopsided rhyme
    c. half rhyme
    d. off rhyme

_____ **9.** Why might Dickinson have used the slant rhyme "Door" and "more" in "The Soul selects her own Society"?
    a. to draw readers' attention to the open door
    b. to stress that the inner self rejects the majority
    c. to establish a regular rhyme scheme
    d. to explain the naturalistic language in the poem

_____ **10.** One reason that poets use slant rhyme is to
    a. match words with exactly identical sounds
    b. create a soothing, rhythmic effect
    c. practice alliteration
    d. emphasize certain words

LITERARY PERIOD TEST

A New American Poetry: Whitman and Dickinson

Applying Skills

This test asks you to use the language skills and strategies you have learned. Before you begin reading, take a minute to remember what you know about summarizing a text, comparing themes, and free verse. Read the following two poems carefully. Then, answer the questions that follow.

Aboard at a Ship's Helm
by Walt Whitman

Aboard at a ship's helm,
A young steersman steering with care.
Through fog on a sea-coast <u>dolefully</u> ringing,
An ocean-bell—O a warning bell, rock'd by the waves.
O you give good notice indeed, you bell by the sea-reefs ringing,
Ringing, ringing, to warn the ship from its wreck-place.

For as on the alert O steersman, you mind the loud <u>admonition</u>,
The bows turn, the freighted ship <u>tacking</u> speeds away under her gray sails,
The beautiful and noble ship with all her precious wealth speeds away gayly
      and safe.
But O the ship, the immortal ship! O ship aboard the ship!
Ship of the body, ship of the soul, voyaging, voyaging, voyaging.

The Moon is distant from the Sea
by Emily Dickinson

The Moon is distant from the Sea—
And yet, with Amber Hands—
She leads Him—<u>docile</u> as a Boy—
Along appointed Sands—

He never misses a <u>Degree</u>—
Obedient to Her Eye
He comes just so far—toward the Town—
Just so far—goes away—

Oh, Signor, Thine, the Amber Hand—
And mine—the distant Sea—
Obedient to the least command
Thine eye impose on me—

Vocabulary Skills: New Words in Context *(25 points; 5 points each)*
Each of the following underlined words has also been underlined in the poems. Use context clues in the poems to help you determine each word's meaning. Then, on the lines provided, write the letter of the word or phrase that *best* completes each sentence.

_____ **1.** In the Whitman poem, a bell is ringing <u>dolefully</u>, or _____.
    a. cheerily   **b.** mournfully   **c.** hopelessly

_____ **2.** The bell's <u>admonition</u> _____ sailors about a nearby reef.
    a. puzzles   **b.** warns   **c.** scolds

_____ **3.** When applied to a ship, <u>tacking</u> means _____.
    a. suddenly sinking   **b.** moving toward land   **c.** changing direction

_____ **4.** In the Dickinson poem, the sea is called <u>docile</u> because it is _____ to the moon.
    a. helpful   **b.** hostile   **c.** submissive

_____ **5.** The <u>Degree</u> referred to in the Dickinson poem is an _____.
    a. assigned direction   **b.** official rank   **c.** academic title

Comprehension *(25 points; 5 points each)*
On the line provided, write the letter of the *best* answer to each of the following items.

_____ **6.** Both the Whitman poem and the Dickinson poem are examples of poetry that
    a. abandons conventional rhyme and meter
    b. stresses the pangs of unrequited love
    c. praises the work of ordinary people
    d. captures the cadence of public speakers

_____ **7.** In the first stanza of the Whitman poem, the speaker describes
    a. the fear in the heart of an inexperienced sailor
    b. a rocky shore that inevitably wrecks ships
    c. a fog-bound ship approaching a reef
    d. the deceptive nature of many warnings

_____ **8.** In the last two lines of the Whitman poem, the speaker suggests that
    a. all dangers can be avoided if we heed the warnings
    b. ocean voyages are filled with excitement
    c. the ship is loaded with pirated gold
    d. the human soul faces a difficult life journey

_____ **9.** In the Dickinson poem, the moon and the sea are metaphors for
    a. uncaring and cold natural forces
    b. a strict teacher and a frightened pupil
    c. a loved one and the speaker
    d. the effect of a rising and falling tide

_____ **10.** An example of slant rhyme in the Dickinson poem is
    a. Hands—Sands
    b. Eye—away
    c. Sea—me
    d. Along—appointed

Reading Skills and Strategies
Summarizing a Text (15 points)

11. From the following options, choose the one you think is the best summary statement of "The Moon is distant from the Sea." On the lines provided, write the letter of the answer you choose, and briefly defend your choice. Use at least two examples from Dickinson's poem to support your ideas.
    a. Just as the sea is "led" by the moon, so is the speaker led by the sea.
    b. Just as the sea is "led" by the moon, so is the speaker led by God.
    c. Just as the sea is "led" by the moon, so is the speaker led by an inner direction.
    d. Just as the sea is "led" by the moon, so is the speaker led by his or her father.

_____

_____

_____

_____

_____

_____

Comparing Themes Across Texts (15 points)

12. On the lines provided, write a brief paragraph in which you agree or disagree with the following statement. Be sure to support your opinion with at least two examples from the poems.

    Both poems deal with the theme of finding direction in life, but the Whitman poem envisions personal direction coming from within, whereas the Dickinson poem envisions direction coming from an external source.

_____

_____

_____

_____

_____

_____

_____

_____

_____

Literary Element: Free Verse *(20 points)*

13. What elements of free verse do you find in "Aboard at a Ship's Helm"? In the left-hand side of the following chart, identify three elements of free verse used by Whitman. Then, give an example of each element from the poem.

Element of Free Verse	Example

LITERARY PERIOD INTRODUCTION TEST

The Rise of Realism
The Civil War and Postwar Period

Pupil's Edition page 408

On the line provided, write the letter of the *best* answer to each of the following items.
(10 points each)

_____ 1. Having seen the horrors of the Civil War firsthand as a Union camp hospital volunteer, Walt Whitman
   a. was still able to retain an optimistic view of the character of Americans
   b. shifted from optimism to pessimism as a result of witnessing the carnage
   c. was overcome with disillusionment after the Battle of Bull Run
   d. was devastated by the death of his wounded brother

_____ 2. Which of the following statements about Herman Melville's response to the Civil War is **not** true?
   a. He believed the fighting during the war to be both heroic and futile.
   b. He wrote a novel about the war based on his visits to battlefields.
   c. His poems about the war reveal his belief in humanity's intrinsic evil.
   d. His poems about the war show a respect for the soldiers of both sides.

_____ 3. Because few major American writers experienced the Civil War firsthand,
   a. they were regarded as cowardly and unpatriotic by both North and South
   b. all of the important poetry and fiction created came from newspaper accounts
   c. no realistic accounts of the soldiers' experiences were written
   d. very little important poetry and fiction emerged directly from this war

_____ 4. A great novel of the Civil War was not written until long after the war had ended because
   a. the proper vehicle for such strong material, the realistic novel, had not yet been fully developed in the United States
   b. it was necessary for the intensity of the country's emotions to subside before such a realistic novel would be accepted by the American public
   c. the writers who viewed the war firsthand lacked the skill to adequately describe what was really happening on the battlefields
   d. no American writers of the period were willing to risk visiting the battle sites during the war

_____ 5. The literary form in which heroes and heroines live idealistic lives beyond the level of everyday life is called the
   a. naturalistic novel
   b. psychological novel
   c. realistic novel
   d. romantic novel

_____ 6. After the Civil War, a generation of writers known as realists sought to
   a. use romance not only to entertain readers, but also to reveal truths to them
   b. accurately portray real life without filtering it through Romanticism
   c. provide an idealistic view of life in order to heal the wounds of the war
   d. accurately portray behavior without seeking explanations for it

_____ 7. Although regional writers realistically portrayed speech patterns and mannerisms of a relatively small geographical area, they
  a. were even more realistic in showing human life as a losing battle
  b. were primarily interested in the impact of social forces on individuals
  c. were often unrealistic in writing about character and social environment
  d. tended to view regional customs with humor and skepticism

_____ 8. The behavior of the characters created by some naturalist writers
  a. was crude, instinctive, and subject to the natural laws of the universe
  b. may have been foolhardy, but usually resulted in happy endings
  c. was usually much more melodramatic than realistic
  d. demonstrated that humans have control over their own destinies

_____ 9. Which of the following statements *best* describes the psychological novels of Henry James?
  a. They show people driven by animal-like instincts.
  b. They open the inner mind to the techniques of fiction.
  c. They contrast innocent Europeans with sophisticated Americans.
  d. They all take place in the United States.

_____ 10. The writings of an ironist may typically
  a. examine human behavior under pressure
  b. examine social institutions with the aim of reforming them
  c. juxtapose human pretensions with the indifference of the universe
  d. demonstrate how the universe helps people achieve their desires

SELECTION TEST

from The Narrative of the Life of Frederick Douglass
Frederick Douglass   Pupil's Edition page 425

Comprehension *(35 points; 5 points each)*
On the line provided, write the letter of the *best* answer to each of the following items.

_____ **1.** During the course of the selection, Douglass shows how he
    a. is consumed by fear
    b. is reduced from defiance to submission
    c. moves from fear to defiance
    d. remains defiant throughout

_____ **2.** Which of the following statements is **not** true about Douglass at the conclusion of the selection?
    a. He regularly suffers physical abuse from white men.
    b. He is still enslaved.
    c. He vows that he is a slave in form only.
    d. He regains his sense of freedom and dignity.

_____ **3.** Douglass walks to Master Thomas's store to
    a. plot revenge
    b. visit friends
    c. seek help
    d. recover from his injuries

_____ **4.** Sandy advises Douglass to carry a root that will
    a. make Covey a more humane, compassionate person
    b. secure his freedom if the root is never removed from his pocket
    c. heal the wounds incurred during whippings
    d. make it impossible for any white man to whip him

_____ **5.** Why does Douglass think the root may bring him good luck?
    a. When he returns to Covey's place, he is given his freedom.
    b. Covey ignored him after he returned.
    c. Covey could not find him in the cornfield.
    d. Covey treats him kindly upon his return.

_____ **6.** When Covey tries to bind Douglass's legs with a rope, Douglass
    a. bows down and begs Covey for mercy
    b. fights back by grabbing Covey by the throat
    c. escapes and runs away to St. Michael's
    d. asks other people for help

_____ **7.** When Covey calls out for Bill to help him subdue Douglass, Bill
    a. refuses to intervene
    b. will not help unless Covey pays him
    c. immediately tackles Douglass
    d. helps Douglass tie up Covey

Literary Element: Douglass's Metaphors *(20 points; 10 points each)*
On the line provided, write the letter of the *best* answer to each of the following items.

_____ 8. Which of the following sets of images is used in Douglass's metaphor at the conclusion
of the selection?
a. embers, a whip, and the arm of slavery
b. a whip, a tomb, and heaven
c. embers, a tomb, and heaven
d. a tomb, a bloody arm, and an irritated wound

_____ 9. The extended metaphor represents
a. freedom and the abolition movement
b. rebirth and resurrection
c. youth and beauty
d. Douglass's decreasing willpower

Vocabulary *(20 points; 2 points each)*
Indicate whether the following pairs of words are synonyms or antonyms by writing an *S* or an *A*
on the line provided.
_____ **10.** intimated : proclaimed
_____ **11.** comply : obey
_____ **12.** interpose : withdraw
_____ **13.** solemnity : lightness
_____ **14.** render : make
_____ **15.** singular : remarkable
_____ **16.** attributed : dissociated
_____ **17.** curry : groom
_____ **18.** expiring : beginning
_____ **19.** afforded : provided

Written Response *(25 points)*

20. On a separate sheet of paper, write one paragraph that describes how Douglass is mistreated
and how he responds to this abuse. Support your ideas with at least three examples from the
selection.

SELECTION TEST

A Pair of Silk Stockings
Kate Chopin

Pupil's Edition page 436

Comprehension *(50 points; 5 points each)*
On the line provided, write the letter of the *best* answer to each of the following items.

_____ 1. Mrs. Sommers initially thinks that a wise use of her fifteen dollars would be to spend the money on
   a. kid gloves for herself
   b. a nutritious lunch
   c. clothes for her children
   d. a matinee at the theater

_____ 2. At the beginning of the story, Mrs. Sommers is characterized as a
   a. dutiful, careful parent
   b. neglectful mother
   c. flighty, irresponsible person
   d. cheerful person

_____ 3. Which of the following statements is true of Mrs. Sommers's past?
   a. She was known for wearing perfectly tailored ensembles.
   b. Her husband deserted her.
   c. Her parents usually provided financial assistance.
   d. She had experienced better days.

_____ 4. Mrs. Sommers is initially drawn to the silk stockings
   a. when she realizes she is touching them as she waits to begin shopping
   b. because she has always worn them and needed a new pair
   c. because the price is too good to resist
   d. when she sees them in a shop window

_____ 5. After Mrs. Sommers buys the stockings, what is her next purchase?
   a. silk undergarments
   b. a pair of boots
   c. two magazines
   d. shoes for her children

_____ 6. What other luxuries does Mrs. Sommers indulge in?
   a. a gallery visit and a newspaper
   b. a new hat and a play
   c. a meal at a nice restaurant and a play
   d. a pair of new gloves and a box of chocolates

_____ 7. Mrs. Sommers's new clothes make her feel
   a. guilty and ashamed of her selfishness
   b. fearful of her family's reaction
   c. self-assured, as if she belongs among the well dressed
   d. like going dancing every day

_____ **8.** At the matinee, Mrs. Sommers
    a. is distracted by guilty thoughts about her spending spree
    b. thoroughly enjoys the performance
    c. departs early because she dislikes the performance
    d. decides to become an actress

_____ **9.** One explanation for Mrs. Sommers's spending spree is that she
    a. thinks it won't matter
    b. is acting on impulse
    c. has plenty of money left at home
    d. has saved for the occasion

_____ **10.** As she rides home on the cable car, Mrs. Sommers
    a. is satisfied and peaceful
    b. feels a wave of remorse
    c. thinks about her childhood
    d. longs for escape from her life

Vocabulary *(20 points; 2 points each)*
For each of the sentences below, select the Word to Own that *best* completes the sentence. Write the Word to Own on the line provided.

judicious	veritable	laborious	fastidious	gaudy
appreciable	acute	reveling	preposterous	poignant

_____ **11.** When fall arrives, the forest is covered by a _____ roof of vibrant colors.

_____ **12.** She experiences _____ pangs of guilt upon recalling how rude she had been to her cousin.

_____ **13.** The difference between what the land sold for and the original purchase price is _____.

_____ **14.** Mimi drives away from the lot, _____ in owning her first brand-new car.

_____ **15.** The curtain rises on a _____ set, complete with outlandish colors and extravagant lighting.

_____ **16.** The cautious accountant uses a _____ approach when hiring new employees.

_____ **17.** The demanding teacher maintains her _____ standards for her students.

_____ **18.** The _____ photograph of mother and child brings tears to the grandfather's eyes.

_____ **19.** After the _____ process of setting the year's budget, Mr. Jones is ready for a break.

_____ **20.** Under the circumstances, the idea of the team's winning a national title seems _____.

Written Response *(30 points)*

21. Why does Mrs. Sommers spend the fifteen dollars in the way she does rather than in the way she had planned? On a separate sheet of paper, write one paragraph explaining your opinion. Support your ideas with at least two examples from the short story.

SELECTION TEST

from Life on the Mississippi
Mark Twain   Pupil's Edition page 452

Comprehension *(25 points; 5 points each)*
On the line provided, write the letter of the *best* answer to each of the following items.

_____ 1. What is Twain reacting to when he declares that he hasn't enough brains to be a pilot so he'll become a roustabout instead?
- **a.** another pilot's threat to throw him through the window for offering unsolicited advice
- **b.** Mr. Bixby's insistence that he must learn the shoal soundings and marks
- **c.** his inability to learn the names of buildings along the river
- **d.** the damage he had done to the boat by allowing it to run over a bluff reef

_____ 2. Why does Twain stay in the pilothouse when Mr. W— takes the wheel?
- **a.** Mr. W— asked him to stay.
- **b.** He wants to learn from Mr. W—.
- **c.** He thinks that Mr. W— will need someone to tell him where the boat is.
- **d.** He doesn't have anything else to do.

_____ 3. Twain gets a lesson in water-reading by
- **a.** steering the boat past a reef under Mr. Bixby's tutelage
- **b.** reciting shoals and marks by memory
- **c.** calling out marks at night
- **d.** watching Mr. W— at the wheel

_____ 4. Which one of the following events indicates to Mr. Bixby that Twain is making progress in his apprenticeship?
- **a.** Mr. Bixby allows Twain to run several miles of the river by himself.
- **b.** Twain learns the names of all the landmarks along the river.
- **c.** Twain learns the shape of the river from St. Louis to New Orleans.
- **d.** Twain differentiates between a bluff reef and a wind reef to Bixby's satisfaction.

_____ 5. When Twain states, "All the grace, the beauty, the poetry had gone out of the majestic river!" he
- **a.** has wearied of Mr. Bixby's "learning" and wants to become a roustabout
- **b.** has come into a fog so thick that he is unable to see the river or its banks
- **c.** bemoans the fact that his mastery of the river has come at a cost
- **d.** has grown tired of the river and wants to leave to pursue his writing

Reading Skills and Strategies: Identifying Comic Devices *(15 points; 5 points each)*
On the line provided, write the letter of the *best* answer to each of the following items.

_____ 6. Which of the following is an example of hyperbole used in the selection?
- **a.** Twain's comparison of the river to a book
- **b.** Twain's exclamation that when he learns the shape of the river, he will be capable of raising the dead
- **c.** Twain's protests that he'll never be able to learn the river's shape
- **d.** Twain's declaration that the river has lost its beauty

_____ **7.** Why is Twain's gun metaphor a comic and apt description of Mr. Bixby?
   a. Mr. Bixby is constantly exploding with anger and sadness.
   b. Mr. Bixby likes guns more than boats.
   c. Twain dislikes Mr. Bixby intensely.
   d. It suits Mr. Bixby's quick wit and temper.

_____ **8.** Twain's statement that he stayed behind with Mr. W— as a matter of convenience is an example of
   a. humorous understatement
   b. comic metaphor
   c. hyperbole
   d. simile

Literary Element: Extended Metaphor *(10 points; 5 points each)*
On the line provided, write the letter of the *best* answer to each of the following items.

_____ **9.** Which of the following is an example in the selection of an extended metaphor?
   a. Twain's comparison of Bixby to a smoothbore gun
   b. Bixby's comparison of Twain to a roustabout
   c. Bixby's comparison of a bluff to a wind reef
   d. Twain's comparison of the river to a house

_____ **10.** When Twain compares the river to a book, he implies the river is
   a. boring
   b. ever-changing and readable
   c. impossible to judge by its cover
   d. written by many authors

Vocabulary *(20 points; 2 points each)*
Match the definition on the left with the Word to Own on the right. Write the letter of the Word to Own on the line provided.

_____ **11.** to settle down
_____ **12.** empty
_____ **13.** lifeless
_____ **14.** doubts; worries
_____ **15.** self-satisfaction
_____ **16.** gloomy; dark
_____ **17.** calmly
_____ **18.** mildly
_____ **19.** kindness
_____ **20.** endless

   a. inanimate
   b. complacency
   c. subside
   d. interminable
   e. serenely
   f. benevolence
   g. misgivings
   h. blandly
   i. void
   j. somber

Written Response *(30 points)*

21. Based on this excerpt, how do you think Twain feels after he achieves his goal of becoming a riverboat pilot? On a separate sheet of paper, write one paragraph describing how he might feel. Support your ideas with at least two examples from the selection.

SELECTION TEST

An Occurrence at Owl Creek Bridge
Ambrose Bierce   **Pupil's Edition page 467**

Comprehension *(35 points; 5 points each)*
On the line provided, write the letter of the *best* answer to each of the following items.

_____ 1. Which one of the following statements about Peyton Farquhar is true?
   a. He betrayed the Confederate forces.
   b. Federal troops shot at him repeatedly.
   c. He was tricked by a Federal spy.
   d. He was a loner who had no family.

_____ 2. What interrupts Farquhar's thoughts about his wife and children?
   a. the ticking of his watch
   b. a train barreling toward the bridge
   c. a hail of bullets
   d. the arrival of Confederate troops

_____ 3. While Farquhar is under water, he thinks he's going to die but
   a. the current is so strong the ropes break
   b. the soldiers rescue him
   c. the river carries him to safety
   d. his hands seem to work independently of his will and free him

_____ 4. The Union soldiers are generally portrayed as
   a. merciless and deceptive
   b. benevolent and forgiving
   c. honorable and friendly
   d. selfish and distracted

_____ 5. After the board is kicked out from under him, Farquhar experiences
   a. an intense sharpening of his senses
   b. despair and grief
   c. a surprising joy and relief
   d. nothing

_____ 6. After Farquhar appears to have escaped from the gunfire while in the river, he
   a. is too exhausted to swim
   b. lands on a bank and runs through the woods
   c. is picked up by a passing riverboat
   d. is recaptured

_____ 7. The surprise ending of the story reveals that Farquhar's actual fate was
   a. a last-minute reprieve
   b. a successful escape
   c. death by drowning
   d. death by hanging

Literary Element: Point of View *(20 points; 10 points each)*
On the line provided, write the letter of the *best* answer to each of the following items.

_____ 8. When Farquhar hears his watch ticking with an exaggerated intensity, Bierce is using the point of view known as
   a. second-person limited
   b. third-person limited
   c. objective
   d. subjective

_____ 9. Which of the following *best* reflects the use of the omniscient point of view?
   a. The writer objectively describes the scene at the plantation.
   b. The writer focuses only on Farquhar and his thoughts and feelings.
   c. The narrator reports that the gray-clad horseman was a Federal scout.
   d. The narrator gives a first-person account of the events.

Vocabulary *(20 points; 2 points each)*
Match the definition on the left with the Word to Own on the right. Write the letter of the Word to Own on the line provided.

_____ 10. central
_____ 11. harmful; evil
_____ 12. guard; sentry
_____ 13. became impatient
_____ 14. dismaying
_____ 15. respect
_____ 16. scrape
_____ 17. regular back-and-forth movement
_____ 18. dangerous
_____ 19. circular movement

   a. sentinel
   b. deference
   c. chafed
   d. perilous
   e. oscillation
   f. pivotal
   g. appalling
   h. gyration
   i. abrasion
   j. malign

Written Response *(25 points)*

20. Throughout the story, Bierce provides hints about the real nature of Farquhar's fate. On a separate sheet of paper, write one paragraph describing how Bierce hints at the truth. Support your ideas with at least two examples from the story.

SELECTION TEST

A Mystery of Heroism
Stephen Crane

Pupil's Edition page 485

Comprehension *(35 points; 5 points each)*
On the line provided, write the letter of the *best* answer to each of the following items.

_____ 1. The story's title includes the word "mystery" probably because
    a. Collins wonders whether there is water in the well
    b. Collins behaves more like a coward than a hero
    c. the story is a type of detective story
    d. heroic behavior is not easy to define

_____ 2. Collins does not consider himself a hero because he
    a. was merely going to the well to satisfy his thirst
    b. was terrified by the risk he took
    c. believes that heroes have no shame in their lives
    d. turns his back on the wounded lieutenant

_____ 3. By the time Collins asks for permission to go to the well,
    a. the lieutenant has died
    b. the well has been destroyed by an explosion
    c. his fellow soldiers have badgered him so much that he feels he cannot back out
    d. his thirst is dictating his actions

_____ 4. Once Collins reaches the well, he
    a. has time to fill each canteen
    b. grows impatient and fills a bucket instead of the canteens
    c. is hit by a stray bullet but continues to get water
    d. is trapped there and cannot immediately return to his company

_____ 5. When the dying lieutenant asks for a drink of water, Collins's initial reaction is to
    a. refuse the request and keep running
    b. carry the wounded man back to his regiment
    c. leave the officer a canteen and keep running
    d. stop immediately and grant his request

_____ 6. Collins's return to his regiment is greeted by
    a. a burst of gunfire
    b. the ire of his colonel
    c. absolute quiet
    d. a roar of approval

_____ 7. At the end of the story, the only thing we know for certain is that
    a. Collins has spilled all the water while returning to his regiment
    b. the bucket is empty and lying on the ground
    c. the wounded lieutenant has drunk all the water
    d. the bucket has been spilled by the skylarking lieutenants

Literary Element: Situational Irony *(20 points; 10 points each)*
On the line provided, write the letter of the *best* answer to each of the following items.

____ 8. Which of the following events from the story is the *best* example of situational irony?
    a. In the midst of battle, an officer screams an order so loudly that it comes out as a shriek.
    b. The colonel and the captain cannot determine whether Collins really wants to fetch the water.
    c. After racing across the battlefield to the well, Collins must wait for the water to slowly fill the canteens.
    d. The terrified Collins returns to give the dying lieutenant a drink of water but finds he cannot do so.

____ 9. Situational irony occurs when
    a. what actually occurs differs from what the reader expects to happen
    b. a character thinks one thing is true but the reader knows that something else is actually true
    c. a character says one thing but actually means something else
    d. a story has a surprise ending

Vocabulary *(20 points; 2 points each)*
Match the definition on the left with the Word to Own on the right. Write the letter of the Word to Own on the line provided.

____ **10.** gesturing while speaking   **a.** conflagration
____ **11.** withdrawal   **b.** stolidity
____ **12.** huge fire   **c.** obliterated
____ **13.** drained of color   **d.** prostrate
____ **14.** foreboding   **e.** ominous
____ **15.** showing no emotion   **f.** gesticulating
____ **16.** lying flat on the ground   **g.** provisional
____ **17.** lazy   **h.** retraction
____ **18.** destroyed   **i.** indolent
____ **19.** temporary   **j.** blanched

Written Response *(25 points)*

20. Is Collins's act ultimately heroic, foolish, or a combination of both? On a separate sheet of paper, write one paragraph explaining your opinion. Support your ideas with at least three examples from the story.

SELECTION TEST

To Build a Fire
Jack London

Pupil's Edition page 496

Comprehension *(25 points; 5 points each)*
On the line provided, write the letter of the *best* answer to each of the following items.

_____ **1.** Which of the following events describes the final outcome of the man's struggle against the frigid weather?
    a. He realizes the danger of traveling in such weather and turns back.
    b. He builds a fire to dry his wet feet, then continues his trek.
    c. He runs all the way to the camp, even though his feet are frozen.
    d. He stops running, falls asleep, and freezes to death.

_____ **2.** What does the man fear from the outset of his journey?
    a. the strange color of the sky
    b. falling through the snow and getting his feet wet
    c. traveling alone in tremendously cold temperatures
    d. his dog's strange behavior

_____ **3.** After he tumbles into the spring, the man
    a. initially succeeds in building a fire
    b. is caught in an avalanche
    c. tries to build a fire to thaw out before eating his lunch
    d. kills the dog to stay warm

_____ **4.** When the fire is extinguished, the man
    a. starts it again with little effort
    b. huddles with his dog to warm his hands and feet
    c. realizes he may have just been given a death sentence
    d. immediately panics and begins running toward camp

_____ **5.** Why is the man unable to run to the camp?
    a. He lacks the endurance to run that far.
    b. He fears getting his feet wet again.
    c. He cannot run because his legs are frozen.
    d. He cannot follow the trail while running.

Reading Skills and Strategies: Analyzing Text Structures—Cause and Effect
(20 points; 10 points each)
On the line provided, write the letter of the *best* answer to each of the following items.

_____ **6.** The events of "To Build a Fire" are organized
    a. in chronological order
    b. as mostly flashback
    c. by emotional content
    d. according to a structure based on comparison/contrast

_____ 7. What event causes the man's final predicament?
    a. He chooses to travel when everything is thawing.
    b. He falls into a hidden spring and can't build a fire.
    c. He stops for lunch and uses up all his matches.
    d. He does not pay attention to his immediate surroundings.

Literary Element: Naturalism *(20 points; 10 points each)*
On the line provided, write the letter of the *best* answer to each of the following items.

_____ 8. Naturalism, as reflected in the story, holds that
    a. animals and human beings can learn to respect each other
    b. nature is a source of comfort and inspiration
    c. close observation of nature requires a scientific approach
    d. human beings are subject to forces beyond their control

_____ 9. Which traits characterize naturalism?
    a. The author recounts events using the first person.
    b. The author employs detachment and objectivity.
    c. The author relies on innuendo and implication.
    d. The author frequently uses foreshadowing and irony.

Vocabulary *(20 points; 2 points each)*
Match the definition on the left with the Word to Own on the right. Write the letter of the Word to Own on the line provided.

_____ 10. firmness
_____ 11. shrank away
_____ 12. compulsory
_____ 13. sticking out
_____ 14. not easily perceived
_____ 15. resulted
_____ 16. difficult to define
_____ 17. extreme
_____ 18. limbs of the body
_____ 19. wavelike motions

    a. intangible
    b. undulations
    c. protruding
    d. solidity
    e. imperative
    f. extremities
    g. recoiled
    h. imperceptible
    i. excruciating
    j. ensued

Written Response *(15 points)*

20. Which of the following statements about London's story do you think *best* reflects naturalist theory?
    a. The man dies because he underestimates the force of the bitter cold.
    b. The man's survival depends on factors over which he has no control.
    c. The dog is better suited to the Yukon's environment than the man is.
    d. Even with a companion, it would have been a dangerous day for the man to travel.

Choose one of the statements above and, on a separate sheet of paper, write a paragraph defending your choice. Support your ideas with at least two examples from the story.

THE AMERICAN LANGUAGE

American Dialects

On the line provided, write the letter of the *best* answer to each of the following items.
(10 points each)

_____ 1. In the 1820s, James Fenimore Cooper said that there were no American dialects because
   a. there were no class or occupational distinctions in the United States
   b. American unity and mobility discouraged the establishment of dialects
   c. not even regional variations could be detected in the country
   d. there never had been dialects in America

_____ 2. Cooper's attitude toward dialects was shared by
   a. Mark Twain
   b. James Russell Lowell
   c. John Steinbeck
   d. Noah Webster

_____ 3. Mark Twain saw local speech as
   a. a way of describing the inhabitants of a region
   b. harmful to a national literature
   c. a rebuke to national unity
   d. a way to poke fun at his characters

_____ 4. Two nineteenth-century views of American speech contrasted
   a. standard usage and informal usage
   b. the unity of American speech and the existence of regional distinctions
   c. British usage and American usage
   d. nationally accepted usage and slang deriving from westward movement

_____ 5. A dialect can be defined as the characteristic language habits of a specific
   a. occupation or profession
   b. age group
   c. speech community
   d. state

_____ 6. Dialects differ *least* from standard English in their
   a. pronunciation
   b. vocabulary
   c. use of slang
   d. grammar

_____ 7. Dialects differ *most* from standard English in their
   a. pronunciation
   b. vocabulary
   c. use of slang
   d. grammar

_____ **8.** In the United States, the greatest number of dialects is still found in the
    a. South
    b. North
    c. West
    d. East

_____ **9.** Scholars divide American speech into three basic types: Northern, Southern, and
    a. Eastern
    b. Western
    c. Midland
    d. standard

_____ **10.** Dialect is an important aspect of literature because
    a. speech patterns are essential aspects of character and setting
    b. different speech patterns create humorous effects
    c. every region has its own speech pattern
    d. regional literature is the most influential school of American writing

LITERARY ELEMENTS TEST

Douglass's Metaphors

Pupil's Edition page 431

On the line provided, write the letter of the *best* answer to each of the following items.
(10 points each)

_____ **1.** A metaphor is a
    a. comparison between two unlike things
    b. comparison using *like* or *as*
    c. figure of speech that exaggerates a situation
    d. person, place, thing, or event that stands for something more than itself

_____ **2.** The "bargain" Frederick Douglass refers to is
    a. the code of slavery
    b. the contract for Douglass to be hired out
    c. the fight
    d. Bill Smith's refusal to fight

_____ **3.** Douglass writes that after the fight Mr. Covey never laid "the weight of his finger" on Douglass in anger. Douglass means that Mr. Covey did not
    a. point out Douglass to a law officer
    b. hire out Douglass to another plantation owner
    c. accuse Douglass of a crime
    d. fight or whip Douglass

_____ **4.** Douglass compares the battle with Mr. Covey to a
    a. natural disaster
    b. rebirth
    c. loss of innocence
    d. cannon burst

_____ **5.** At the end of the selection, Douglass refers to slavery as a
    a. prison sentence
    b. battle
    c. nightmare
    d. career

_____ **6.** When Douglass states that the battle rekindled the dying embers of a fire, he suggests all of the following **except** that
    a. he felt reborn
    b. he had almost given up hope for freedom
    c. he wanted to fight Mr. Covey again
    d. his sense of pride returned

_____ **7.** "The bloody arm of slavery" likens slavery to
    a. a disciplined soldier
    b. a cruel overseer
    c. an indifferent plantation owner
    d. a skillful surgeon

_____ **8.** Which comparison does Douglass make to describe his experiences?
    a. slavery to a battle
    b. a tomb to death
    c. freedom to a resurrection
    d. freedom to an angel

_____ **9.** Douglass uses metaphors to describe
    a. the people around him
    b. Mr. Covey's rope
    c. Mr. Covey's plantation
    d. a turning point in his life

_____ **10.** What is the effect of Douglass's metaphors?
    a. They create a feeling of uncertainty.
    b. They provide the narrative with humor.
    c. They make his points about slavery more powerful.
    d. They give the narrative a limited point of view.

LITERARY PERIOD TEST

The Rise of Realism: The Civil War and Postwar Period

Applying Skills

The following selection comes from the early part of Mark Twain's novel *Adventures of Huckleberry Finn*. Before you begin reading, take a minute to remember what you know about analyzing text structure, point of view, and humor. Read the selection carefully, and then answer the questions that follow. At this point in the novel (Chapter 5), Huck has been taken away from his irresponsible, drunken father and placed with a pious widow who is attempting to "civilize" him. Huck's father has heard that Huck has received some money, and the old man comes creeping into Huck's room one night in search of it. When Huck goes to his room and lights his candle, "there sat Pap—his own self!"

Pap Starts in on a New Life
by Mark Twain

I had shut the door to. Then I turned around, and there he was. I used to be scared of him all the time, he tanned[1] me so much. I reckoned I was scared now, too; but in a minute I see I was mistaken—that is, after the first jolt, as you may say, when my breath sort of hitched, he being so unexpected; but right away after I see I warn't scared of him worth bothering about.

He was most fifty, and he looked it. His hair was long and tangled and greasy, and hung down, and you could see his eyes shining through like he was behind vines. It was all black, no gray; so was his long, mixed-up whiskers. There warn't no color in his face, where his face showed; it was white; not like another man's white, but a white to make a body sick, a white to make a body's flesh crawl—a tree-toad white, a fish-belly white. As for his clothes—just rags, that was all. He had one ankle resting on t'other knee; the boot on that foot was busted, and two of his toes stuck through, and he worked them now and then. His hat was laying on the floor—an old black slouch with the top caved in, like a lid.

I stood a-looking at him; he set there a-looking at me, with his chair tilted back a little. I set the candle down. I noticed the window was up; so he had clumb in by the shed. He kept a-looking me all over. By and by he says:

"Starchy clothes—very. You think you're a good deal of a big-bug, *don't* you?"

"May I am, maybe I ain't," I says.

"Don't give me none o' your lip," says he. "You've put on considerable many frills since I been away. I'll take you down a peg before I get done with you. You're educated, too, they say—can read and write. You think you're better'n your father, now don't you, because he can't? *I'll* take it out of you. Who told you you might meddle with such hi-falut'n foolishness, hey?—who told you you could?"

"The widow. She told me."

"The widow, hey?—and who told the widow she could put in her shovel about a thing that ain't none of her business?"

"Nobody told her."

"Well, I'll learn her how to meddle. And looky here—you drop that school, you hear? I'll learn people to bring up a boy to put on airs over his own father and let on to be better'n what *he* is. You lemme catch you fooling around that school again, you hear? Your mother couldn't read, and she couldn't write, nuther, bother she died. None of the family couldn't before *they* died. I can't, and here you're a-swelling yourself up like this. I ain't the man to stand it—you hear? Say, lemme hear you read."

---

[1] **tanned:** whipped

I took up a book and begun something about General Washington and the wars. When I'd read about a half a minute, he fetched the book a whack with his hand and knocked it across the house. He says:

"It's so. You can do it. I had my doubts when you told me. Now looky here; you stop that putting on frills. I won't have it. I'll lay for you, my smarty; and if I catch you about that school I'll tan you good. First you know you'll get religion, too. I never see such a son."

He took up a little blue and yaller picture of some cows and a boy, and says:

"What's this?"

"It's something they give me for learning my lessons good."

He tore it up, and says:

"I'll give you something better—I'll give you a cowhide."

He set there a-mumbling and a-growling a minute, and then he says:

Ain't you a sweet-scented <u>dandy</u>, though? A bed; and bed-clothes; and a look'n'-glass; and a piece of carpet on the floor—and your own father got to sleep with the hogs in the tanyard. I never see such a son. I bet I'll take some o' these frills out o' you before I'm done with you. Why, there ain't no end to your airs—they say you're rich. Hey?—how's that?"

"They lie—that's how."

"Looky here—mind how you talk to me; I'm a-standing about all I can stand now—so don't gimme no sass. I've been in town two days, and I hain't heard nothing but about you bein' rich. I heard about it away down the river, too. That's why I come. You git me that money tomorrow—I want it.

"I hain't got no money."

"It's a lie. Judge Thatcher's got it. You git it. I want it."

"I hain't got no money, I tell you. You ask Judge Thatcher; he'll tell you the same."

"All right. I'll ask him; and I'll make him pungle,[2] too, or I'll know the reason why. Say, how much you got in your pocket? I want it."

"I hain't got only a dollar, and want that to—"

"It don't make no difference what you want it for—you just shell it out."

He took it and bit it to see if it was good, and then he said he was going downtown to get some whiskey, said he hadn't had a drink all day. When he had got out on the shed he put his head in again, and cussed me for putting on frills and trying to do better than him; and when I reckoned he was gone he came back and put his head in again, and told me to mind about that school, because he was going to lay for me and lick me if I didn't drop that.

Next day he was drunk, and he went to Judge Thatcher's and bullyragged him, and tried to make him give up the money; but he couldn't, and then he swore he'd make the law force him.

The judge and the widow went to law to get the court to take me away from him and let one of them be my <u>guardian</u>; but it was a new judge that had just come, and he didn't know the old man; so he said courts mustn't interfere and separate families if they could help it; said he'd druther not take a child away from its father. So Judge Thatcher and the widow had to quit on the business.

That pleased the old man till he couldn't rest. He said he'd cowhide me till I was black and blue if I didn't raise some money for him. I borrowed three dollars from Judge Thatcher, and Pap took it and got drunk, and went a-blowing around and cussing and whooping and carrying on; and he kept it up all over town, with a tin pan, till most midnight; then they jailed him, and the next day they had him before the court, and jailed him again for a week. But he said *he* was satisfied; said he was boss of his son, and he'd make it warm for *him*.

When he got out the new judge said he was a-going to make a man of him. So he took him to his own house, and dressed him up clean and nice, and had him to breakfast and dinner and supper with the family, and was just old pie to him, so to speak. And after supper he talked to him about <u>temperance</u> and such things till the old man cried, and said he'd been a fool, and fooled away his life; but now he was a-going to turn over a new leaf and be a man nobody wouldn't be ashamed of, and he hoped the judge would help him and not look down on him. The judge said

---

[2]**pungle:** pay the money

he could hug him for them words; so *he* cried, and his wife she cried again; Pap said he'd been a man that had always been misunderstood before, and the judge said he believed it. The old man said that what a man wanted that was down was <u>sympathy</u>, and the judge said it was so; so they cried again. And when it was bedtime the old man rose up and held out his hand, and says:

"Look at it, gentleman and ladies all; take a-hold of it; shake it. There's a hand that was the hand of a hog; but it ain't so no more; it's the hand of a man that's started in on a new life, and'll die before he'll go back. You mark them words—don't forget I said them. It's a clean hand now; shake it—don't be afeared."

So they shook it, one after the other, all around, and cried. The judge's wife she kissed it. Then the old man he signed a pledge—made his mark. The judge said it was the holiest time on record, or something like that. Then they tucked the old man into a beautiful room, which was the spare room, and in the night some time he got powerful thirsty and clumb out on to the porch roof and slid down a stanchion and traded his new coat for a jug of forty-rod, and clumb back again and had a good old time; and toward daylight he crawled out again, drunk as a fiddler, and rolled off the porch and broke his left arm in two places, and was most froze to death when somebody found him after sun-up. And when they come to look at that spare room they had to take soundings before they could <u>navigate</u> it.

The judge felt kind of sore. He said he reckoned a body could reform the old man with a shotgun, maybe, but he didn't know no other way.

Vocabulary Skills: New Words in Context *(20 points; 4 points each)*
Each of the underlined words below has also been underlined in the selection. Re-read those passages and use context clues and prior knowledge to help you select an answer. On the line provided, write the letter of the word or words that *best* completes each sentence.

_____ **1.** A <u>dandy</u> is a man who pays too much attention to his _____.
    a. education
    b. appearance
    c. diet

_____ **2.** If you serve as a minor's <u>guardian</u>, you are his or her _____.
    a. guide
    b. legal caretaker
    c. captor

_____ **3.** A person who believes in <u>temperance</u> practices _____ in the consumption of alcoholic beverages.
    a. abstinence
    b. inebriation
    c. recklessness

_____ **4.** Someone who yearns for <u>sympathy</u> typically wants _____.
    a. discipline
    b. congruity
    c. compassion

_____ **5.** To <u>navigate</u> is to _____ a course.
    a. divert
    b. mobilize
    c. steer

Vocabulary

Affixes *(20 points; 4 points each)*
Use your knowledge of affixes to determine the meaning of the words in the left-hand column.
On the line provided, write the letter indicating the definition of each of the following words.

_____ **6.** inexplicable

_____ **7.** protuberant

_____ **8.** disjunction

_____ **9.** excavator

_____ **10.** congregate

a. state of being separated off

b. characteristic of being collected

c. someone who digs out earth

d. not able to be explained

e. showing as bulging forward

Comprehension *(20 points; 4 points each)*
On the line provided, write the letter of the *best* answer to each of the following items.

_____ **11.** What is Huck's initial reaction to his father's unexpected appearance?
    a. He is furious.
    b. He panics and hollers for help.
    c. He is scared.
    d. He does not care one way or another.

_____ **12.** The primary reason Pap has come to see his son is that he
    a. is concerned about Huck's well-being
    b. has heard that Huck is rich
    c. wants to warn Huck about becoming a dandy
    d. wants to give Huck a tanning for attending school

_____ **13.** What does Pap think about Huck's ability to read?
    a. He is proud of his son and wants Huck to teach him how to read.
    b. He accuses Huck of trying to better himself.
    c. He tries to prove that Huck cannot really read.
    d. He says he will approve of it if Huck will give him money.

_____ **14.** Which of the following statements about Pap's conversion is *not* true?
    a. Pap cries openly and proclaims that he is going to change.
    b. Pap signs a temperance pledge.
    c. Pap trades his new coat for a jug of whiskey.
    d. Pap becomes a church member and gets a job.

_____ **15.** When Pap is found with a broken arm and the judge sees the condition of his room,
    a. the judge is mad because he has been fooled
    b. the judge and his wife invite Pap to work for them
    c. Huck feels sorry for him and gives him more money
    d. the court awards custody of Huck to Judge Thatcher

Reading Skills and Strategies
Analyzing Text Structures *(10 points)*

16. In the boxes below, briefly describe the chronology of Pap's actions after he left Huck's room and before the judge invited him to dinner. Be sure to record the events in the order in which they occur. The first box has been filled in for you as an example.

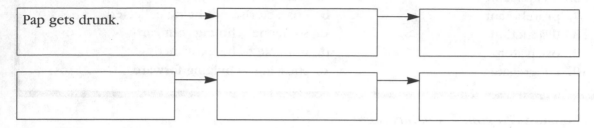

Pap gets drunk.

Identifying Comic Devices *(20 points)*

17. Like the narrator in Twain's *Life on the Mississippi*, Huck recounts a dramatic series of events with humor. On a separate sheet of paper, identify the comic devices each narrator uses and explain how these devices create humor. Use at least two examples from each selection to support your ideas.

Literary Element: Point of View *(10 points)*

18. Which of the following statements best captures why Twain chose to use Huck's point of view in the novel? Choose what you believe is the *strongest* response. On the lines provided, write the letter of the answer you choose and briefly defend your choice. Use at least one example from the selection to support your ideas.
  a. Huck's casual, conversational style lightens up otherwise serious events.
  b. Twain wants the reader to see events through Huck's eyes.
  c. The story would not keep the reader's interest if it were told from the third-person point of view.
  d. Using an objective voice simply is not natural for Twain.

_____

_____

_____

_____

_____

_____

_____

_____

_____

_____

LITERARY PERIOD INTRODUCTION TEST

The Moderns

On the line provided, write the letter of the *best* answer to each of the following items.
(10 points each)

_____ 1. Until the beginning of the twentieth century, all of the following were part of the American dream **except** a
  a. respect for the mysterious workings of the subconscious mind
  b. belief that the country's abundance and bounty were limitless
  c. trust in the ultimate triumph of any self-reliant individual
  d. faith in America's progress toward prosperity

_____ 2. After World War I, American writers began to
  a. try to tighten their connections with the past
  b. grow cynical about traditional authority and values
  c. urge the country to build economic opportunities
  d. abandon their art and find new ways of making a living

_____ 3. The modernist movement challenged American writers to
  a. adopt Marxism as a philosophical basis for their work
  b. set their stories and poems in the South or Midwest
  c. find new themes, subjects, and styles for their work
  d. avoid the influences and ideas of European writers

_____ 4. A growing interest in psychoanalysis led writers to
  a. doubt the value and sincerity of their work
  b. rely on doctors to help them find meaning in life
  c. criticize works that described characters' feelings
  d. try to capture their characters' thought processes

_____ 5. During the Jazz Age, many American writers and artists
  a. supported Prohibition in their work
  b. openly criticized the music of the period
  c. lived as expatriates in France
  d. embraced the idea of America as Eden

_____ 6. Ernest Hemingway created major characters who
  a. express themselves in flamboyant ways
  b. avoid the challenges of day-to-day life
  c. are willing to do anything to achieve their goals
  d. behave honorably in a world without purpose

_____ 7. Some American poets were inspired by modernist European painters and began to use their imagery and symbolism, while others looked to
  a. American painters for style and subjects
  b. traditional forms and ordinary speech
  c. ancient Greek and Roman myths for themes
  d. forms they admired in modern British drama

____ **8.** Poets of the Harlem Renaissance wrote American poetry that involved
    a. traditional verse forms
    b. ghetto speech and rhythms from jazz and blues
    c. references to ancient African forms of poetry
    d. discussions of the decline of American cities

____ **9.** Many American modernist writers
    a. maintained a vision of America as Eden
    b. embraced the boundless optimism of earlier times
    c. believed nature had outlived its usefulness
    d. focused on obscure questions and issues

____ **10.** American modernist writers managed to
    a. avoid fundamental questions asked by writers of the past
    b. destroy our illusions about American dreams and ideals
    c. create a literature that reflects many American voices
    d. focus only on the positive aspects of American culture

SELECTION TEST

A Wagner Matinée
Willa Cather

Pupil's Edition page 539

Comprehension *(35 points; 5 points each)*

On the line provided, write the letter of the *best* answer to each of the following items.

_____ 1. On greeting his aunt, Clark is struck by how
  a. eager she is to attend concerts again
  b. unfriendly and distant she acts
  c. easily she adjusts to life in Boston
  d. shabby she looks and how exhausted she seems

_____ 2. Which sentence *best* describes Clark's view of his Uncle Howard?
  a. He is a cruel man who treats Georgiana badly.
  b. He is unable to give Georgiana a comfortable life.
  c. He is a cultured man who misses the cities of the East.
  d. He is an ambitious and prosperous farmer.

_____ 3. How is Georgiana a victim of circumstance?
  a. She fell in love with Howard, married him, and moved to an isolated farm.
  b. She has chosen not to cultivate her love of music while living in Nebraska.
  c. She wants Clark to learn how to play several different musical instruments.
  d. She is determined to take voice and musical composition lessons.

_____ 4. When Clark was a boy, Georgiana warned him not to
  a. choose a spouse too quickly, or he may be hurt
  b. love something too much, or it may be taken from him
  c. return to Boston, for he may be unhappy with city life
  d. give up his studying, or he would end up poor and miserable

_____ 5. When the horns play in the *Tannhäuser,* Georgiana clutches Clark's sleeve and he realizes
  a. how much Georgiana dislikes brass instruments
  b. that Georgiana may be ill
  c. how silent the plains are
  d. that Georgiana's hands are too arthritic to play the piano

_____ 6. Which statement *best* summarizes why Georgiana cries during the concert?
  a. She is suddenly homesick for Nebraska and her family.
  b. She remembers how important music is to her.
  c. She dislikes being exposed to a snobbish atmosphere.
  d. She is happy that she gave up her career as a pianist.

_____ 7. Clark sympathizes with his aunt because
  a. long ago she shared her love of music with him
  b. he remembers his own difficulties in returning to Boston
  c. he, too, has few opportunities to attend cultural events
  d. Howard has written to him about Georgiana's decline

Literary Element: Setting *(20 points; 10 points each)*
On the line provided, write the letter of the *best* answer to each of the following items.

_____ **8.** In the descriptions of the two settings—Nebraska and Boston—the narrator
    a. explains his aunt's reasons for permanently returning to the city
    b. contrasts the purity of one with the decadence of the other
    c. contrasts the bleakness of one with the liveliness of the other
    d. explains major reasons for the Westward Expansion movement

_____ **9.** What does Georgiana's reaction to the setting of the concert reveal?
    a. She does not enjoy the concert.
    b. She misses the cultural opportunities of the East.
    c. Her love of music has decreased.
    d. She is furious with Howard.

Vocabulary *(20 points; 2 points each)*
Match the definition on the left with the Word to Own on the right. Write the letter of the Word to Own on the line provided.

_____ **10.** at a slant   **a.** deluge
_____ **11.** escaping   **b.** eluding
_____ **12.** dull; inactive   **c.** grotesque
_____ **13.** anxious uncertainty   **d.** inert
_____ **14.** countless   **e.** legacy
_____ **15.** strange; absurd   **f.** myriad
_____ **16.** deeply respectful   **g.** obliquely
_____ **17.** inheritance   **h.** pious
_____ **18.** rush; flood   **i.** reverential
_____ **19.** devoted to one's religion   **j.** trepidation

Written Response *(25 points)*

20. "A Wagner Matinée" is written from the point of view of Clark, and we see Georgiana's reactions to the concert through his eyes. On a separate sheet of paper, describe what he perceives as Georgiana's reaction to the concert. Make at least two references to details in the story to support your ideas.

SELECTION TEST

His Father's Earth
Thomas Wolfe   **Pupil's Edition page 549**

Comprehension *(35 points; 5 points each)*
On the line provided, write the letter of the *best* answer to each of the following items.

_____ **1.** In his imaginary experience of circus life, the boy sees himself as
   a. escaping from an unhappy family life
   b. suffering from the unkind treatment of circus workers
   c. taking care of the circus workers
   d. learning to be a circus performer

_____ **2.** The boy's vision enables him to
   a. have a deeper understanding of what home is
   b. understand his parents' problems
   c. acquire money for the circus workers
   d. experience reality

_____ **3.** The vision of exciting travel contrasts with
   a. the ease of the circus's routine
   b. dangers in the outside world
   c. an image of returning home eagerly
   d. the hardships of urban life

_____ **4.** The birdsong represents the
   a. boy's spiritual awakening
   b. the chaos of the circus
   c. the adventure the boy finds in traveling
   d. the harmony the boy finds in the circus

_____ **5.** All of the following are realistic aspects of the boy's imaginings **except**
   a. the hunger and hard work of the circus crew
   b. building homes
   c. traveling
   d. gathering crops

_____ **6.** The father reacts to the boy's homecoming with
   a. joy and acceptance
   b. rebukes and criticism
   c. questions and concerns
   d. lack of attention or interest

_____ **7.** When he returns home, the boy realizes all of the following **except** that
   a. he cannot go back to the innocence of his childhood
   b. his father has had the same experiences that he has had
   c. an individual is small when compared with the world
   d. he understands youths who have hope, but feel lonely

Literary Element: Description *(20 points; 10 points each)*
On the line provided, write the letter of the *best* answer to each of the following items.

_____ **8.** The descriptions of food convey
   a. admiration for the father's skills as a farmer
   b. a picture of the poverty and hunger in America
   c. the idea that the abundance of American resources cannot last long
   d. a sense of personal nourishment and fulfillment

_____ **9.** Birdsong is described in a way that makes it seem
   a. like the plaintive cries of animals
   b. as exciting as the sensations of circus life
   c. ordinary compared with life on the road
   d. like an ominous foreshadowing of tragedy

Vocabulary *(20 points; 2 points each)*
Match the definition on the left with the Word to Own on the right. Write the letter of the Word to Own on the line provided.

_____ **10.** abundant; plentiful   **a.** exulted
_____ **11.** topped   **b.** frugal
_____ **12.** guess   **c.** garnished
_____ **13.** rejoiced greatly   **d.** intermittent
_____ **14.** weak, as from exhaustion   **e.** languid
_____ **15.** views   **f.** nominal
_____ **16.** very small   **g.** opulent
_____ **17.** pausing occasionally   **h.** prodigal
_____ **18.** extremely abundant   **i.** surmise
_____ **19.** thrifty; economical   **j.** vistas

Written Response *(25 points)*

20. Consider the titles of two of Wolfe's novels: *Look Homeward, Angel* and *You Can't Go Home Again*. On a separate sheet of paper, describe how "His Father's Earth" is also about an idea of home. Make at least two references to details in the story to support your ideas.

SELECTION TEST

Design / Nothing Gold Can Stay / Once by the Pacific / Neither Out Far Nor In Deep / Birches / The Death of the Hired Man

Robert Frost

OPEN
BOOK   **Pupil's Edition pages 560–576**

Comprehension *(20 points; 4 points each)*

On the line provided, write the letter of the *best* answer to each of the following items.

_____ 1. In "Design," the overall imagery suggests that
    a. the moth is not actually dead
    b. evil may masquerade as innocence
    c. the spider is aware of the speaker
    d. all of nature is beautiful

_____ 2. The gold in "Nothing Gold Can Stay" is a symbol of
    a. the magnificence of autumn leaves   **c.** human greed and selfishness
    b. sunrise in the Garden of Eden   **d.** fleeting beauty and perfection

_____ 3. In "Neither Out Far Nor In Deep," one reason people look at the ocean rather than at the land may be because they are
    a. intrigued by mystery   **c.** fascinated by a sinking ship
    b. disgusted by worldly events   **d.** longing for an ocean voyage

_____ 4. Which poem expresses pessimism about our ability to grasp the calamity that awaits humankind?
    a. "Nothing Gold Can Stay"   **c.** "Once by the Pacific"
    b. "Neither Out Far Nor In Deep"   **d.** "The Death of the Hired Man"

_____ 5. According to Frost, the boy who swings on birch trees experiences
    a. a frightening near-death vision
    b. the pleasures of both heaven and earth
    c. the wrath of an indignant landowner
    d. a variety of minor injuries

Reading Skills and Strategies

On the line provided, write the letter of the *best* answer to each of the following items.

Understanding Blank Verse *(30 points; 10 points each)*

_____ 6. Which of the following pairs of lines is an example of blank verse?
    a. "He's worn out. He's asleep beside the stove. / When I came up from Rowe's I found him here . . ."
    b. "The people along the sand / All turn and look one way."
    c. "There would be more than ocean-water broken / Before God's last *Put out the Light* was spoken."
    d. "So dawn goes down to day. / Nothing gold can stay."

____ 7. Which of the following *best* describes blank verse?
   a. rhymed iambic pentameter
   b. unrhymed iambic pentameter
   c. free verse with occasional internal rhyme
   d. iambic pentameter with irregular line breaks

____ 8. Frost uses which of the following two meters?
   a. trochaic tetrameter and anapestic monometer
   b. iambic hexameter and dactylic dimeter
   c. strict iambic and loose iambic
   d. loose heptameter and strict dimeter

Drawing Inferences About Characters *(20 points; 10 points each)*

____ 9. In "The Death of the Hired Man," the characters' feelings are revealed by
   a. how the characters react to death
   b. the characters' different definitions of work
   c. the observations of the third-person narrator
   d. what the characters say to one another

____ 10. In "The Death of the Hired Man," one can infer that Silas hopes to maintain dignity because he
   a. leaves his former employers alone
   b. asks for money only from people who can afford to help him
   c. claims to have come to do some tasks
   d. stays with his brother rather than with friends

Literary Element: Dialogue in Verse *(10 points)*
On the line provided, write the letter of the *best* answer to each of the following items.

____ 11. Why does Frost use blank verse in "The Death of the Hired Man"?
   a. to prove that blank verse is better than free verse
   b. to make the dialogue sound natural
   c. to avoid iambic pentameter and strict rhyme schemes
   d. to use complicated end rhymes

Written Response *(20 points)*

12. Some readers view Frost's poems as being *pessimistic*—that is, as dwelling on the downside of life. Other readers view the poems as being *realistic*—that is, as balancing negative and positive aspects. Which of these two views is closest to your own opinion of Frost's work? On a separate sheet of paper, respond to this question. Make at least two references to details in Frost's poems to support your ideas.

SELECTION TEST

Bells for John Whiteside's Daughter
John Crowe Ransom
Shine, Perishing Republic
Robinson Jeffers

Pupil's Edition page 577

Pupil's Edition page 580

Comprehension *(35 points; 5 points each)*
On the line provided, write the letter of the *best* answer to each of the following items.

____ **1.** In "Bells for John Whiteside's Daughter," Ransom seeks to convey the
   a. relief the geese feel when their tormentor dies
   b. contrast between a still corpse and an active child
   c. reasons that justify the death of a young person
   d. futility of mourning those who have passed away

____ **2.** The speaker remembers John Whiteside's daughter mostly for her
   a. quiet obedience to her elders
   b. deep insights into the meaning of life
   c. beauty and grace
   d. mischievous ways

____ **3.** In her coffin, John Whiteside's daughter seems to be in a "brown study," which is
   a. a seriousness unlike the lively way she acted in life
   b. a dark and somber room that reflects the family's sorrow
   c. an apt comment on the unhappiness of her youth
   d. symbolic of the way she studied geese

____ **4.** In "Shine, Perishing Republic," Jeffers views America as
   a. full of powerful instincts for change and renewal
   b. a place where democratic ideals have been realized
   c. a thickening, decaying, and rotting empire
   d. fighting off onslaughts of foreign forces

____ **5.** Jeffers seems to feel that his children
   a. are willing and complacent victims of technology
   b. may hate him for his love of the natural world
   c. can escape destruction by opting for a rural life
   d. have discovered a way of life that is better than his

____ **6.** Which of the following sentences *best* states a similar theme for both "Bells for John Whiteside's Daughter" and "Shine, Perishing Republic"?
   a. In the light of eternity, human life has no real purpose.
   b. Humankind is corrupt and is causing its own destruction.
   c. Immortality is guaranteed to those who live exemplary lives.
   d. The finest lives are those lived in accordance with nature.

____ **7.** What is one thing that the narrator in "Shine, Perishing Republic" has lost?
   a. hatred of large cities
   b. love of meteors and mountains
   c. admiration for American society
   d. devotion to his religion

Literary Element: Tone *(30 points; 15 points each)*
On the line provided, write the letter of the *best* answer to each of the following items.

_____ **8.** In "Bells for John Whiteside's Daughter," the two contrasting tones are
   a. amusement and solemnity
   b. pessimism and optimism
   c. sarcasm and sorrow
   d. amazement and disillusionment

_____ **9.** In "Shine, Perishing Republic," Robinson Jeffers combines the tones of
   a. humor and irritation
   b. hope and wonder
   c. cynicism and anguish
   d. optimism and pessimism

Written Response *(35 points)*

10. Although both Ransom and Jeffers deal with the subjects of loss and death, the tones they use are different. On a separate sheet of paper, contrast the tones in "Bells for John Whiteside's Daughter" and "Shine, Perishing Republic." Make at least one reference to a specific image in each poem to support your ideas.

| SELECTION TEST |

Winter Dreams
F. Scott Fitzgerald   **Pupil's Edition page 586**

Comprehension *(25 points; 5 points each)*
On the line provided, write the letter of the *best* answer to each of the following items.

_____ 1. Dexter Green can *best* be described as
    a. ambitious and full of desires
    b. judgmental and comical
    c. courageous and helpful
    d. honest and trustworthy

_____ 2. What is Dexter's eventual attitude toward Judy Jones's flirtations with men?
    a. Dexter is outraged that Judy flirts with men.
    b. Dexter often criticizes Judy for flirting with men.
    c. Dexter enjoys watching Judy flirt with men.
    d. Dexter does not condemn Judy for flirting with men.

_____ 3. What happens to Dexter and Judy's engagement?
    a. Dexter breaks off the engagement.
    b. Dexter never intended to marry Judy.
    c. Judy breaks off the engagement.
    d. Judy discovers that Dexter is married.

_____ 4. At the end of the story, Devlin tells Dexter that
    a. Judy's husband does not treat her well
    b. Judy and her husband are divorced
    c. Judy still dates a number of men
    d. Judy cannot stand her husband

_____ 5. Which of the following word pairs describes Judy?
    a. sensitive and compassionate   **c.** uneducated and poor
    b. confident and condescending   **d.** sophisticated and kind

Reading Skills and Strategies
On the line provided, write the letter of the *best* answer to each of the following items.

Drawing Inferences About Characters *(10 points; 5 points each)*

_____ 6. Which of the following actions shows that Dexter is spellbound by Judy?
    a. He cuts in on Judy at a dance.
    b. He becomes engaged to Irene Scheerer.
    c. He gets back together with Judy in spite of his engagement.
    d. He joins the Army instead of going to New York.

_____ 7. On Dexter's return to the golf course as a golfer, what do his actions suggest about his feelings?
    a. He is uncomfortable with his newly privileged position.
    b. Proud and arrogant, he looks down on the caddies.
    c. He wishes he had learned the course better in his youth.
    d. He has gone golfing in the hope of impressing Judy.

Understanding Paradoxes *(10 points; 5 points each)*

_____ **8.** Why is it paradoxical that Judy's smile has "no root in mirth, or even amusement"?
  a. Her smile is an invitation to be kissed.
  b. She smiles at the chicken livers and at Dexter.
  c. Smiles usually indicate happiness.
  d. Her smile is an indication of her boredom.

_____ **9.** Why is it paradoxical that Judy calls everyone "darling"?
  a. She truly cares for no one.
  b. She can't remember anyone's name.
  c. She is trying to irritate Irene.
  d. She knows it annoys men.

Literary Element: Motivation *(20 points; 10 points each)*
On the line provided, write the letter of the *best* answer to each of the following items.

_____ **10.** What is Dexter's motivation for pursuing Judy?
  a. He wants to work for her father.
  b. He perceives her as being a symbol of "the best."
  c. He is the only man she is interested in.
  d. She seems shy and lonely.

_____ **11.** What is Judy's possible motivation for asking Dexter to marry her?
  a. She is deeply in love with Dexter and wants to start a family.
  b. She had a quarrel with Irene and wants revenge.
  c. She is attracted to men who seem inaccessible or challenging.
  d. She is jealous of Irene and passionately in love with Dexter.

Vocabulary *(20 points; 2 points each)*
Match the definition on the left with the Word to Own on the right. Write the letter of the Word to Own on the line provided.

_____ **12.** joyfulness	**a.** reserve	
_____ **13.** variance; difference	**b.** turbulence	
_____ **14.** irregular behavior	**c.** malicious	
_____ **15.** celebration	**d.** plaintive	
_____ **16.** feeling of alarm or agitation	**e.** petulance	
_____ **17.** intentionally hurtful	**f.** elation	
_____ **18.** expressing sadness	**g.** ludicrous	
_____ **19.** self-restraint	**h.** divergence	
_____ **20.** irritability; impatience	**i.** mirth	
_____ **21.** laughable; absurd	**j.** perturbation	

Written Response *(15 points)*

22. On a separate sheet of paper, complete the following statement. Then, give at least two examples or ideas from the story to support the statement.

At the end of the story, tears stream down Dexter's face because . . .

SELECTION TEST

The Leader of the People
John Steinbeck

Comprehension *(25 points; 5 points each)*
On the line provided, write the letter of the *best* answer to each of the following items.

_____ 1. Which of the following statements about Jody's father is true?
  a. He insists that Jody ask his permission before doing anything on the ranch.
  b. He never gives in during a confrontation with anyone, including his wife.
  c. He will not allow Jody to kill mice despite Jody's constant pleading.
  d. He is rather carefree, an attitude that annoys his family when there is work to be done.

_____ 2. At the end of Steinbeck's story, Grandfather says that if he had not been the leader of the people
  a. the whole group would have died of disease
  b. another person would have been the leader
  c. the American Indians would have been treated more fairly
  d. the horses would have been stolen

_____ 3. According to Grandfather, some men hated the ocean because in the past the
  a. ocean did not provide sufficient drinking water
  b. men realized that they had lost their way
  c. men were afraid of the unpredictability of the ocean
  d. ocean prevented them from continuing westward

_____ 4. What does Jody think of Grandfather's stories?
  a. Jody is afraid of them.   **c.** Jody dislikes them.
  b. Jody thinks they are thrilling. **d.** Jody believes they are too long.

_____ 5. Which of the following statements *best* describes the climax of the story?
  a. Grandfather overhears Jody's father saying he doesn't want to hear the stories.
  b. Jody's mother says that the stories might be all that Grandfather has left.
  c. Grandfather accepts that he has to settle at the continent's edge.
  d. Jody's father indulges Grandfather by listening to the stories again and again.

Reading Skills and Strategies: Interpreting Figures of Speech *(20 points; 10 points each)*
On the line provided, write the letter of the *best* answer to each of the following items.

_____ 6. Which of the following quotations from the story is a metaphor?
  a. ". . . . his white eyebrows overhung his eyes like mustaches."
  b. "Jody thought of the wide plains and of the wagons. . . ."
  c. "Jody tried to leap into the middle of his shadow. . . ."
  d. "Across his mind marched the great phantoms. . . ."

_____ 7. The five most common figures of speech are
  a. metonymy, synecdoche, repetition, personification, and hyperbole
  b. kenning, conceit, parallelism, metaphor, and simile
  c. personification, hyperbole, metaphor, oxymoron, and simile
  d. onomatopoeia, oxymoron, anagram, euphemism, and paradox

Literary Element: Conflict *(20 points; 10 points each)*
On the line provided, write the letter of the *best* answer to each of the following items.

_____ **8.** Which of the following conflicts in the story is also its theme?
    a. fear vs. courage
    b. reality vs. dreams
    c. strength vs. weakness
    d. old age vs. childhood

_____ **9.** Jody's father feels conflict in relation to Grandfather because Grandfather
    a. insists upon putting iron plates in the wagon wheels
    b. constantly changes the ending of his story
    c. continues to tell the same stories over and over
    d. insists upon taking over the farm whenever he comes to visit

Vocabulary *(20 points; 2 points each)*
Match the definition on the left with the Word to Own on the right. Write the letter of the Word to Own on the line provided.

_____ **10.** improper	**a.** immune
_____ **11.** proud and overly confident	**b.** rancor
_____ **12.** assembled	**c.** arrogant
_____ **13.** unhappily	**d.** marshaling
_____ **14.** protected	**e.** unseemly
_____ **15.** opening	**f.** cleft
_____ **16.** anger	**g.** disconsolately
_____ **17.** leading; guiding	**h.** contemptuously
_____ **18.** scornfully	**i.** humoring
_____ **19.** indulging	**j.** convened

Written Response *(15 points)*

20. On a separate sheet of paper, describe two conflicts that occur in "The Leader of the People." Describe the personalities of the characters involved. Do you think that the conflicts are resolved peacefully, angrily, or not at all? Use at least two examples from the story to support your opinion.

SELECTION TEST

The Secret Life of Walter Mitty
James Thurber   Pupil's Edition page 624

Comprehension *(25 points; 5 points each)*
On the line provided, write the letter of the *best* answer to each of the following items.

_____ 1. Which of the following statements *best* describes Mrs. Mitty?
a. She does all the shopping for the household.
b. She cannot make decisions.
c. She is always working.
d. She constantly tells Walter what to do.

_____ 2. When Walter imagines that he is on the witness stand, he
a. brilliantly argues for his innocence in the murder of Gregory Fitzhurst
b. proudly admits that he could have killed Gregory Fitzhurst with his left hand
c. successfully demonstrates that the district attorney murdered Gregory Fitzhurst
d. acts as his own lawyer in the trial for the murder of Gregory Fitzhurst

_____ 3. Walter imagines that he fixes an anesthetizer machine in the operating room using
a. a fountain pen   c. a puppy biscuit
b. a glove   d. a pencil

_____ 4. In all of his fantasies, Walter imagines that he is
a. an outlaw narrowly escaping from the authorities
b. a man who shows control in difficult situations
c. a person who knows exactly how to follow orders
d. a hero who saves lives

_____ 5. When Walter is questioned about the gun, his attitude can *best* be described as
a. arrogant and fearless
b. frightened and intimidated
c. confused and depressed
d. excited and hysterical

Reading Skills and Strategies: Analyzing Text Structures—Cause/Effect
(20 points; 10 points each)
On the line provided, write the letter of the *best* answer to each of the following items.

_____ 6. The use of cause and effect in "The Secret Life of Walter Mitty" is unusual because
a. Walter's wife is often the cause
b. the effects often come before the causes
c. the effects are wild fantasies and the causes are mundane
d. Walter is not a realistic human being

_____ 7. Walter's courtroom drama is triggered by
a. his sudden recollection of what he needs at the A & P
b. his overhearing a newsboy talking about a trial
c. an article he reads in the hairdresser's shop
d. something that goes wrong during surgery

Elements of Literature   *Formal Assessment* **123**

Literary Element: Parody *(20 points; 10 points each)*
On the line provided, write the letter of the *best* answer to each of the following items.

_____ 8. James Thurber's descriptions of Walter's fantasies can be seen as parodies because they
   a. humorously imitate real life
   b. humorously imitate action-adventure stories
   c. seriously imitate twentieth-century drama
   d. seriously imitate mystery novels

_____ 9. Which of the following details is part of one parody in the story?
   a. Walter waits for his wife to get her hair done.
   b. Walter hits the district attorney.
   c. Walter attempts to take the chains off his car.
   d. Walter asks for puppy biscuits at the A & P.

Vocabulary *(20 points; 2 points each)*
Match the definition on the left with the Word to Own on the right. Write the letter of the Word to Own on the line provided.

_____ **10.** arrogant   **a.** craven
_____ **11.** troubled   **b.** bedlam
_____ **12.** wild confusion   **c.** rakishly
_____ **13.** place or condition of noise or confusion   **d.** haggard
_____ **14.** violent ripping apart   **e.** distraught
_____ **15.** suggestively   **f.** insolent
_____ **16.** very fearful; cowardly   **g.** cannonading
_____ **17.** artillery fire   **h.** insinuatingly
_____ **18.** wasted or worn in appearance   **i.** rending
_____ **19.** dashingly; jauntily   **j.** pandemonium

Written Response *(15 points)*

20. Do you think that Walter Mitty is trying to escape from reality? If so, what reality is he trying to escape from? On a separate sheet of paper, state and explain your opinion. Make at least two references to the story to support your ideas.

SELECTION TEST

A Worn Path
Eudora Welty   **Pupil's Edition page 634**

Comprehension *(35 points; 5 points each)*
On the line provided, write the letter of the *best* answer to each of the following items.

_____ 1. On her journey, Phoenix encounters
   a. an old woman with a cane
   b. a hunter and his dog
   c. a young girl with a plate
   d. an alligator under a log

_____ 2. The incidents with the thorn bush and the scarecrow indicate that Phoenix
   a. has trouble seeing
   b. fears nothing
   c. has trouble walking
   d. drifts in and out of consciousness

_____ 3. Throughout her journey, Phoenix
   a. wants to turn back
   b. tries to remember where she is going
   c. is determined to keep going
   d. thinks only of her grandson

_____ 4. How is Phoenix able to remember the way to the doctor's office?
   a. After many trips to the doctor, her feet remember where to take her.
   b. She asks many helpful people for directions.
   c. She is able to find her way with the help of some schoolchildren.
   d. She is able to find her way with the help of a large black dog.

_____ 5. When Phoenix arrives at the doctor's office, what does the attendant think?
   a. She thinks that Phoenix is in the wrong building.
   b. She thinks that Phoenix is insane.
   c. She supposes that Phoenix is from the country.
   d. She supposes that Phoenix is a "charity case."

_____ 6. Phoenix is going to use her two nickels to buy
   a. a paper windmill
   b. some throat medicine
   c. a new dress
   d. a new cane

_____ 7. Phoenix imagines that she sees
   a. a buzzard in a cornfield
   b. a log across the creek
   c. her dress caught in a bush
   d. a boy with a slice of marble cake

Literary Element: Theme *(20 points; 10 points each)*
On the line provided, write the letter of the *best* answer to each of the following items.

____ **8.** The main theme of "A Worn Path" can *best* be described as the
  a. The persistent temptation to steal is a test of faith.
  b. Incredible physical strength can result from age and wisdom.
  c. An overwhelming presence of nature can threaten human lives.
  d. Strong devotion helps people continue on a difficult journey.

____ **9.** The main theme of the story can *best* be compared to
  a. an endless road to nowhere
  b. a long trail with obstacles and challenges
  c. a high-speed chase down a freeway
  d. a bumpy dirt road through a wheat field

Vocabulary *(20 points; 2 points each)*
Match the definition on the left with the Word to Own on the right. Write the letter of the Word to Own on the line provided.

____ **10.** continuing

____ **11.** groove made by a plow

____ **12.** purposeful

____ **13.** serious

____ **14.** lighted up

____ **15.** pattern; arrangement

____ **16.** deeply thoughtful

____ **17.** formal

____ **18.** assigned

____ **19.** freely swinging weight that regulates a clock's movement

a. intent

b. radiation

c. solemn

d. persistent

e. meditative

f. appointed

g. pendulum

h. illumined

i. furrow

j. ceremonial

Written Response *(25 points)*

20. On a separate sheet of paper, write a brief essay describing Phoenix's character. What kind of person is she? Make at least two references to details in the story to support your description.

Elements of Literature

SELECTION TEST

Richard Cory
Miniver Cheevy
Edwin Arlington Robinson

OPEN
BOOK

Pupil's Edition page 645
Pupil's Edition page 646

Comprehension *(80 points; 10 points each)*
On the line provided, write the letter of the *best* answer to each of the following items.

_____ **1.** The basic irony in "Richard Cory" is that a wealthy, enviable gentleman
   a. is detested by ordinary people
   b. doesn't understand human suffering
   c. finds nothing to live for
   d. won't talk to his neighbors

_____ **2.** Richard Cory's eventual fate
   a. results from business failures
   b. shows his underlying villainy
   c. was predictable, given his everyday behavior
   d. comes as a surprise to the townspeople

_____ **3.** "Richard Cory" contains strong visual images of
   a. life in a small New England town
   b. impoverished people living on the street
   c. fashions and customs of a bygone era
   d. the darkness of a midsummer night

_____ **4.** The final mystery of Richard Cory's life revolves around
   a. what unspeakable sadness he kept hidden
   b. why he took frequent strolls into town
   c. how he managed to impress other people
   d. what kind of treasures he had

_____ **5.** The irony of Miniver Cheevy's story is that he
   a. enjoys thinking about ancient times
   b. dreams of great deeds while failing to act
   c. has a thorough knowledge of medieval history
   d. fails to use his wealth wisely

_____ **6.** Miniver Cheevy can *best* be characterized as the type of person who
   a. blames his parents for the woes he suffers
   b. likes to discuss his goals with friends
   c. feels he is out of place and misunderstood
   d. strikes out violently when he is criticized

____ **7.** To comfort himself, Cheevy
    a. writes about knighthood
    b. dresses in regal clothing
    c. teaches Greek history
    d. relies on alcohol

____ **8.** Richard Cory and Miniver Cheevy are most alike in that they both have
    a. secret miseries
    b. antisocial attitudes
    c. slim physiques
    d. comfortable homes

Written Response *(20 points)*

9. In both "Richard Cory" and "Miniver Cheevy," the characters seem to yearn for things they feel they lack in life. On a separate sheet of paper, describe what you think the characters long for. Support your ideas with at least one example from each poem.

SELECTION TEST

Soldier's Home
Ernest Hemingway   Pupil's Edition page 652

Comprehension *(35 points; 5 points each)*
On the line provided, write the letter of the *best* answer to each of the following items.

_____ **1.** Which of the following sentences *best* states the theme of "Soldier's Home"?
  a. Family and friends want returning soldiers to find good jobs.
  b. Most civilians never appreciate the heroism of soldiers.
  c. Wartime combat is so devastating that it changes one completely.
  d. Soldiers return home with little respect for their neighbors.

_____ **2.** Krebs can *best* be described as a person who
  a. deeply distrusts everyone around him
  b. looks forward to taking up peacetime activities
  c. has lost his goals and the energy to pursue them
  d. has suffered injuries that leave him physically weak

_____ **3.** When he returns home, Krebs finds that he
  a. can talk only to his sister about the war
  b. has to lie to be listened to
  c. wants to read adventure books
  d. does not want a girlfriend

_____ **4.** Krebs has returned home too late to
  a. find a comfortable place to live
  b. feel any interest about wartime events
  c. receive news of the whereabouts of his fellow soldiers
  d. receive an elaborate welcome from the town

_____ **5.** Krebs's sister Helen seems to
  a. need his love and approval
  b. grow embarrassed by his behavior
  c. resent his long absence from home
  d. be jealous of the attention he gets

_____ **6.** Krebs's father thinks that Krebs
  a. is lazy
  b. would like to re-enlist in the army
  c. should take the car out from time to time
  d. should come to work for him

_____ **7.** After the conversation with his mother, Krebs decides to go away because he
  a. wants to avoid any kind of conflict
  b. hears of a job opportunity in Kansas City
  c. realizes that his parents no longer love him
  d. yearns to find a rural area and settle down

Reading Skills and Strategies: Reading for Details *(20 points; 10 points each)*
On the line provided, write the letter of the *best* answer to each of the following items.

_____ **8.** What does Krebs seem to need *most* when he returns home?
     a. an executive job at his father's office
     b. solitude and understanding
     c. further military training
     d. stimulation and excitement

_____ **9.** What is Krebs *most* nostalgic about?
     a. the Rhine River Valley
     b. the library
     c. being in Europe
     d. playing pool

Vocabulary *(20 points; 2 points each)*
Match the definition on the left with the Word to Own on the right. Write the letter of the Word to Own on the line provided.

_____ **10.** feeling discomfort in the stomach   **a.** alliances
_____ **11.** close associations for common objectives   **b.** apocryphal
_____ **12.** of questionable authority; false   **c.** atrocity
_____ **13.** with great care   **d.** consequences
_____ **14.** battles   **e.** elaborately
_____ **15.** scheming   **f.** engagements
_____ **16.** uncontrolled excitement   **g.** exaggeration
_____ **17.** horrible; brutal   **h.** hysteria
_____ **18.** results of an action   **i.** intrigue
_____ **19.** overstatement   **j.** nauseated

Written Response *(25 points)*

20. Krebs thinks a great deal about lies. On a separate sheet of paper, explain why Krebs feels that he is lying. Make at least two references to details in the story to support your ideas.

SELECTION TEST

The Love Song of J. Alfred Prufrock
T. S. Eliot

OPEN
BOOK

Pupil's Edition page 663

Comprehension *(45 points; 15 points each)*
On the line provided, write the letter of the *best* answer to each of the following items.

_____ **1.** Which of the following statements *best* reflects Prufrock's view of himself?
    a. I am a victim of bad luck.   **c.** Women have always admired me.
    b. I am unable to take risks.   **d.** Youth is adventurous; old age is dull.

_____ **2.** Prufrock thinks of the frolicking mermaids as creatures who
    a. live in a world of freedom and immortality
    b. lure him toward death and destruction
    c. laugh at the peculiarities of romanticism
    d. know that the ocean is safer than the land

_____ **3.** Prufrock seems to be a man who has
    a. suffered a hard life in London   **c.** avoided opportunities for change
    b. had a pleasant home and family life   **d.** treated other people with malice

Reading Skills and Strategies
On the line provided, write the letter of the *best* answer to each of the following items.

Identifying Main Ideas and Supporting Details *(10 points)*

_____ **4.** Which of the following sentences *best* states the main idea of the poem?
    a. The modern world has no need of intellectual people.
    b. Modern life is spiritually bankrupt.
    c. In modern times, heroes are not needed.
    d. Modern people are generous and kind.

Understanding Rhythm, Rhymes, Metaphors, and Illusions *(10 points)*

_____ **5.** The majority of allusions that Eliot makes in the poem are
    a. scientific   **c.** musical
    b. political   **d.** biblical

Literary Element: Dramatic Monologue *(10 points)*
On the line provided, write the letter of the *best* answer to the following item.

_____ **6.** Prufrock's dramatic monologue enables the reader to
    a. see logical, sequential connections between ideas
    b. understand the lives of many other people
    c. glimpse the defining events in Prufrock's childhood
    d. follow the stream of Prufrock's rambling thoughts

Written Response *(25 points)*

7. Prufrock expresses a general sense of despair. On a separate sheet of paper, identify the passage or image in the poem that you think most vividly communicates this feeling of despair. Give at least one reason why this passage or image impresses you.

SELECTION TEST

The Life You Save May Be Your Own
Flannery O'Connor   Pupil's Edition page 673

Comprehension *(25 points; 5 points each)*
On the line provided, write the letter of the *best* answer to each of the following items.

_____ 1. The elder Lucynell allows Shiftlet to live with them because she wants him to
     a. repair the car   **c.** marry her daughter
     b. fix a fence   **d.** pay the mortgage

_____ 2. The mother and Shiftlet are similar because they both
     a. exploit other people
     b. have a sense of humor
     c. protect animals
     d. understand Shiftlet's goal

_____ 3. The climax of the story occurs when Shiftlet
     a. leaves Lucynell in The Hot Spot
     b. gets the ancient car to start
     c. tells the hitchhiker about his mother
     d. notices a highway warning sign

_____ 4. Shiftlet's dissatisfaction with his marriage ceremony is probably a result of the fact that
     a. he would prefer to marry the elder Lucynell
     b. he is already married and is breaking the law by marrying again
     c. the elder Lucynell has made fun of his physical disabilities
     d. he only married the younger Lucynell in order to get the car

_____ 5. The young Lucynell can *best* be described as a
     a. cruel character who takes pleasure in hurting people
     b. trusting soul who is content with her life on the farm
     c. suspicious person who distrusts most adults
     d. wise character who cannot be surprised by anything

Reading Skills and Strategies: Making Predictions *(10 points; 5 points each)*
On the line provided, write the letter of the *best* answer to each of the following items.

_____ 6. Shiftlet's refusal to answer the elder Lucynell's question about where he's from enables the reader to predict that
     a. he will eventually answer the question
     b. the young Lucynell will ask him where he's from
     c. the elder Lucynell will repeat the question many times
     d. he will behave like a person who has something to hide

_____ 7. When Shiftlet says that "'people don't care how they lie,'" we can predict that he
     a. is devoted to the truth
     b. will lie a great deal
     c. has never told a lie
     d. occasionally tells harmless "white" lies

Literary Elements
On the line provided, write the letter of the *best* answer to each of the following items.

Foreshadowing *(10 points; 5 points each)*

_____ 8. Near the beginning of the story, Shiftlet suggests to the mother that he may be a
liar. This is an example of foreshadowing because it
a. shows that Shiftlet knows himself well
b. hints at the deception to come
c. reveals the mother's goals
d. indicates that Shiftlet likes the daughter

_____ 9. The boy at The Hot Spot looks darkly at Shiftlet after the man first speaks. His
glance foreshadows
a. the awakening of young Lucynell
b. the terrible conversation they have
c. the return of the elder Lucynell
d. Shiftlet's continuing, rewarding journey

The Four "Modes" of Fiction *(5 points)*

_____ 10. Which of the following elements in "The Life You Save May Be Your Own" is in
keeping with the ironic mode of fiction?
a. Shiftlet is neither admirable nor heroic.
b. Shiftlet enjoys conversation.
c. The young Lucynell marries Shiftlet.
d. The young Lucynell is described as looking like an angel.

Vocabulary *(20 points; 2 points each)*
Match the definition on the left with the Word to Own on the right. Write the letter of the Word
to Own on the line provided.

_____ 11. regretted a. amble
_____ 12. very eager; hungry b. gaunt
_____ 13. like a loud burst of laughter c. guffawing
_____ 14. leisurely pace d. irked
_____ 15. firing of many shots at once e. listed
_____ 16. very thin f. morose
_____ 17. humid and still g. ravenous
_____ 18. annoyed; irritated h. rued
_____ 19. tilted i. sultry
_____ 20. gloomy j. volley

Written Response *(30 points)*

21. The end of the story describes a violent storm filled with strange clouds, crashing thunder,
and pelting rain. On a separate sheet of paper, explain what this storm may symbolize. Make
at least two references to details in the story to support your ideas.

SELECTION TEST

Richard Bone
"Butch" Weldy
Fiddler Jones
Petit, the Poet
Mrs. George Reece
Edgar Lee Masters

OPEN
BOOK

Pupil's Edition page 692

Comprehension *(75 points; 5 points each)*
On the line provided, write the letter of the *best* answer to each of the following items.

_____ 1. Richard Bone describes himself as a hypocrite because he continued working at a job that required him to
   a. report history   **c.** support the war
   b. praise the rich   **d.** write lies

_____ 2. Richard Bone implies that he carved what he was told to because
   a. he was paid to carve whatever people wanted
   b. he does not want to hurt people's feelings
   c. he knew the people who had died
   d. printers write what they are told

_____ 3. At the end of "Richard Bone," Bone compares himself to the
   a. undertaker   **c.** preacher
   b. historian   **d.** newspaper editor

_____ 4. The first line of the poem "'Butch' Weldy," which states that "Butch" settled down and "got religion," refers to
   a. "Butch's" life before he caused Fiddler Jones's death
   b. a time after Fiddler Jones's death when "Butch" stopped drinking
   c. the time after "Butch's" accident
   d. "Butch's" being drunk for most of his life

_____ 5. The trial in "'Butch' Weldy" is
   a. "Butch's" trial for causing Fiddler Jones's death
   b. Old Rhodes's son being tried for causing Fiddler Jones's death
   c. "Butch's" suit against Rhodes to get compensation for his accident
   d. the "trial" his life has become since his injuries in the explosion at work

_____ 6. When "Butch" Weldy says, "I didn't know him at all," he refers to
   a. Old Rhodes
   b. Old Rhodes's son
   c. the man who left the blow-fire burning
   d. the Circuit Judge

_____ 7. In "Fiddler Jones," Fiddler Jones
   a. cannot resist dancing
   b. does not like the way his life has gone
   c. carves cemetery headstones for a living
   d. has trouble getting his farming done

_____ **8.** Fiddler Jones
  a. did not know how to farm
  b. heard music in everything
  c. was lazy at heart
  d. resented "Butch" Weldy for causing his death

_____ **9.** Fiddler Jones
  a. never got richer
  b. envied Cooney Potter's success
  c. lost his forty acres
  d. died a broken man

_____ **10.** In "Petit, the Poet," Petit does not pay attention to
  a. life in the village
  b. the poets Homer and Whitman
  c. triolets, villanelles, and rondels
  d. the pines in the wood

_____ **11.** To Petit, seed pods represent
  a. rebirth
  b. nature and growth
  c. the people of the village
  d. his work and his life

_____ **12.** Petit is preoccupied with
  a. rhythm and rhyme
  b. symphonies
  c. weaving
  d. the woodlands

_____ **13.** "Butch" Weldy and George Reece both suffer at the hands of
  a. their defense attorney
  b. Jack the Fiddler
  c. the bank president
  d. the tank yard owner

_____ **14.** In "Mrs. George Reece," Mrs. Reece recommends
  a. living life to the fullest
  b. saving money
  c. going to school
  d. memorizing a verse

_____ **15.** Mrs. Reece
  a. finds excuses for her behavior
  b. takes responsibilities seriously
  c. seeks revenge
  d. tutors students

Written Response (25 points)

16. A common theme in literature is how people or characters react to their pasts. On a separate sheet of paper, describe how this theme applies to three of the characters: Richard Bone, "Butch" Weldy, Fiddler Jones, Petit, or Mrs. George Reece. Use at least one idea or image from each of the three poems bearing their names to support your conclusions.

SELECTION TEST

Recuerdo
Edna St. Vincent Millay

Pupil's Edition page 698

Comprehension *(50 points; 10 points each)*
On the line provided, write the letter of the *best* answer to each of the following items.

_____ 1. The main setting of "Recuerdo" is
    a. a trip on a ferryboat
    b. an elopement celebration
    c. an endurance contest
    d. a salon in Greenwich Village

_____ 2. Who is the "we" in the poem?
    a. a speaker and her lover
    b. the speaker and a friend
    c. a speaker and a sister
    d. the speaker and a brother

_____ 3. Which of the following poetic devices does Millay use repeatedly in the poem?
    a. personification
    b. hyperbole
    c. parallelism
    d. allusion

_____ 4. The main subject of the poem is
    a. the generosity of youth
    b. an interesting afternoon
    c. New York City in the 1920s
    d. the power of love

_____ 5. The poet's use of repetition in the poem creates a
    a. lilting, happy mood
    b. contrast with the poet's feeling in the present
    c. contrast with the woman they meet
    d. sense of the motion and rhythm of the ferry

Reading Skills and Strategies: Appreciating Imagery *(30 points; 15 points each)*
On the line provided, write the letter of the *best* answer to each of the following items.

_____ 6. Millay intends the image of the weeping woman to have a
    a. negative connotation
    b. positive connotation
    c. neutral connotation
    d. strict denotation

_____ 7. The positive images in Millay's poem include all of the following **except**
    a. fruit
    b. the moon
    c. fire
    d. tombstones

Written Response *(20 points)*

8. *Recuerdo* means "remembrance." On a separate sheet of paper, discuss what elements evoke a happy memory for the speaker. Make at least two references to details in the poem to support your ideas.

SELECTION TEST

The Jilting of Granny Weatherall
Katherine Anne Porter   Pupil's Edition page 703

Comprehension *(25 points; 5 points each)*
On the line provided, write the letter of the *best* answer to each of the following items.

____ 1. Granny Weatherall's attitude can *best* be described as
    a. resolute and determined   **c.** sarcastic
    b. sweetly nostalgic   **d.** humorous

____ 2. The story is told from the point of view of
    a. Doctor Harry   **c.** Ellen Weatherall
    b. Cornelia   **d.** George

____ 3. Granny Weatherall's marriage to John was evidently
    a. filled with conflict   **c.** disappointing and dreary
    b. long and successful   **d.** a source of material wealth

____ 4. Which of the following would be the most accurate subtitle for the story?
    a. "A Dutiful Child"   **c.** "An Incurable Wound"
    b. "A Doctor's Success"   **d.** "The Fear of Life"

____ 5. Which of the following situations in the story is ironic?
    a. Granny Weatherall is happy that Cornelia remembered her manners and offered Father Connolly a chair.
    b. Granny Weatherall believes that what happened with her first fiancé, George, was a positive experience.
    c. Granny Weatherall believes she is expressing herself as she is dying, but all anyone hears is mumbling.
    d. Granny Weatherall makes an eloquent speech while she is on her deathbed.

Reading Skills and Strategies: Reading Closely *(10 points; 5 points each)*
On the line provided, write the letter of the *best* answer to each of the following items.

____ 6. When Granny Weatherall sees Hapsy coming into the room, others around her perceive that
    a. Granny Weatherall is looking a bit under the weather
    b. Hapsy was actually leaving the room
    c. it is Granny's daughter Lydia who is coming into the room
    d. the weather is starting to get worse

____ 7. When Granny Weatherall notes that the doctor has returned after only five minutes, what has really happened is that
    a. the doctor never actually returned
    b. an entire day had passed
    c. it was actually the doctor's brother
    d. she had imagined the first visit

Literary Element: Stream of Consciousness *(20 points; 10 points each)*
On the line provided, write the letter of the *best* answer to each of the following items.

_____ 8. Porter chose to use the stream-of-consciousness style of narration in order to
   a. express the thoughts of people gathered around a deathbed
   b. point out the injustices Granny Weatherall has suffered
   c. vividly describe the hard life of a pioneer
   d. allow the reader to get inside Granny's head

_____ 9. Porter's use of the stream-of-consciousness technique allows the reader to
   a. admire Granny Weatherall's accurate memory
   b. contrast Granny Weatherall's thoughts with reality
   c. sympathize with Hapsy and Lydia
   d. realize that the doctor was absent for five minutes

Vocabulary *(20 points; 2 points each)*
Match the definition on the left with the Word to Own on the right. Write the letter of the Word to Own on the line provided.

_____ 10. excessive pride

_____ 11. something showy, frivolous, or needless

_____ 12. cold and damp

_____ 13. rejected (as a lover)

_____ 14. annoy

_____ 15. diminished

_____ 16. skilled in saying the right thing

_____ 17. aura; halo

_____ 18. extra amount

_____ 19. contested

a. clammy
b. disputed
c. dwindled
d. frippery
e. jilted
f. margin
g. nimbus
h. plague
i. tactful
j. vanity

Written Response *(25 points)*

20. At the end of the story, the dying Granny Weatherall asks God to give her a "sign." On a separate sheet of paper, explain what kind of sign Granny is looking for, what the response is, and how this response reflects the central event in her past.

SELECTION TEST

A Rose for Emily
William Faulkner

Pupil's Edition page 715

Comprehension *(25 points; 5 points each)*
On the line provided, write the letter of the *best* answer to each of the following items.

_____ 1. The emotions a reader might be expected to feel toward Emily include
    a. amusement and gratitude   **c.** contempt and disappointment
    b. pity and horror   **d.** approval and satisfaction

_____ 2. After her father dies, Emily
    a. moves to another town   **c.** becomes a supporter of the arts
    b. sees many suitors   **d.** refuses to acknowledge his death

_____ 3. The last time the townspeople see Homer Barron alive, he is
    a. buying a suit of clothes   **c.** proposing marriage to Emily
    b. drinking with other men   **d.** entering Emily's house

_____ 4. The strand of gray hair discovered at the end of the story signifies that
    a. Emily has apparently lain beside the skeleton
    b. Emily has forgotten about her family
    c. Homer Barron kept a lock of Emily's hair
    d. Emily was much older than Homer Barron

_____ 5. How does Colonel Sartoris influence Emily?
    a. He makes her think about future suitors.
    b. He makes her feel as if she's above the law.
    c. He makes her feel as if the world is ending.
    d. He makes her think about military maneuvers.

Reading Skills and Strategies: Taking Notes on a Character *(10 points; 5 points each)*
On the line provided, write the letter of the *best* answer to each of the following items.

_____ 6. What does Emily's father do to influence the development of her character?
    a. He drives off suitors and prevents her from marrying.
    b. He refuses to allow her to use the family name.
    c. He forces her to work in the family business.
    d. He forgets to leave anything to Emily in his will.

_____ 7. Which of Homer Barron's actions has the greatest effect on the development of Emily's character?
    a. He takes her on rides in a buggy.
    b. He visits her at her house.
    c. He returns to town after an absence.
    d. He enrages her by rejecting her.

Literary Element: Setting *(20 points; 10 points each)*
On the line provided, write the letter of the *best* answer to each of the following items.

____ **8.** The social environment described in the story is
    a. an idealized view of Southern society
    b. an inconsequential backdrop to the main action
    c. a reflection of indifference to one's neighbors
    d. a crucial part of the story's setting

____ **9.** The small-town setting of the story helps the reader to understand
    a. the unimportance of social class and gentility to Emily
    b. the history of the Civil War
    c. the tolerant attitudes of the townspeople toward Northerners
    d. why the thwarting of Emily's desire to marry Homer Barron mattered so much

Vocabulary *(20 points; 2 points each)*
Match the definition on the left with the Word to Own on the right. Write the letter of the Word to Own on the line provided.

____ **10.** shaky; trembling from old age   **a.** acrid

____ **11.** extremely poor person   **b.** archaic

____ **12.** short decorative drapery   **c.** circumvent

____ **13.** eternity   **d.** doddering

____ **14.** full of hate; venomous   **e.** pauper

____ **15.** bitter; irritating   **f.** perpetuity

____ **16.** old-fashioned   **g.** tranquil

____ **17.** proved correct   **h.** valance

____ **18.** to get the better of by craft or ingenuity   **i.** vindicated

____ **19.** calm; quiet   **j.** virulent

Written Response *(25 points)*

20. In what ways is Emily affected by the shadows of the past? On a separate piece of paper, explain how Emily is affected by her father and by the Grierson family's sense of its position in society. Make at least two references to details in the story to support your ideas.

SELECTION TEST

Go Down, Death
James Weldon Johnson
America
Claude McKay

OPEN
BOOK

Pupil's Edition page 737

Pupil's Edition page 744

Comprehension *(45 points; 5 points each)*
On the line provided, write the letter of the *best* answer to each of the following items.

_____ 1. The speaker in "Go Down, Death" comforts Sister Caroline's family by explaining that Sister Caroline is
   a. resting with Jesus
   b. joining the natural world
   c. bound to recover
   d. being reunited with departed friends

_____ 2. Death responds to God's urgent command with
   a. a brief argument
   b. swift and silent obedience
   c. long-winded agreement
   d. a humorous delay

_____ 3. The speaker in Johnson's poem characterizes Jesus as a
   a. weeping friend
   b. beautiful child
   c. stern judge
   d. loving parent

_____ 4. Johnson wrote "Go Down, Death" in the style of
   a. political orators
   b. jazz musicians
   c. old-time preachers
   d. blues singers

_____ 5. All of the following images appear in McKay's poem **except**
   a. a tiger
   b. an eagle
   c. a flood
   d. treasure

_____ 6. The theme of McKay's poem "America" concerns the speaker's mixed feelings about
   a. the Russian revolution
   b. Southern Gothic literature
   c. the Harlem Renaissance
   d. life in the United States

_____ 7. The central conflict in McKay's poem takes place between
   a. the speaker's contradictory observations and feelings
   b. the king of the state and the leader of a group of rebels
   c. the speaker's past dreams and present reality
   d. a rich man and a poor man

_____ 8. The speaker in "America" draws strength from
   a. the beauty found in nature
   b. the support of established writers
   c. America's vastness and energy
   d. the belief that things will get better

_____ 9. The speaker in McKay's poem envisions America's future as
   a. a sad and necessary decline
   b. the rise of a superpower
   c. a vastly improved and just nation
   d. a disastrous social experiment

Literary Elements

On the line provided, write the letter of the *best* answer to each of the following items.

Personification *(20 points; 10 points each)*

_____ **10.** In "Go Down, Death," Death is personified as a
   a. preacher in heaven   **c.** rescuer on horseback
   b. cruel and devious angel   **d.** huge comet in the sky

_____ **11.** In "America," America is personified as a
   a. granite mountain that the speaker wants to climb
   b. woman who feeds the speaker bitterness
   c. tiger that eats bread with the speaker
   d. rich treasure that disappears in the sand

Free Verse and the Orator's Style *(20 points; 10 points each)*

_____ **12.** Both James Weldon Johnson and Walt Whitman use repetition, parallelism, and
   sound effects to
   a. create rhymes, figurative language, and regular meter
   b. personify emotions, thoughts, and natural objects
   c. create rhythm
   d. convince the reader that death is a terrifying event

_____ **13.** Both James Weldon Johnson and Walt Whitman use all of the following elements in
   their poems **except**
   a. slang   **c.** natural rhythms of speech
   b. irregular line lengths   **d.** strict meter

Written Response *(15 points)*

14. What is the attitude of the speaker in "America" toward his country? On a separate sheet of
paper, write the letter of the answer you choose and defend your choice. There is more than
one possible correct answer. Use at least one example from the poem to support your ideas.
   a. He is angered by his country's injustices.
   b. He imagines that one day his country will fall.
   c. He stands in awe of the greatness of his country.
   d. He does not care about his country.

SELECTION TEST

Tableau
Incident
Countee Cullen

OPEN
BOOK

Pupil's Edition page 747

Pupil's Edition page 748

Comprehension *(60 points; 6 points each)*
On the line provided, write the letter of the *best* answer to each of the following items.

_____ **1.** In "Tableau," the boys are walking together because they
  a. are trying to cause trouble   **c.** are following local custom
  b. hope to provoke social change   **d.** enjoy each other's company

_____ **2.** How do other people react to the behavior of the two boys in "Tableau"?
  a. They cheer on the two boys.   **c.** They ignore the boys' presence.
  b. They are upset by the display.   **d.** They quietly approve of the friendship.

_____ **3.** In the last stanza of "Tableau," the boys
  a. angrily confront the adults of the town   **c.** sadly go their separate ways
  b. happily continue walking   **d.** speak to each other loudly

_____ **4.** "Tableau" seems to present a simple picture, but the larger focus of the poem is the
  a. boys' walking across the street
  b. reaction of other children
  c. state of race relations
  d. poet's childhood dreams

_____ **5.** Cullen uses lightning as imagery in the last stanza to illustrate all of the following **except**
  a. the power of the boys' friendship
  b. the destruction the boys' relationship will bring
  c. the courage of the two boys
  d. the enlightened attitude of the boys

_____ **6.** There is irony in the apparently simple title "Incident" because the poem describes
  a. an event with serious consequences   **c.** a series of historical events
  b. more than one personal event   **d.** the poet's experience

_____ **7.** While riding through Baltimore, the speaker in "Incident" at first feels
  a. frightened, yet fascinated   **c.** puzzled and homesick
  b. eager, yet timid   **d.** happy and optimistic

_____ **8.** Upon seeing another boy, the speaker in "Incident"
  a. attempts to scare him   **c.** tries to be friendly
  b. is reminded of his brother **d.** strikes up a conversation

_____ 9. In "Incident," the encounter with the boy in Baltimore
     a. has a strong impression on the speaker
     b. has no particular effect on the speaker
     c. provokes the speaker to lash out in anger
     d. is remembered fondly by the speaker

_____ 10. How do the rhythm and rhyme contribute to the theme of "Incident"?
     a. They give the poem a singsong effect.
     b. Their simplicity contrasts with the serious theme of the poem.
     c. They make the poem easy to read.
     d. They show that the Baltimorean is young and will grow out of his prejudice.

Written Response *(40 points; 20 points each)*

11. What is the theme of "Incident"? On a separate sheet of paper, write the letter of the answer you choose and defend your choice. There is more than one possible correct answer. Use at least one example from the poem to support your ideas.
     a. Children can be as mean as adults.
     b. A cruel word can leave a lasting impression.
     c. Public transportation is dangerous.
     d. Other: _____

12. How are interactions between people of different races portrayed in the two Cullen poems you have read? On a separate sheet of paper, compare and contrast the two portrayals. Make at least two references to examples from each of the poems to support your ideas.

SELECTION TEST

from Dust Tracks on a Road
Zora Neale Hurston

Pupil's Edition page 751

Comprehension *(25 points; 5 points each)*

On the line provided, write the letter of the *best* answer to each of the following items.

_____ 1. Which of the following quotations from *Dust Tracks on a Road* demonstrates the use of slang?
   a. "I used to take a seat on top of the gatepost and watch the world go by."
   b. "Not only was I barefooted, but my feet and legs were dusty."
   c. "She would cut her eyes and give us a glare that meant trouble . . ."
   d. "They came and went, came and went."

_____ 2. Upon seeing cars and carriages pass by her house, Zora Neale would
   a. ask the travelers for a ride
   b. follow them with her bike
   c. run to inform her parents
   d. try to race the cars on foot

_____ 3. Zora Neale's grandmother feared her granddaughter's boldness would
   a. cause her to fall off the gatepost
   b. make her unpopular at school
   c. provoke white people to harm her
   d. one day cause a traffic accident

_____ 4. The students' good behavior in school is most influenced by
   a. their wish to impress their teachers
   b. the threat of Mrs. Calhoun's palmetto switch
   c. the absence of visitors in the classroom
   d. the hope that visitors will recognize them

_____ 5. What is Zora Neale's reaction to the gifts given to her by the visitors from Minnesota?
   a. She is grateful but disappointed because she'd hoped for more.
   b. She is embarrassed that the women singled her out.
   c. It is one of the most joyful experiences of her life.
   d. She is suspicious of the women's generosity.

Reading Skills and Strategies: Analyzing an Autobiography *(30 points; 15 points each)*

On the line provided, write the letter of the *best* answer to each of the following items.

_____ 6. Zora Neale ignores her grandmother's warning, which shows that Zora Neale is
   a. frightened, weak, and insecure
   b. ignorant, uneducated, and closed-minded
   c. outgoing, independent, and brazen
   d. irritable, angry, and impatient

_____ 7. By reading the class reader from cover to cover, Zora Neale shows that she is
   a. worried that the other students will mock her
   b. obsessed with pleasing her parents and the teacher
   c. afraid she won't get straight A's
   d. self-motivated and ambitious

Vocabulary (20 points; 2 points each)

Match the definition on the left with the Word to Own on the right. Write the letter of the Word to Own on the line provided.

____	**8.** think; imagine	**a.** hail
____	**9.** deeply	**b.** brazenness
____	**10.** stepping	**c.** caper
____	**11.** greet	**d.** exalted
____	**12.** foolish prank	**e.** realm
____	**13.** greed	**f.** avarice
____	**14.** kingdom	**g.** tread
____	**15.** boldness	**h.** profoundly
____	**16.** lifted up	**i.** resolved
____	**17.** made a decision; determined	**j.** conceive

Written Response (25 points)

18. Sometimes a person's heroes or heroines tell you a lot about that person. On a separate sheet of paper, describe the kind of literary characters that attract Hurston. Then explain why you think she is drawn to these characters. Make at least two references to details in the selection to support your ideas.

SELECTION TEST

The Weary Blues
Harlem
Langston Hughes

OPEN
BOOK

Pupil's Edition page 761
Pupil's Edition page 764

Comprehension *(60 points; 10 points each)*
On the line provided, write the letter of the *best* answer to each of the following items.

_____ 1. The song performed in "The Weary Blues" addresses
    a. all people who are unhappy
    b. the plight of underpaid musicians
    c. the musician's poor health
    d. men without children

_____ 2. The musician in "The Weary Blues" feels tired because he
    a. works all night
    b. receives low wages
    c. can't find satisfaction
    d. suffers from lack of sleep

_____ 3. At the end of "The Weary Blues," the musician
    a. sleeps like the dead
    b. meets the poet
    c. smiles at the audience
    d. passes around a hat

_____ 4. According to the speaker in "Harlem," conditions for people living in Harlem
    a. improved after the birth of the blues
    b. have deteriorated since they moved there
    c. have not changed much over the years
    d. will become better as time passes

_____ 5. The speaker in "Harlem" uses "we" to refer to
    a. residents of Manhattan
    b. people selling bread in Harlem
    c. people who remember the Depression
    d. African Americans in Harlem

_____ 6. In the final stanza of "Harlem," people
    a. thoughtfully observe the outside world
    b. recall World War II
    c. talk about the civil rights movement
    d. decide to leave the neighborhood

Literary Element: Rhythm *(10 points; 5 points each)*
On the line provided, write the letter of the *best* answer to each of the following items.

_____ 7. Rhythms in "The Weary Blues"
    a. are highly regular
    b. reflect the rhythms of blues music
    c. require piano in the background
    d. are those of the traditional sonnet

_____ 8. The type of poetry that could *best* accommodate the "syncopated" rhythm referred to in "The Weary Blues" is
    a. the sonnet
    b. free verse
    c. the villanelle
    d. blank verse

Literary Element: Tone *(10 points; 5 points each)*
On the line provided, write the letter of the *best* answer to answer each of the following items.

____ 9. The tone of a work refers to the
    a. atmosphere created by the work
    b. emotions of the narrator
    c. attitude of the writer
    d. way in which a writer uses language

____ 10. "Harlem" conveys all of the following **except**
    a. caution
    b. anger
    c. frustration
    d. cynicism

Written Response *(20 points)*

11. Are the situations described in the two Langston Hughes poems similar or different? On a separate sheet of paper, compare and contrast the hardship(s) described by the speaker in "Harlem" with the musician's experience(s) in "The Weary Blues." Make at least two references to examples from both poems to support your ideas.

SELECTION TEST

The River-Merchant's Wife: A Letter
Ezra Pound

OPEN
BOOK

Pupil's Edition page 774

Comprehension *(40 points; 10 points each)*
On the line provided, write the letter of the *best* answer to each of the following items.

_____ 1. In "The River-Merchant's Wife: A Letter," the speaker recalls how she first met her husband
  a. when they were children
  b. on their wedding day
  c. during courtship
  d. five months before

_____ 2. The speaker describes her behavior during the early days of the marriage as
  a. coy and flirtatious
  b. joyful and lighthearted
  c. shy and somber
  d. reckless and nervous

_____ 3. The couple became separated when the husband
  a. fell ill and went to a hospital
  b. left home on business
  c. died unexpectedly
  d. was kidnapped

_____ 4. In her loneliness, the speaker finds it painful even to watch
  a. a pair of butterflies
  b. purple plums
  c. the swirling river
  d. chattering monkeys

Reading Skills and Strategies: Identifying Images *(20 points; 10 points each)*
On the line provided, write the letter of the *best* answer to each of the following items.

_____ 5. The image of the wife pulling flowers as a child is meant to communicate that
  a. she dislikes flowers
  b. she is mischievous
  c. she will marry a merchant
  d. her life will be sorrowful

_____ 6. The image of the monkeys making sorrowful sounds is meant to communicate that
  a. the monkeys are angry
  b. good fortune awaits
  c. the wife is sad
  d. life is difficult

Literary Element: The Objective Correlative *(20 points; 10 points each)*
On the line provided, write the letter of the *best* answer to each of the following items.

_____ 7. Which of the following details is the *best* example of an objective correlative in the poem?
  a. the butterflies
  b. Cho-fu-Sa
  c. the gate
  d. the village

_____ 8. Which of the following quotations from the poem is the *best* example of an objective correlative?
  a. "And I will come out to meet you"
  b. "The monkeys make sorrowful noise overhead"
  c. "At sixteen you departed"
  d. "Please let me know beforehand"

Written Response *(20 points)*

9. Various images in "The River-Merchant's Wife: A Letter" contribute to the overall mood of the poem. On a separate sheet of paper, describe what you think the mood of the poem is. Select two images and explain how you think they help create that mood.

SELECTION TEST

The Red Wheelbarrow
The Great Figure
Spring and All
William Carlos Williams

OPEN
BOOK

Pupil's Edition page 779

Pupil's Edition page 781

Comprehension *(75 points; 5 points each)*
On the line provided, write the letter of the *best* answer to each of the following items.

_____ 1. "The Red Wheelbarrow" depicts a
    a. realistic scene
    b. series of fantastic images
    c. character's sorrow
    d. historically important moment

_____ 2. The speaker in "The Red Wheelbarrow"
    a. makes allusions to musical compositions
    b. emphasizes the importance of images
    c. regrets past actions
    d. offers an opinion about life

_____ 3. To describe the images in "The Red Wheelbarrow," Williams uses
    a. colors and simple language
    b. references to Imagist theory
    c. elaborate figures of speech
    d. sounds and rhythms

_____ 4. "The Red Wheelbarrow" has all of the following characteristics **except** that it
    a. uses common speech   **c.** uses a set rhyme scheme
    b. focuses on images   **d.** uses free verse

_____ 5. What does the title of "The Great Figure" literally refer to?
    a. vast size   **c.** a famous person
    b. the number 5   **d.** a Greek statue

_____ 6. The scene of "The Great Figure" is a
    a. dense forest in New Jersey
    b. beautiful but deserted town
    c. rainy night on a city street
    d. busy day in a large city

_____ 7. The images in "The Great Figure" primarily appeal to readers' senses of
    a. touch and hearing   **c.** sight and hearing
    b. smell and touch   **d.** smell and sight

_____ 8. The poem "The Great Figure" creates an overall impression of
    a. dramatic action
    b. peace and quiet
    c. dangerous menace
    d. an ordinary workday

_____ 9. Williams uses all of the following images in "The Great Figure" **except**
   a. clanging gongs   **c.** howling sirens
   b. tolling bells   **d.** rumbling wheels

_____ 10. In "Spring and All," Williams contrasts
   a. blue clouds and brown fields
   b. dried weeds and standing water
   c. brown trees and purple bushes
   d. hospitals and roads

_____ 11. One of the points Williams makes in "Spring and All" is that
   a. disease can take people by surprise at any time
   b. people are resistant to change
   c. from seeming death comes life
   d. spring is a time when love blossoms

_____ 12. In "Spring and All," Williams creates the feeling of spring through all of the
   following **except**
   a. the images of fields and water
   b. the chill of the wind
   c. an air of lifelessness and death
   d. bright colors

_____ 13. In "Spring and All," spring brings all of the following **except**
   a. uncertainty   **c.** determination
   b. creativity   **d.** dignity

_____ 14. The poem "Spring and All" is about the coming of spring, and, on a symbolic level,
   a. recovery in a hospital
   b. people as actors on the stage of life
   c. the speaker's life as a poet
   d. the birth of babies

_____ 15. Williams's poems can *best* be described as
   a. ornate
   b. deceptively simple
   c. sophisticated in rhyme scheme
   d. surreal

Written Response *(25 points)*

16. "The Red Wheelbarrow," "The Great Figure," and "Spring and All" share an ability to surprise the reader by creating a sense of expectation early in the poems. On a separate sheet of paper, describe how two of the poems by Williams foster an element of surprise. Make references to at least one example in each poem to support your ideas.

SELECTION TEST

Anecdote of the Jar
Disillusionment of Ten O'clock
Wallace Stevens

OPEN
BOOK

Pupil's Edition page 784

Comprehension *(50 points; 10 points each)*
On the line provided, write the letter of the *best* answer to each of the following items.

_____ 1. Which of the following words *best* describes the effect that the jar's placement has on the wilderness in Stevens's poem "Anecdote of the Jar"?
    a. spoiling   **c.** uplifting
    b. taming   **d.** distracting

_____ 2. An interpretation of "Anecdote of the Jar" is that
    a. people can control nature
    b. the appearance of nature is shaped by our imagination
    c. people should try to preserve the wilderness
    d. the wilderness will take over the land

_____ 3. The jar in Stevens's poem is generally described
    a. as a beautiful, fragile object   **c.** as a piece of scientific equipment
    b. with long, descriptive adjectives   **d.** in terms of its physical appearance

_____ 4. In "Disillusionment of Ten O'clock," Stevens asserts that most people
    a. do not seek out exciting adventures   **c.** dream in color
    b. respond positively to pure colors   **d.** do not have an active imagination

_____ 5. Wallace Stevens's poetry is particularly concerned with the relationship between
    a. people and nature   **c.** business and art
    b. the mind and the body   **d.** reality and the imagination

Reading Skills and Strategies: Analyzing Metaphor *(20 points; 10 points each)*
On the line provided, write the letter of the *best* answer to each of the following items.

_____ 6. The jar in "Anecdote of the Jar" can be seen as a metaphor for
    a. the slovenly wilderness of Tennessee
    b. the crushing boredom of nature
    c. humanity's interaction with nature
    d. humanity's love of wilderness areas

_____ 7. The implied symbol of the white night-gowns in "Disillusionment of Ten O'clock" is
    a. young children   **c.** married couples
    b. the lack of imagination   **d.** the importance of history

Written Response *(30 points)*

8. In "Ancedote of the Jar" and "Disillusionment of Ten O'clock," Stevens uses implied metaphors and symbols. On a separate piece of paper, discuss Stevens's use of metaphors and symbols. Refer to at least four metaphors or symbols used in the poems to support your answer.

SELECTION TEST

Poetry
Marianne Moore

Pupil's Edition page 787

Comprehension *(75 points; 15 points each)*
On the line provided, write the letter of the *best* answer to each of the following items.

_____ 1. In "Poetry," the speaker claims that grasping hands, dilating eyes, and rising hair are important because
    a. a sophisticated interpretation can be applied to them
    b. they are derivative
    c. they are useful
    d. they are new and exotic

_____ 2. What is "all this fiddle" that the speaker refers to in Moore's poem?
    a. poetry   **c.** interpretations
    b. adjectives   **d.** contempt

_____ 3. According to "Poetry," a good poet would
    a. symbolize love as a heart
    b. read Homer for inspiration
    c. dismiss the importance of textbooks and papers
    d. present imaginary places with real details

_____ 4. In "Poetry," the bat holding on upside down could be seen as a metaphor for
    a. school books and business letters
    b. derivative and unintelligible poetry
    c. baseball fans, critics, and statisticians
    d. hands that grasp and eyes that dilate

_____ 5. According to "Poetry," the *best* subject matter for poetry is
    a. bats, elephants, and wolves
    b. raw and genuine
    c. gardens and nature
    d. unintelligible

Written Response *(25 points)*

6. Which of the following statements *best* describes the message of Moore's "Poetry"? On a separate sheet of paper, write the letter of the answer you choose, and then defend your choice. There is more than one possible answer. Use at least one example from the selection to support your ideas.
    a. All poetry should focus on the natural world.
    b. If you say you dislike poetry, you probably just dislike certain types of poetry.
    c. Poets should write with imagination about topics that are useful.
    d. Other: _____

SELECTION TEST

Chicago
Carl Sandburg
what if a much of a which of a wind somewhere i have never travelled, gladly beyond
E. E. Cummings

Pupil's Edition page 792

Pupil's Edition page 797

Pupil's Edition page 798

Comprehension *(70 points; 10 points each)*
On the line provided, write the letter of the *best* answer to each of the following items.

_____ 1. "Chicago" opens with a description of the city's reputation as a center for
    a. computer software and other high-tech industries
    b. railroads, manufacturing, and stockyards
    c. music, theater, and cultural activities
    d. immorality and political corruption

_____ 2. In Sandburg's poem, the speaker compares Chicago to a
    a. hog that refuses to be slaughtered
    b. painted woman under a gas lamp
    c. fighter who has never lost a battle
    d. mighty, steam-driven locomotive

_____ 3. In the poem "Chicago," the speaker's attitude toward Chicago is
    a. admiring and affectionate   **c.** sad and repulsed
    b. indifferent and nonchalant   **d.** ambivalent and wary

_____ 4. In "what if a much of a which of a wind," the images describe
    a. a tornado in the Midwest   **c.** a gravitational problem
    b. the destruction of the universe   **d.** global weather changes

_____ 5. Cummings's poem "what if a much of a which of a wind" expresses the speaker's confidence in
    a. natural phenomena   **c.** humanity
    b. poetry   **d.** the rational mind

_____ 6. The speaker of "somewhere i have never travelled, gladly beyond" compares himself to
    a. a flower
    b. a small, frail hand
    c. silent eyes
    d. the color red

_____ 7. The speaker of "somewhere i have never travelled, gladly beyond" fears
    a. travelling
    b. being weak
    c. being rejected
    d. intense stares

Literary Element: Apostrophe *(10 points; 5 points each)*
On the line provided, write the letter of the *best* answer to each of the following items.

_____ **8.** "Chicago" makes use of apostrophe in that the
      a. speaker addresses the city as if it were a person
      b. poem contains inflated language and imagery
      c. poem features experimental use of punctuation
      d. speaker expresses his dislike of the city

_____ **9.** The use of apostrophe in "Chicago"
      a. shows possession   **c.** makes the poem confusing
      b. reveals the speaker's anxiety   **d.** gives the poem immediacy

Written Response *(20 points)*

10. Despite their differences, "Chicago," "what if a much of a which of a wind," and "somewhere i
have never travelled, gladly beyond" are similar in several ways. On a separate sheet of paper,
write a paragraph in which you compare the three poems. You should be able to find at least
two ways that the poems are similar. Make references to at least one example in each poem to
support your ideas.

THE AMERICAN LANGUAGE

American Slang

Pupil's Edition page 801

On the line provided, write the letter of the *best* answer to each of the following items.
(10 points each)

____ 1. Slang or its equivalent
   a. is a product of laziness and silliness
   b. flourishes only among the uneducated
   c. is as ancient as language itself
   d. is easier to understand than standard English

____ 2. The early words for slang—*cant* and *argot*—associated slang with
   a. formal studies
   b. kinship
   c. age groups
   d. occupation

____ 3. According to anthropologists, the main function of slang is to
   a. simplify language use
   b. define members of a group
   c. communicate meaning
   d. develop more colorful language

____ 4. Another explanation for the popularity of slang is that
   a. slang always refers to concrete objects
   b. people enjoy inventing informal, playful language
   c. slang generally derives from musical concepts
   d. using slang is a sign of economic success

____ 5. Most slang words and expressions
   a. disappear quickly
   b. are adopted by most people
   c. become a permanent part of the language
   d. communicate effectively

____ 6. For those who do not use it, the response to slang is often
   a. approval
   b. fear and trembling
   c. fascination
   d. highly critical

____ 7. Why has the United States been a particularly fertile ground for slang since the 1830s?
   a. Americans have developed a keen interest in language.
   b. Americans have found standard English difficult.
   c. The informality of slang is associated with democratic ideals.
   d. Slang has been taught in American schools.

_____ **8.** Slang words and phrases develop
  a. at the suggestion of professional linguists
  b. in exactly the same way as other additions to the language
  c. only when used by a particular occupational group
  d. because they are colorful rather than useful

_____ **9.** Backwoodsmen of the nineteenth century were responsible for introducing slang words that were
  a. variations of existing words
  b. standard words clipped to form shortened words
  c. borrowed from another language
  d. imaginative and wild inventions

_____ **10.** Certain words are considered slang for generations because they
  a. are confined to a small group
  b. fulfill only general purposes
  c. seem so informal
  d. are pure poetry

LITERARY ELEMENTS TEST

Free Verse and the Orator's Style	Pupil's Edition page 742
The Four "Modes" of Fiction	Pupil's Edition page 683
The Objective Correlative	Pupil's Edition page 777

On the line provided, write the letter of the *best* answer to each of the following items. *(10 points each)*

Free Verse and the Orator's Style

____ 1. Whitman uses all of the following elements in his free verse **except**
    a. standardized line length
    b. sound effects
    c. simple language
    d. repetition

____ 2. Whitman's use of free verse includes parallel structure, which is
    a. a word or line that is repeated several times in a poem
    b. the repetition of words or phrases that have similar grammatical forms
    c. the repetition of the same consonant sounds in words that occur close together
    d. a series of related figures of speech used to describe an object or a place

The Four "Modes" of Fiction

____ 3. All of the following are elements of tragedy **except**
    a. a main character who falls from grace
    b. a simple, straightforward plot
    c. a struggle with evil
    d. a noble hero

____ 4. Which mode of fiction *best* describes Ernest Hemingway's story "Soldier's Home"?
    a. romance
    b. comedy
    c. tragedy
    d. irony

____ 5. In a typical comedy, the two central characters
    a. dislike each other
    b. play practical jokes on each other
    c. write jokes about each other
    d. want to marry each other

____ 6. Which mode of fiction *best* describes Flannery O'Connor's story "The Life You Save May Be Your Own"?
    a. comedy
    b. tragedy
    c. irony
    d. romance

The Objective Correlative

____ 7. When poets use the objective correlative, they focus mainly on the readers'
     a. educational background
     b. objective thoughts
     c. philosophies
     d. emotions

____ 8. Which of the following quotations from "The River-Merchant's Wife: A Letter" is the *best* example of an objective correlative?
     a. "The leaves fall early this autumn, in wind."
     b. "While my hair was still cut straight across my forehead . . ."
     c. "At fifteen I stopped scowling,"
     d. "Why should I climb the lookout?"

____ 9. The objective correlative can *best* be compared to
     a. narrative
     b. a tragedy
     c. shorthand
     d. a sonata

____ 10. The image of different mosses growing deeply in "The River-Merchant's Wife: A Letter" is an objective correlative that
     a. reveals the speaker's educational background in Chokan
     b. expresses the speaker's sorrow over her husband's absence
     c. expresses the speaker's philosophy about fear
     d. expresses the speaker's objective thoughts about anger

LITERARY PERIOD TEST

The Moderns

Applying Skills

This test asks you to use the language skills and strategies you have learned. Before you begin reading, take a minute to remember what you know about semantic feature analysis, main idea, supporting detail, and tone. Read the poems, and then answer the questions that follow.

Daybreak in Alabama
by Langston Hughes

When I get to be a <u>composer</u>
I'm gonna write me some music about
Daybreak in Alabama
And I'm gonna put the purtiest songs in it
5   Rising out of the ground like a swamp mist
And falling out of heaven like soft dew.
I'm gonna put some tall tall trees in it
And the scent of pine needles
And the smell of red clay after rain
10   And long red necks
And poppy colored faces
And big brown eyes
Of black and white black white black people
And I'm gonna put white hands
15   And black hands and brown hands and yellow hands
And red clay earth hands in it
Touching everybody with kind fingers
And touching each other natural as dew
In that dawn of music when I
20   Get to be a composer
And write about daybreak
In Alabama.

The Planet on the Table
by Wallace Stevens

Ariel was glad he had written his poems.
They were of a remembered time
Or of something seen that he liked.
Other makings of the sun
5   Were waste and <u>welter</u>
And the ripe shrub <u>writhed</u>.
His self and the sun were one
And his poems, although makings of his self,
Were no less makings of the sun.
10   It was not important that they survive.
What mattered was that they should bear
Some <u>lineament</u> or character,

"Daybreak in Alabama" from *Selected Poems* by Langston Hughes. Copyright 1948 by Alfred A. Knopf, Inc.; renewed © 1976 by the Executor of the Estate of Langston Hughes. Reprinted by permission of **Alfred A. Knopf, Inc.**

"The Planet on the Table" from *Collected Poems* by Wallace Stevens. Copyright 1954 by Wallace Stevens. Reprinted by permission of **Alfred A. Knopf, Inc.**

Some <u>affluence</u>, if only half-perceived
In the poverty of their words,
15   Of the planet of which they were part.

Vocabulary Skills: New Words in Context (20 points; 4 points each)

Each of the following underlined words has also been underlined in the selection. Re-read those passages and use context clues to help you select an answer. On the line provided, write the letter of the word or phrase that *best* completes each sentence.

_____ **1.** A <u>composer</u> is a
    a. trumpet player
    b. painter
    c. songwriter
    d. collector

_____ **2.** <u>Welter</u> could be
    a. a disordered jumble
    b. rich growth
    c. brightly colored paper
    d. useful products

_____ **3.** A snake that <u>writhed</u> probably
    a. became stronger
    b. twisted and turned
    c. grew heartily
    d. stood out

_____ **4.** <u>Lineament</u> is *best* described as a
    a. type of cloth
    b. muscle pain
    c. healing balm
    d. distinctive feature

_____ **5.** <u>Affluence</u> refers to the planet's
    a. abundance
    b. rivers
    c. land mass
    d. size

Vocabulary: Semantic Features Analysis (20 points; 5 points each)

On the line provided, write the letter of the *best* answer to each of the following items.

_____ **6.** The meanings of synonymous words such as *tradition, duty, care,* and *obligation* can be best distinguished by analyzing their
    a. semantic features
    b. vowel sounds
    c. suffixes and prefixes
    d. syllabic structure

_____ **7.** To determine a word's exact denotation it is best to
    a. consult a thesaurus
    b. follow a pronunciation guide
    c. consult a dictionary
    d. review its etymology

_____ **8.** When chosen with precision, several synonyms in a series will often
    a. mean exactly the same thing
    b. make a sentence overly wordy
    c. fill out a sentence so that it seems worth paying attention to
    d. build a meaning richer than the meaning of any one word alone

_____ **9.** An analysis of the connotations of synonyms demonstrates that
    a. synonyms are completely interchangeable
    b. synonyms seldom mean exactly the same thing
    c. connotations add variety but do not affect the meanings of words
    d. the meanings of synonyms do not overlap

Comprehension *(20 points; 4 points each)*
On the line provided, write the letter of the *best* answer to each of the following items.

_____ **10.** In Hughes's poem, which of the following things is **not** something the composer says he is going to put into his music?
   a. tall trees
   b. swamp mist
   c. the smell of red clay after rain
   d. the scent of pine needles

_____ **11.** To what does Hughes compare the color of people's faces?
   a. daybreak
   b. music
   c. clay
   d. poppies

_____ **12.** In Hughes's poem, to what could "daybreak in Alabama" refer?
   a. a beautiful sunset
   b. westward migration
   c. a natural disaster
   d. change for the better

_____ **13.** The subject of Stevens's poem is the
   a. writing of poetry
   b. solar system
   c. speaker's disillusionment
   d. richness of language

_____ **14.** In "The Planet on the Table," which of the following statements is **not** true about the poems that Ariel writes?
   a. It is not essential that they survive.
   b. They were of a forgotten time.
   c. Ariel is happy that he wrote them.
   d. They were creations of the sun.

Reading Skills and Strategies
Identifying Main Ideas and Supporting Details *(10 points)*

15. From the following options, choose the one you think is the main idea of "The Planet on the Table." On the lines provided, write the letter of the answer you choose and briefly defend your choice. Use at least two details from the poem to support your ideas.
    a. The makings of the sun are the things of the natural world, while the makings of the poet are poems that reflect his imagined world.
    b. A poet should write about pleasant things instead of writing about "waste and welter."
    c. The makings of the sun will die and decompose, but the makings of the poet's mind will be eternal.
    d. Poems should be true to the inner world of the poet's mind.

_____

_____

_____

_____

Identifying Images *(10 points)*

16. In the chart below, list three images from "Daybreak in Alabama" that appeal to three different senses and note the sense to which each image appeals. Then, offer an interpretation of what you think these images add up to in the poem.

Image	Sense
Interpretation	

Literary Element: Tone *(20 points)*

17. What tone is used by each of the poets in these selections—detached, cynical, philosophical, solemn, playful, ironic, or passionate? What language in the poems helps determine the author's tone? On a separate sheet of paper, write two paragraphs in which you answer these questions for each of the poems. Use at least two examples from the poems to support your ideas.

LITERARY PERIOD INTRODUCTION TEST

American Drama

On the line provided, write the letter of the *best* answer to each of the following items.
(10 points each)

_____ 1. The first important figure in American drama is generally considered to be
     a. Samuel Beckett
     b. Edward Albee
     c. Eugene O'Neill
     d. William Inge

_____ 2. Most of American drama in the 1800s can be described as
     a. mild and sentimental, rarely challenging accepted traditions
     b. shockingly realistic and psychologically accurate
     c. musical comedies with little or no plot
     d. western melodramas with distinct heroes and villains

_____ 3. Ibsen, Strindberg, and Chekhov were innovative
     a. European playwrights who realistically presented characters and situations
     b. American playwrights who presented the psychological complexities of their characters
     c. New York producers of Absurdist dramas who present new European plays
     d. European playwrights who were heavily influenced by the plays of Edward Albee and Clifford Odets

_____ 4. The Provincetown Players and the Washington Square Players
     a. founded the Theater of the Absurd in the latter part of the twentieth century
     b. placed themselves in opposition to the established commercial theater
     c. were famous for participating only in one-act plays
     d. joined together to present an electrifying performance of *The Bald Soprano*

_____ 5. Which of the following statements is **not** true of Arthur Miller and Tennessee Williams?
     a. Miller is concerned with social matters; Williams is concerned with personal matters.
     b. Williams uses delicate, elegant language; Miller uses spare, plain language.
     c. Miller has been called the "playwright of our souls"; Williams has been called the "playwright of our social concerns."
     d. Miller's characters are ordinary people; Williams's characters are psychologically complex human beings.

_____ 6. The plays of Miller and Williams
     a. focus primarily on social responsibility
     b. rely heavily on realism
     c. usually feature female protagonists
     d. involve colorful, visually dramatic sets

_____ 7. Current American drama
     a. uses little dialogue and features fantastic characters
     b. focuses on moral and religious teachings
     c. revolts against realism
     d. de-emphasizes stage effects and imaginative sets

____ **8.** Expressionist drama aims to
    a. shock the audience by portraying characters with unrealistic conflicts
    b. make the audience focus on themselves rather than on the stage
    c. keep drama within the confines of a "beginning, middle, end" pattern
    d. reveal the inner consciousness of characters

____ **9.** Many Absurdist plays may be only one act because
    a. they present only one view of a situation
    b. they present an image which needs little development
    c. they enable theaters to produce more plays in a year
    d. short plays cost less to produce than long plays

____ **10.** The leading American Absurdist playwright is
    a. William Inge
    b. Tennessee Williams
    c. Edward Albee
    d. Arthur Miller

SELECTION TEST

The Crucible, Act One
Arthur Miller

Comprehension *(40 points; 5 points each)*

On the line provided, write the letter of the *best* answer to each of the following items.

_____ **1.** The best definition of the word "crucible" as it applies to the play is
   a. the hollow at the bottom of an ore furnace where molten lead collects
   b. a container made of a substance that can resist great heat
   c. a lamp burning before a cross
   d. a severe test or trial

_____ **2.** In the Overture, Salem is described as all of the following **except** a
   a. place inhabited by fanatics
   b. few dark houses
   c. prosperous village
   d. location that ships out products of increasing value

_____ **3.** Before the action of the play begins, Betty Parris and her friends
   a. have been chasing boys and flirting with them
   b. have had affairs with some of the men in town
   c. have been caught dancing in the woods
   d. have been guilty of blasphemy and witchcraft themselves

_____ **4.** Which of the following statements best describes Tituba?
   a. She leads the girls astray.
   b. She is from Boston, and Reverend Parris distrusts her.
   c. She commonly performs minor acts of witchcraft.
   d. She is a slave from Barbados who is devoted to Betty.

_____ **5.** Who is Reverend Parris's niece?
   a. Susanna Walcott
   b. Abigail Williams
   c. Mary Warren
   d. Mercy Lewis

_____ **6.** What does Abigail Williams believe about her dismissal from the Proctor's service?
   a. Elizabeth Proctor was hard to please.
   b. Elizabeth Proctor drank and blamed Abigail for her drinking.
   c. John Proctor did not fire her, but Elizabeth Proctor did.
   d. John Proctor liked her and did not want her to work.

_____ **7.** What is Ann Putnam's greatest grief?
   a. Her daughter Ruth is about to die.
   b. Seven of her children died in infancy.
   c. She is worried about Ruth's bad behavior.
   d. She knows her husband is unfaithful.

_____ 8. Why is the Reverend John Hale summoned?
  a. He is to settle the dispute between Parris and Parris's parishioners.
  b. The parishioners want him to come and preach instead of Parris.
  c. He has legal training and will help with the disputes over property.
  d. He is an expert on witchcraft and can help Salem.

Reading Skills and Strategies: Interpreting a Text *(15 points; 5 points each)*
On the line provided, write the letter of the *best* answer to each of the following items.

_____ 9. Arthur Miller gives us valuable information about Abigail's character when he says in a stage direction that she
  a. hates Reverend Parris
  b. has a great capacity for lying
  c. likes men too much
  d. has too much influence over the other girls

_____ 10. Betty is likely to be in a trancelike state because
  a. she fears punishment for being caught dancing in the woods
  b. she has been spoiled by her father and is trying to get his attention
  c. she feels upset about losing her mother
  d. she does not like Tituba and wants to get her in trouble

_____ 11. A possible motivation for later accusations of witchcraft is suggested by all of the following **except**
  a. John Proctor's disapproval of Reverend Parris
  b. Putnam's land dispute with Giles Corey
  c. Abigail's interest in John Proctor
  d. Hale's statement that Betty is a witch

Literary Element: Motivation *(15 points; 5 points each)*
On the line provided, write the letter of the *best* answer to each of the following items.

_____ 12. When Abigail threatens Betty, Abigail is motivated by her
  a. jealousy of Betty's pampered life as the daughter of a minister
  b. need for attention in the village because she is an orphan
  c. fear of the villagers knowing everything they did in the woods
  d. fear that Tituba will be accused of witchcraft

_____ 13. Abigail accuses Goody Good and Goody Osburn of witchcraft because
  a. she is angry with John Proctor for rejecting her
  b. the accusations seem to be a way to cause Parris trouble
  c. something evil happened to the girls in the forest
  d. she can persuade Mrs. Putnam and not be punished

_____ 14. Giles Corey says that his wife has been reading strange books because he
  a. is angry and wants his wife to be punished
  b. wants to see if Reverend Hale knows about witches
  c. wants to ask about something he thinks is important
  d. thinks his wife may be a witch

Written Response *(30 points)*

15. Tituba, Abigail, and Betty name people whom they claim accompanied the Devil. On a separate sheet of paper, explain why these three declare that they saw certain people with the Devil. Then, describe what circumstances motivate them to name specific individuals. Support your reasons with at least two references to Act One.

SELECTION TEST

The Crucible, Act Two
Arthur Miller

Comprehension *(55 points; 5 points each)*
On the line provided, write the letter of the *best* answer to each of the following items.

____ **1.** Mary Warren
   a. accuses Elizabeth Proctor of being a witch
   b. claims that she is an official of the court trying witches
   c. lies to Reverend Hale
   d. does not like either Elizabeth or John Proctor

____ **2.** When he comes in from planting, what suggestion does John Proctor make to his wife concerning the house?
   a. He wants her to make Mary Warren clean it.
   b. He says that the house is dark and dreary.
   c. He says because their family is larger, they need more room.
   d. He suggests that she bring in some flowers.

____ **3.** Elizabeth is afraid that her husband
   a. thinks that she is a witch
   b. is still interested in Abigail Williams
   c. is drawn to Mary Warren
   d. is too harsh with Abigail Williams

____ **4.** The people who have been accused of being witches by the court may save themselves from hanging by
   a. praying and saying the Lord's Prayer
   b. accusing other people of being witches
   c. confessing to being witches
   d. denying that they are witches and reciting Biblical passages

____ **5.** What reason does John Proctor give Reverend Hale for his absence from church?
   a. He does not think Reverend Parris is godly.
   b. He needs the time to work his farm.
   c. His children have been frequently ill.
   d. God does not require constant church attendance.

____ **6.** Hale comes to the Proctors' house
   a. to get John's help to stop the witch trials
   b. to find out why Elizabeth has not been at church
   c. to ask the Proctors some questions
   d. because he knows that the girls are all lying about seeing witches

____ **7.** Which commandment does John forget when Hale asks him to recite the Ten Commandments?
   a. Thou shalt not covet thy neighbor's goods.
   b. Thou shalt not bear false witness.
   c. Thou shalt not steal.
   d. Thou shalt not commit adultery.

____ **8.** What is Hale's advice to the Proctors as he prepares to leave their house?
   a. He tells both of them to stay away from Abigail Williams.
   b. He tells them to go to church and baptize their youngest child.
   c. He counsels them to stay away from Salem.
   d. He urges Elizabeth to discharge Mary Warren from their service.

_____ **9.** What is unusual about the doll that Mary Warren makes for Elizabeth?
    a. It has a needle stuck in its stomach.
    b. It looks like Abigail.
    c. Mary made it from corn shucks and shells.
    d. It looks like Elizabeth.

_____ **10.** Ezekiel Cheever is
    a. a judge in the court   **c.** a deputy magistrate
    b. the clerk of the court   **d.** a doctor in the town

_____ **11.** As Elizabeth is led away to jail, what does John demand of Mary Warren?
    a. that she stay away from the witch trials in the town
    b. that she inform the court that Abigail is lying
    c. that she take care of the Proctor children until Elizabeth returns
    d. that she stop lying and accusing people of being witches

Reading Skills and Strategies: Interpreting a Text *(10 points; 5 points each)*
On the line provided, write the letter of the *best* answer to each of the following items.

_____ **12.** One of the chief conflicts established in Act Two is between
    a. John and Elizabeth Proctor
    b. Elizabeth Proctor and Mary Warren
    c. John Proctor and John Hale
    d. John Proctor and Ezekiel Cheever

_____ **13.** Marshal Herrick is shamefaced when he appears at the Proctors' house because he
    a. is drunk
    b. has accused Rebecca Nurse and Martha Corey of witchcraft
    c. comes to take away Elizabeth
    d. comes to ask John for money

Literary Element: Motivation *(10 points; 5 points each)*
On the line provided, write the letter of the *best* answer to each of the following items.

_____ **14.** Mary Warren's motivation for joining the girls in their accusations of witchcraft is
    a. her hatred of John and Elizabeth Proctor
    b. that she has been mistreated by some of the women in the village
    c. that she is a lonely girl who craves friends and attention
    d. that she wants power over others

_____ **15.** Elizabeth says that Abigail accuses her of being a witch because Abigail
    a. is bored and the witchcraft trials are fun for her
    b. is still angry at Elizabeth because she made her work so hard
    c. is afraid that she herself will be accused of being a witch
    d. wants to get rid of Elizabeth so she can have John

Written Response *(25 points)*

16. In Act Two, several ironies, or discrepancies between appearance and reality, emphasize the evil of the events surrounding the Salem witchcraft trials. On a separate piece of paper, describe at least three examples of irony from Act Two and explain why they are ironic.

SELECTION TEST

The Crucible, Act Three
Arthur Miller

Pupil's Edition page 863

Comprehension *(55 points; 5 points each)*

On the line provided, write the letter of the *best* answer to each of the following items.

_____ 1. Deputy Governor Danforth
    a. seems proud and does not like his authority challenged
    b. is eager to hear Giles Corey's defense of his wife
    c. believes that the girls accusing the women of witchcraft are frauds
    d. is an ignorant, humorless man who refuses to listen to evidence

_____ 2. When John Proctor appears at the General Court with evidence that the accusations are frauds,
    a. he is accused of being a witch by Judge Hathorne
    b. Ezekiel Cheever says that John plows on Sundays
    c. he is not allowed to see Elizabeth
    d. Hale accepts his deposition

_____ 3. What is the deal that Danforth tries to make with John Proctor?
    a. The court will read his deposition if he acknowledges that he is a witch.
    b. If he presents the deposition in open court, Danforth will hear it.
    c. If he will drop charges, Danforth will not try Elizabeth for a year.
    d. If John can get one hundred villagers to sign the deposition, Danforth will hear it.

_____ 4. In Act Three the person who begins to have doubts about the rightness of the witch trials is
    a. Ezekiel Cheever   **c.** Thomas Putnam
    b. Judge Hathorne   **d.** Reverend John Hale

_____ 5. Who is the richest man in the village who can afford to buy the land forfeited by George Jacobs if Jacobs hangs as a witch?
    a. Deputy Governor Danforth   **c.** Thomas Putnam
    b. Giles Corey   **d.** Ezekiel Cheever

_____ 6. What does Judge Hathorne ask Mary Warren to do in court that she cannot do?
    a. pray   **c.** send out her spirit
    b. faint   **d.** recite the Ten Commandments

_____ 7. What does Abigail Williams do as soon as Danforth begins to question her?
    a. She begins to cry and behave hysterically.
    b. She says that Elizabeth Proctor sent her spirit out.
    c. She says that they must all beware of the Devil.
    d. She threatens Danforth.

_____ 8. What secret does John Proctor reveal to prove the girls are lying?
    a. He says that Abigail seeks vengeance.
    b. He confesses that he does not like Reverend Parris or the church.
    c. He says that Abigail told him that she was going to accuse Elizabeth.
    d. He says that he promised to marry Abigail if anything happened to Elizabeth.

_____ 9. What does John tell the court about his wife?
    a. She is about to confess.
    b. She will charge Abigail with murder.
    c. She will not lie.
    d. She is pregnant.

_____ 10. How do the girls in the courtroom terrorize Mary Warren?
    a. They give her a poppet that looks like her.
    b. They repeat everything that she says.
    c. They tell the court that she has cast a spell on John.
    d. They say that they see the Devil talking to her.

_____ 11. Who is taken to jail at the end of Act Three?
    a. Martha Corey and John Proctor   **c.** Giles Corey and John Proctor
    b. Mary Warren and Martha Corey   **d.** Elizabeth Proctor and Mary Warren

Reading Skills and Strategies: Interpreting a Text *(10 points, 5 points each)*
On the line provided, write the letter of the *best* answer to each of the following items.

_____ 12. Parris's concerns about the depositions presented suggest all of the following **except** that he
    a. wants to see justice done
    b. believes he can advance his career if the trial goes well
    c. believes he can get rid of the people who oppose him
    d. is worried about people finding out the truth

_____ 13. Abigail triumphs for all of the following reasons **except**
    a. Danforth believes her and not John
    b. Mary Warren rejoins the girls
    c. Elizabeth lies to save her husband
    d. John denounces the trials

Literary Element: Motivation *(10 points; 5 points each)*
On the line provided, write the letter of the *best* answer to each of the following items.

_____ 14. Danforth does not want to find out that the girls' accusations are false because he
    a. will not be able to acquire the victims' land
    b. will be blamed for the deaths of innocent people
    c. is afraid people will think him ignorant of the law
    d. does not want his involvement with Abigail revealed

_____ 15. Elizabeth's motivation for lying about John's affair with Abigail is that
    a. she is embarrassed and does not want anyone to know
    b. the villagers will think she has been a bad wife
    c. she is afraid that John will be arrested as a witch
    d. she loves John and wants to protect him

Written Response *(25 points)*

16. In Act Three, John Proctor, Francis Nurse, Giles Corey, Mary Warren, and the Reverend Hale all take bold measures that could get them into serious trouble. Choose three of these characters. On a separate piece of paper, describe what each of these three characters does to influence the court proceedings, and what risks each character runs. Support your ideas with at least three references to what the characters do in Act Three and what happens to them as a result.

SELECTION TEST

The Crucible, Act Four
Arthur Miller   Pupil's Edition page 878

Comprehension *(55 points; 5 points each)*
On the line provided, write the letter of the *best* answer to each of the following items.

_____ 1. At the opening of Act Four Ezekiel Cheever reveals that
     a. Mr. Herrick is too often drunk
     b. there is much confusion and disagreement in the town
     c. Tituba and Sarah Good are about to be hanged
     d. Reverend Parris wanders about because he has lost his mind

_____ 2. What news does Reverend Parris give the court in Act Four?
     a. The women accused of witchcraft are about to confess.
     b. Mercy Lewis and Abigail Williams have stolen Parris's money and disappeared.
     c. Tituba and Sarah Good have cast a spell on Marshal Herrick.
     d. None of the accused have conversed or associated with the Devil.

_____ 3. Which two men urge Deputy Governor Danforth to postpone the witch trials because a
     rebellion in the town seems possible?
     a. Ezekiel Cheever and John Hale   **c.** John Hale and Reverend Parris
     b. John Proctor and John Hale   **d.** Reverend Parris and Judge Hathorne

_____ 4. What does John Hale urge Elizabeth Proctor to do?
     a. persuade her husband to confess to witchcraft
     b. admit that she lied about Abigail and John
     c. promise to get the other women to confess
     d. plead her own case because she is pregnant

_____ 5. How does Giles Corey die?
     a. He refuses to confess, and finally he is hanged as a witch.
     b. He dies of a broken heart when he hears that his wife is dead.
     c. He dies of guilt because he accused his wife of reading strange books.
     d. He is not hanged, but instead is crushed with stones.

_____ 6. John tells Elizabeth that he has not confessed to being a witch because
     a. he says that he has confessed to too many lies
     b. Danforth and Parris want to use him as an example
     c. he does not want to confess a lie to contemptible people
     d. he is afraid that Danforth will hang Elizabeth for spite

_____ 7. Elizabeth blames herself
     a. for Mary Warren's lies   **c.** for John's reluctance to confess
     b. for John's affair with Abigail   **d.** John's imprisonment

_____ 8. Elizabeth tells John that she "kept a cold house." Keeping "a cold house" means that she
     a. never invited anyone to visit them
     b. frequently let the fire go out
     c. was not a loving or proper wife
     d. refused to keep flowers or pretty things in the house

_____ **9.** What does John want from Elizabeth?
   a. her approval for his confession to witchcraft
   b. her assurance that she loves him
   c. her promise to trust him
   d. her own confession to witchcraft

_____ **10.** What is one thing that John cannot do?
   a. get Martha Corey and Rebecca Nurse to confess
   b. sign his name to a lie
   c. allow his lie to be made public
   d. let Elizabeth lie for him

_____ **11.** In his confession John admits to
   a. thinking evil thoughts about Parris   **c.** sending out his spirit on Abigail Williams
   b. seeing Goody Osburn with the Devil   **d.** seeing the Devil

Reading Skills and Strategies: Interpreting a Text *(10 points, 5 points each)*
On the line provided, write the letter of the *best* answer to each of the following items.

_____ **12.** Danforth does not want to postpone the hangings because
   a. he does not want the people convicted of witchcraft to confess
   b. the townspeople are looking forward to the hangings
   c. the townspeople have put pressure on him to hang those convicted of witchcraft
   d. people will think Danforth doubts the validity of the trials

_____ **13.** When John goes to the gallows and Elizabeth says that her husband has his "goodness now," she means that
   a. he was always a good man in spite of his sins
   b. she has forgiven him for his affair with Abigail
   c. by tearing up his confession, he feels that he has regained his honor
   d. he is an example to all others accused of witchcraft

Literary Elements: Motivation *(10 points; 5 points each)*
On the line provided, write the letter of the *best* answer to each of the following items.

_____ **14.** Why does Elizabeth refuse to influence John's decision whether to confess?
   a. She feels he must face his own conscience and make his own decision.
   b. She cannot feel guilty if he refuses to confess.
   c. She cannot feel guilty if he does confess.
   d. She feels that he cannot blame anyone but himself if he does not confess.

_____ **15.** Which of the following is a strong motivation for John to tear up his confession?
   a. His fear of eternal damnation if he swears to a lie.
   b. He wants to be courageous like Rebecca Nurse and Martha Corey.
   c. He believes that he has to pay for his sin of adultery with Abigail.
   d. He believes that if he does not confess, he will save Elizabeth's life.

Written Response *(25 points)*

16. In Act Four, John Proctor's sense of his public self and of his private self come into conflict. On a separate piece of paper, describe the conflict Proctor faces, the factors that help him come to a decision, and the decision he makes. Support your ideas with at least three references to the play.

AMERICAN LANGUAGE TEST

Euphemisms

On the line provided, write the letter of the *best* answer to each of the following items.
(10 points each)

_____ 1. The Victorian Age was known for
  a. the many new words that came into the language
  b. its extreme concern with respectability
  c. excessive preoccupation with monetary concerns
  d. glorification of the Dutch monarchy

_____ 2. A euphemism is a word or phrase
  a. that has a pleasant musical sound
  b. derived from Greek or Latin
  c. that is substituted for one considered offensive
  d. that expresses strong emotion

_____ 3. Words become offensive because
  a. people consider them so
  b. of their inherent nature
  c. of their derivation from a foreign language
  d. of their association with certain foods

_____ 4. The Puritans created a favorable environment for euphemisms by
  a. wiping out profanity completely
  b. creating a society that was hostile to vulgar speech
  c. trying to create a distinctly American form of English
  d. penalizing nonconformity in language

_____ 5. A mixture of profane and overly delicate language was prevalent in communities of
  a. Puritans
  b. Victorians
  c. pioneers
  d. political activists

_____ 6. "The language of anticipation" reflects an outlook characterized by
  a. religiosity
  b. realism
  c. pessimism
  d. optimism

_____ 7. Early American euphemisms reflected democratic ideals in their
  a. titles for people and occupations
  b. terms for geographical areas
  c. striving for national uniformity
  d. concern for using words coined in this country

____ **8.** The English language is composed mostly of
   a. Anglo-Saxon and Greek words
   b. Anglo-Saxon and Latin words
   c. Anglo-Saxon and German words
   d. Latin and Greek words

____ **9.** Latinate words tend to
   a. sound educated and sophisticated
   b. metamorphose into slang words
   c. be difficult to understand
   d. be shorter than French words

____ **10.** Euphemisms are often used to
   a. make language simpler
   b. obscure meaning
   c. provoke argument
   d. evoke emotion

LITERARY ELEMENTS TEST

Drama

On the line provided, write the letter of the *best* answer to each of the following items.
(10 points each)

_____ 1. A play is not finished in the same way that a poem or novel is because
    a. it must have a definite beginning, middle, and end
    b. it has to be beautifully written
    c. after it is written, it still needs to be brought to life on stage
    d. after it is written, the playwright must find more funding

_____ 2. A play primarily engages the enthusiasm of directors, actors, and technicians through
    a. colorful sets
    b. gesture and movement
    c. special theatrical effects
    d. the story

_____ 3. The playwright makes the audience concerned for a character by
    a. creating a simple psychological story
    b. describing the gestures and facial expressions of the characters
    c. focusing on a conflict that involves something important to the character
    d. devising a complicated plot involving several major characters

_____ 4. The protagonist of a play is the
    a. major character who usually drives the action forward
    b. character that the audience finds the most appealing
    c. most interesting and memorable character in the drama
    d. character who eventually gets what she or he wants

_____ 5. Exposition gives the audience
    a. the physical setting of the play
    b. background information
    c. the play's final conclusion
    d. the play's psychological realism

_____ 6. Most of the plays that are produced in the United States today are
    a. produced with the hope that they will make money
    b. put on with the intention of shocking the public
    c. produced on Broadway
    d. written by the play's producer and given to the director

_____ 7. Playwrights must usually find an agent who
    a. directs the play and screens the actors
    b. ensures that the play is suitable for Broadway
    c. submits a play to producers who are likely to consider it
    d. takes charge of set design, costume design, and music

_____ 8. The producer does all of the following **except**
   a. advance money to finance a play
   b. meet with agents who represent playwrights
   c. work with a playwright on changes to a play
   d. supervise the technical production of a play

_____ 9. Which of the following statements is **not** true about staging a play?
   a. Theater is a collaborative medium.
   b. A director and actors "take away" a play from its author.
   c. The director has complete control over the production of a play.
   d. Rehearsals are both pleasant and tense.

_____ 10. Which of the following statements is **not** true of the theater?
   a. Producers seldom take risks on a play.
   b. Thousands of plays are copyrighted each year.
   c. The audience can contribute to a good performance.
   d. Producers seldom visit regional theaters.

LITERARY PERIOD TEST

Drama

Applying Skills

This test asks you to use the language skills and strategies you have learned. The following scene is taken from Tennessee Williams's play, *The Glass Menagerie*. The characters appearing in this scene are as follows: Amanda Wingfield; her daughter, Laura Wingfield, who survived a childhood illness which left one of her legs shorter than the other; and Amanda's son, Tom Wingfield, who narrates the play. Before you begin reading, take a minute to remember what you know about analogies, conflict, motivation, and interpreting a text. Read the passage, and then answer the questions that follow.

FROM *The Glass Menagerie*
by Tennessee Williams
Scene 1

The Wingfield apartment is in the rear of the building, one of those vast hive-like conglomerations of cellular living-units that flower at warty growths in overcrowded urban centers of lower middle-class population and are symptomatic of the impulse of this largest and fundamentally enslaved section of American society to avoid fluidity and differentiation and to exist and function as one interfused mass of <u>automatism</u>.

The apartment faces an alley and is entered by a fire escape, a structure whose name is a touch of accidental poetic truth, for all of these huge buildings are always burning with the slow and implacable fires of human desperation. The fire escape is part of what we see—that is, the landing of it and steps descending from it.

The scene is memory and is therefore nonrealistic. Memory takes a lot of poetic license. It omits some details; others are exaggerated, according to the emotional value of the articles it touches, for memory is seated predominantly in the heart. The interior is therefore rather dim and poetic.

At the rise of the curtain, the audience is faced with the dark, grim rear wall of the Wingfield tenement. This building is flanked on both sides by dark, narrow alleys which run into murky canyons of tangled clotheslines, garbage cans, and the sinister latticework of neighboring fire escapes. It is up and down these side alleys that exterior entrances and exits are made during the play. At the end of TOM'S *opening commentary, the dark tenement wall slowly becomes transparent and reveals the interior of the ground-floor Wingfield apartment.*

Nearest the audience is the living room, which also serves as a sleeping room for LAURA, *the sofa unfolding to make her bed. Just beyond, separated from the living room by a wide arch or second proscenium with transparent faded portieres[1] (or second curtain), is the dining room. In an old-fashioned whatnot[2] in the living room are seen scores of transparent glass animals. A blown-up photograph of the father hangs on the wall of the living room, to the left of the archway. It is the face of a very handsome young man in a doughboy's First World War cap. He is gallantly smiling, ineluctably smiling, as if to say "I will be smiling forever."*

Also hanging on the wall, near the photograph, are a typewriter keyboard chart and a Gregg shorthand diagram. An upright typewriter on a small table stands beneath the charts.

The audience hears and sees the opening scene in the dining room through both the transparent fourth wall of the building and the transparent gauze portieres of the dining-room arch. It is during this revealing scene that the fourth wall slowly ascends, out of sight. This transparent exterior wall is not brought down again until the very end of the play, during TOM'S *final speech.*

---

[1] **portieres** (pôr • tyerz´): curtains covering a doorway, used instead of a door.
[2] **whatnot:** open shelves for holding small objects ("whatnots").

The narrator is an undisguised convention of the play. He takes whatever license with dramatic convention is convenient to his purposes.

[TOM *enters, dressed as a merchant sailor, and strolls across to the fire escape. There he stops and lights a cigarette. He addresses the audience.*]

Tom. Yes, I have tricks in my pocket, I have things up my sleeve. But I am the opposite of a stage magician. He gives you illusion that has the appearance of truth. I give you truth in the pleasant disguise of illusion. To begin with, I turn back time. I reverse it to that quaint period, the thirties, when the huge middle class of America was <u>matriculating</u> in a school for the blind. Their eyes had failed them, or they had failed their eyes, and so they were having their fingers pressed forcibly down on the fiery Braille alphabet of a dissolving economy. In Spain there was revolution. Here there was only shouting and confusion. In Spain there was Guernica. Here there were disturbances of labor, sometimes pretty violent, in otherwise peaceful cities such as Chicago, Cleveland, Saint Louis . . . This is the social background of the play.

[*Music begins to play.*]

The play is memory. Being a memory play, it is dimly lighted, it is sentimental, it is not realistic. In memory everything seems to happen to music. That explains the fiddle in the wings. I am the narrator of the play, and also a character in it. The other characters are my mother, Amanda, my sister, Laura, and a gentleman caller who appears in the final scenes. He is the most realistic character in the play, being an <u>emissary</u> from a world of reality that we were somehow set apart from. But since I have a poet's weakness for symbols, I am using this character also as a symbol; he is the long delayed but always expected something that we live for. There is a fifth character in the play who doesn't appear except in this larger-than-life-size photograph over the mantel. This is our father who left us a long time ago. He was a telephone man who fell in love with long distances; he gave up his job with the telephone company and skipped the light fantastic out of town . . . The last we heard of him was a picture postcard from Mazatlán, on the Pacific coast of Mexico, containing a message of two words: "Hello—Goodbye!" and no address. I think the rest of the play will explain itself. . . .

[AMANDA'S *voice becomes audible through the portieres.*]

[*Legend on screen:* "Où sont les neiges?"3]

[TOM *divides the portieres and enters the upstage area.* AMANDA *and* LAURA *are seated at a drop-leaf table. Eating is indicated by gestures without food or utensils.* AMANDA *faces the audience.* TOM *and* LAURA *are seated in profile. The interior has lit up softly and through the screen we see* AMANDA *and* LAURA *seated at the table.*]

Amanda (*calling*). Tom?

Tom. Yes, Mother.

Amanda. We can't say grace until you come to the table!

Tom. Coming, Mother. (*He bows slightly and withdraws, reappearing a few moments later in his place at the table.*)

Amanda (*to her son*). Honey, don't *push* with your *fingers*. If you have to push with something, the thing to push with is a crust of bread. And chew—chew! Animals have secretions in their stomachs which enable them to digest food without <u>mastication</u>, but human beings are supposed to chew their food before they swallow it down. Eat food leisurely, son, and really enjoy it. A well-cooked meal has lots of delicate flavors that have to be held in the mouth for appreciation. So chew your food and give your salivary glands a chance to function!

---

3 **Où sont les neiges?":** French, for "Where are the snows?" This is a reference to a famous line by the fifteenth-century French poet, François Villon. The complete line "Où sont les neiges d'antan?" is a sad question about the passing of time: "But where are the snows of yesteryear?"

[TOM *deliberately lays his imaginary fork down and pushes his chair back from the table.*]

Tom. I haven't enjoyed one bite of this dinner because of your constant directions on how to eat it. It's you that make me rush through meals with your hawklike attention to every bite I take. Sickening—spoils my appetite—all this discussion of animals' secretion—salivary glands—mastication!

Amanda (*lightly*). Temperament like a Metropolitan star! [TOM *rises and walks toward the living room.*]

You're not excused from the table.

Tom. I'm getting a cigarette.

Amanda. You smoke too much.

[LAURA *rises.*]

Laura. I'll bring in the blanc mange.⁴

[TOM *remains standing with his cigarette by the portieres.*]

Amanda (*rising*). No, sister—you be the lady this time and I'll be the servant.

Laura. I'm already up.

Amanda. Resume your seat, little sister—I want you to stay fresh and pretty—for gentlemen callers!

Laura (*sitting down*). I'm not expecting any gentlemen callers.

Amanda (*crossing out to the kitchenette, airily*). Sometimes they come when they are least expected! Why, I remember one Sunday afternoon in Blue Mountain—

[*She enters the kitchenette.*]

Tom. I know what's coming!

Laura. Yes. But let her tell it.

Tom. Again?

Laura. She loves to tell it.

[AMANDA *returns with a bowl of dessert.*]

Amanda. One Sunday afternoon in Blue Mountain—your mother received—*seventeen*—gentlemen callers! Why, sometimes there weren't chairs enough to accommodate them all. We had to send the servant over to bring in folding chairs from the parish house.

Tom (*remaining at the portieres*). How did you entertain those gentlemen callers?

Amanda. I understood the art of conversation!

Tom. I bet you could talk.

Amanda. Girls in those days *knew* how to talk, I can tell you.

Tom. Yes?

[*Image on screen:* AMANDA *as a girl on a porch, greeting callers.*]

Amanda. They knew how to entertain their gentlemen callers. It wasn't enough for a girl to be possessed of a pretty face and a graceful figure—although I wasn't slighted in either respect. She also needed to have a nimble wit and a tongue to meet all occasions.

Tom. What did you talk about?

Amanda. Things of importance going on in the world! Never anything coarse or common or vulgar. [*She addresses* TOM *as though he were seated in the vacant chair at the table though he remains by the portieres. He plays this scene as though reading from a script.*] My callers were gentlemen—all! Among my callers were some of the most prominent young planters of the Mississippi Delta—planters and sons of planters!

[TOM *motions for music and a spot of light on* AMANDA. *Her eyes lift, her face glows, her voice becomes rich and elegiac.*]

[*Screen legend:* "Où sont les neiges d'antan?"]

There was young Champ Laughlin who later became vice-president of the Delta Planters Bank. Hadley Stevenson who was drowned in Moon Lake and left his widow one hundred and fifty thousand in Government bonds. There were the Cutrere brothers, Wesley and Bates. Bates was one of my bright particular beaux! He got in a quarrel with that wild Wainwright boy. They shot it out on

---

⁴ **blanc mange** (blə mänzhˊ): a dessert shaped in a mold.

the floor of Moon Lake Casino. Bates was shot through the stomach. Died in the ambulance on the way to Memphis. His widow was also well-provided for, came into eight or ten thousand acres, that's all. She married him on the rebound—never loved her—carried my picture on him the night he died! And there was that boy that every girl in the Delta had set her cap for! That beautiful, brilliant young Fitzhugh boy from Greene County!

Tom. What did he leave his widow?

Amanda. He never married! Gracious, you talk as though all of my old admirers had turned up their toes to the daisies!

Tom. Isn't this the first you've mentioned that still survives?

Amanda. That Fitzhugh boy went North and made a fortune—came to be known as the Wolf of Wall Street! He had the Midas touch, whatever he touched turned to gold! And I could have been Mrs. Duncan J. Fitzhugh, mind you! But—I picked your *father!*

Laura (*rising*). Mother, let me clear the table.

Amanda. No, dear, you go in front and study your typewriter chart. Or practice your shorthand a little. Stay fresh and pretty!—It's almost time for your gentlemen callers to start arriving. [*She flounces girlishly toward the kitchenette.*] How many do you suppose we're going to entertain this afternoon?

[TOM *throws down the paper and jumps up with a groan.*]

Laura (*alone in the dining room*). I don't believe we're going to receive any, Mother.

Amanda (*reappearing, airily*). What? No one—not one? You must be joking!

[LAURA *nervously echoes her laugh. She slips in a fugitive manner through the half-open portieres and draws them gently behind her. A shaft of very clear light is thrown on her face against the faded tapestry of the curtains. Faintly the music of "The Glass Menagerie" is heard as she continues lightly:*]

Not one gentleman caller? It can't be true! There must be a flood, there must have been a tornado!

Laura. It isn't a flood, it's not a tornado, Mother. I'm just not popular like you were in Blue Mountain. . . .

[TOM *utters another groan.* LAURA *glances at him with a faint, apologetic smile. Her voice catches a little.*] Mother's afraid I'm going to be an old maid.

[*The scene dims out with "The Glass Menagerie" music.*]

Vocabulary Skills: New Words in Context (20 points; 4 points each)

Each of the following underlined words has also been underlined in the selection. Re-read those passages and use context clues to help you select an answer. On the line provided, write the letter of the word or phrase that *best* completes each sentence.

_____ **1.** A society characterized by underline automatism is
  a. compassionate, or concerned for others
  b. overly proud and arrogant, or egotistical
  c. lacking in creativity, or machinelike

_____ **2.** A person who is matriculating is
  a. enrolling   **b.** dancing   **c.** protesting

_____ **3.** An emissary is someone who
  a. has a position in the military
  b. is sent to carry out a purpose or mission
  c. owns a number of large corporations

_____ **4.** Mastication is the act of
  a. studying   **b.** complaining   **c.** chewing

_____ 5. When Amanda <u>flounces</u>, she
    a. struggles with great difficulty
    b. moves with quick, flinging motions
    c. steps forward slowly and cautiously

Vocabulary

Doing Analogies *(20 points; 5 points each)*
    On the line provided, write the letter of the *best* answer to each of the following items.

_____ 6. The relationship of the words "driver : truck" is best indicated by the phrase
    a. . . . is driven by . . .
    b. . . . controls a . . .
    c. . . . is a mode of transportation for . . .
    d. . . . is bigger than . . .

_____ 7. The set of words below which has a part and whole relationship (. . . is a part of . . .) is
    a. engine : car   c. house : office
    b. circus : clown   d. bouquet : flowers

_____ 8. Which set of words below does **not** have a function relationship (. . . is used to . . .)?
    a. spoon : stir   c. knife : danger
    b. needle : sew   d. ruler : measure

_____ 9. The relationship of the words "wind : erosion" is best described as a
    a. degree relationship   c. part and whole relationship
    b. classification relationship   d. cause and effect relationship

Comprehension *(20 points; 4 points each)*
On the line provided, write the letter of the *best* answer to each of the following items.

_____ 10. The Wingfield family lives in a
    a. wealthy neighborhood
    b. poverty-stricken community
    c. lower middle-class urban area
    d. secluded rural area

_____ 11. Amanda does not want Laura to clear the table or get dessert because she
    a. wants Laura to recover from her illness
    b. wants Laura to look fresh for male visitors
    c. thinks Laura is superior to the rest of the family
    d. believes that Laura is an incompetent person

_____ 12. Tom says that he cannot enjoy his dinner because
    a. he is suffering from indigestion
    b. his knife and spoon are only imaginary
    c. his mother's health worries him
    d. his mother criticizes his eating habits

____ **13.** Which of the following statements *best* describes Tom's attitude toward the story of Amanda's seventeen gentlemen callers?
    a. He doesn't want to hear her tell it again, but listens anyway.
    b. He is shocked by Amanda's past behavior, but hides his surprise.
    c. He openly admires his mother's unique gift for storytelling.
    d. He refuses to listen to Amanda's constant lies and exaggerations.

____ **14.** The dialogue involving Tom, Laura, and Amanda suggests that
    a. Amanda's husband will probably reunite with his family.
    b. Amanda wants to relive her past through her daughter.
    c. Laura has a number of admirers, just like her mother.
    d. Laura is withholding a secret from her mother.

Literary Elements
Conflict (10 points)

15. There is a conflict of some kind between each pairing of the three characters in this selection. In the chart below, indicate what conflict exists between each pairing and support each of your ideas with a detail from the selection.

Pairing	Conflict	Support from the Selection
Amanda/Laura		
Laura/Tom		
Tom/Amanda		

Motivation (10 points)

____ **16.** Laura has very little dialogue in this scene, but what she says reveals what motivates her. On a separate piece of paper, write a comment about what motivates Laura in each of the selected passages listed below.
    a. "I'm already up."
    b. "Yes. But let her tell it."
    c. "I don't believe we're going to receive any, Mother."

Reading Skills and Strategies: Interpreting a Text (20 points)
17. Amanda's character is revealed not only through her words but through her actions and her effects on Tom and Laura. On a separate sheet of paper, write two paragraphs about what Amanda's actions reveal about her and what is revealed about her by Tom and Laura's reactions.

LITERARY PERIOD INTRODUCTION TEST

Contemporary Literature
Pupil's Edition page 904

On the line provided, write the letter of the *best* answer to each of the following items.
(10 points each)

_____ 1. Contemporary writers like Kurt Vonnegut and Joseph Heller have described war as
    a. an expression of patriotic loyalty
    b. a reflection of the madness of modern life
    c. the ultimate test of masculinity
    d. a logical response to personal frustrations

_____ 2. According to the introduction, the chief drawback of the spread of technology is
    a. dehumanization of the individual
    b. decreased life expectancy
    c. extinction of some animals
    d. sluggish economic activity

_____ 3. U.S. involvement in the Vietnam War
    a. established the concept of war as glorious and heroic
    b. lasted for two years
    c. greatly enhanced the United States's image abroad
    d. sharply divided the American public

_____ 4. In general, postmodern literature can be viewed as
    a. closely resembling modernist works of the 1930s
    b. open to multiple interpretations, and it frequently comments on itself
    c. lacking in meaning other than what the reader brings to it
    d. realistic and known for its reliance on the past

_____ 5. Short stories like Donald Barthelme's "Sentence" and "Game" and novels like Walter
    Abish's *Alphabetical Africa* are notable for their
    a. conventional viewpoints and detached tones
    b. familiar characters and themes
    c. nontraditional forms and structures
    d. focus on different worlds and cultures

_____ 6. One of the characteristics of postmodern fiction is the use of
    a. linear, chronological plots and standard methods of character development
    b. nontraditional forms that blur the boundaries between fiction and nonfiction
    c. themes advancing the idea that life is limited
    d. imitation and the nostalgic pursuit of the past

_____ 7. New Journalists like Truman Capote and Joan Didion attracted attention by
    a. using historical characters in fictional stories
    b. using old-fashioned language to describe cultural events
    c. asserting the writer's personal presence in nonfiction pieces
    d. mixing realistic narrative devices with elements of magic and dreams

_____ **8.** Nonfiction has become as much of an art form as fiction or poetry because
   a. journalists and other nonfiction writers now receive improved training in writing
   b. contemporary nonfiction often incorporates literary elements such as suspense, symbolism, and characterization
   c. writers care more about accuracy than about providing an entertaining story
   d. critics and the general public have become disillusioned with other forms of entertainment

_____ **9.** Postmodern poetry can be described as
   a. an attempt to follow Ezra Pound's insistence that the image is the core of the poem
   b. a reflection of the conformity and boredom that is seen in society as a whole
   c. a frank and often brutal re-creation of the poet's travel experiences
   d. a rebellion against impersonal poetry that emphasizes intellectual analysis

_____ **10.** Since the 1970s, American poetry has
   a. been characterized by diverse voices and styles
   b. become increasingly narrow in subject matter
   c. reflected a more elitist perspective
   d. been appreciated for its simplicity and earnestness

SELECTION TEST

from **Night**
Elie Wiesel

Comprehension *(40 points; 5 points each)*
On the line provided, write the letter of the *best* answer to each of the following items.

_____ 1. The people in the boxcar do all of the following to silence Madame Schächter **except**
    a. bind and gag her   **c.** threaten to throw her out
    b. beat her   **d.** reason with her

_____ 2. Initially, why do Madame Schächter's actions trouble the people in the boxcar?
    a. They worry that the boxcar is on fire.
    b. It awakens them to the terrors of deportation.
    c. They cannot stand the noise and the disturbance.
    d. They are trying to get to sleep.

_____ 3. The head of the block counsels the prisoners to
    a. look straight at the SS guards   **c.** not be afraid
    b. stand straight   **d.** answer the doctors' questions

_____ 4. The prisoners run hard so that
    a. their numbers will not be written down
    b. they will be nominated for special treatment
    c. they will be selected
    d. they can be granted exercise privileges outside the block

_____ 5. Before Wiesel leaves, his father wants to give him
    a. his ration of food   **c.** his pair of boots
    b. a knife and a spoon   **d.** his soup cup

_____ 6. Akiba Drumer asks his fellow prisoners to
    a. find his son and tell him what had happened
    b. save him from selection
    c. help him recover his faith
    d. say prayers after he is dead

_____ 7. Wiesel remembers seeing Rabbi Eliahou's son
    a. stopping to catch his breath during the run to the camp
    b. being shot by one of the SS guards
    c. letting distance grow between him and his father while running
    d. among the dead outside the shed

_____ 8. Juliek brings with him a
    a. violin   **c.** photograph of his family
    b. prayer book   **d.** drawing pad

Literary Element: Atmosphere—Witnessing the Scene *(15 points; 5 points each)*
On the line provided, write the letter of the *best* answer to each of the following items.

____ 9. Wiesel creates a sense of foreboding in the boxcar segment through all of the following **except**
  a. the smell of burning flesh
  b. the tall chimney against the black sky
  c. the snarling German shepherds
  d. the sight of flames

____ 10. After the prisoners are examined by the SS doctors, Wiesel shatters the optimistic atmosphere of the scene by
  a. depicting the guard writing down numbers
  b. contrasting those selected with those not selected
  c. showing the triumph of Yossi, Tibi, and Wiesel
  d. describing his laughter and his thoughts

____ 11. Wiesel's clawing for air creates an atmosphere of
  a. desperation   **c.** frustration
  b. anger   **d.** doom

Vocabulary *(20 points; 4 points each)*
Match the definition on the left with the Word to Own on the right. Write the letter of the Word to Own on the line provided.

____ 12. roaming about searching   **a.** abyss
____ 13. gulf or void   **b.** encumbrance
____ 14. hindrance; burden   **c.** conscientiously
____ 15. diligently; thoroughly   **d.** semblance
____ 16. mere empty show; pretense   **e.** scouring

Written Response *(25 points)*

17. Throughout the excerpt from *Night,* Wiesel describes the prisoners' behaviors and thoughts that arise under extraordinary circumstances. On a separate sheet of paper, describe their actions and their thinking. Make at least two references to details in the excerpt to support your description. Then, explain why you think these behaviors and thoughts occur.

SELECTION TEST

The Death of the Ball Turret Gunner
Randall Jarrell

Pupil's Edition page 932

A Noiseless Flash
from Hiroshima
John Hersey

Pupil's Edition page 936

Comprehension *(25 points; 5 points each)*
On the line provided, write the letter of the *best* answer to each of the following items.

_____ 1. Jarrell's ball turret gunner entered the armed forces
    a. after careful decision   **c.** without much thought
    b. under protest   **d.** as a fierce patriot

_____ 2. The first three words of the last line
    a. illustrate the speaker's growing confusion
    b. provide chilling confirmation of the sense of doom
    c. clarify that the poem is a work of nonfiction
    d. are an example of figurative language

_____ 3. The tone of the poem can *best* be described as
    a. humorous   **c.** condescending
    b. patriotic   **d.** elegiac

_____ 4. A main theme of "A Noiseless Flash" is that
    a. chance alone determined who survived the attack
    b. many individuals anticipated the nuclear holocaust
    c. people respond methodically in emergencies
    d. all people suffer equally in war

_____ 5. The six people Hersey focuses on can *best* be characterized as
    a. exceptional cases   **c.** ordinary people
    b. wealthy civilians   **d.** heroic soldiers

Reading Skills and Strategies: Reading Closely for Details *(10 points; 5 points each)*
On the line provided, write the letter of the *best* answer to each of the following items.

_____ 6. In "A Noiseless Flash," Hersey states that Japanese radar operators thought there would
be no attack on the morning of August 6, 1945, because
    a. the American bombers had been seen going in another direction
    b. the bombers usually attacked at night
    c. they spotted only three planes
    d. the war had supposedly ended

_____ 7. What does Father Kleinsorge do immediately after he hears the air raid siren in "A
Noiseless Flash"?
    a. He begins to read Mass.
    b. He changes into a military uniform.
    c. He stretches out on his cot.
    d. He wanders around the garden.

Literary Element: Subjectivity and Objectivity *(20 points; 10 points each)*
On the line provided, write the letter of the *best* answer to each of the following items.

_____ 8. All of the following are examples of objective reporting **except**
    a. historical data   **c.** various statistics
    b. direct quotations   **d.** fictional characters

_____ 9. If "A Noiseless Flash" had been written subjectively, the author
    a. would not have been concerned with facts
    b. could have clearly expressed his own opinions
    c. could not have used quotations
    d. would have had to use the first-person point of view

Vocabulary *(20 points; 2 points each)*
Match the definition on the left with the Word to Own on the right. Write the letter of the Word to Own on the line provided.

_____ 10. preoccupied; haunted   **a.** rendezvous
_____ 11. designed to cause fires   **b.** abstinence
_____ 12. prolonged   **c.** obsessed
_____ 13. meeting   **d.** philanthropies
_____ 14. one who believes in noble goals; a dreamer **e.** incendiary
_____ 15. charitable gifts   **f.** debris
_____ 16. rubble; broken pieces   **g.** hedonistic
_____ 17. pleasure-loving; self-indulgent   **h.** sustained
_____ 18. staying away   **i.** convivial
_____ 19. jovial; sociable   **j.** idealist

Written Response *(25 points)*

20. *Hiroshima* has been called a nonfiction novel. On a separate sheet of paper, write a paragraph that explains how, based on the excerpt you have read, this book can be categorized as both fiction and nonfiction. Use at least two examples from "A Noiseless Flash" to support your opinion.

SELECTION TEST

For the Union Dead
Robert Lowell   **Pupil's Edition page 949**
Game
Donald Barthelme   **Pupil's Edition page 956**

Comprehension *(20 points; 5 points each)*
On the line provided, write the letter of the *best* answer to each of the following items.

_____ 1. "For the Union Dead" can *best* be described as being about
     a. the importance of the Civil War
     b. modernity
     c. growing up
     d. social ideals and disillusionment

_____ 2. Colonel Shaw was a
     a. Revolutionary War hero
     b. former mayor of Boston
     c. white leader of a black Union regiment
     d. famous Confederate officer

_____ 3. The subject of "Game" can *best* be described as
     a. survival of the fittest
     b. the dehumanization of individuals
     c. the profound childishness of adults
     d. the need for discipline in the armed forces

_____ 4. The men in "Game" are distressed by
     a. their opposing religious beliefs
     b. the lack of enough food and water to survive
     c. the realization that relief is not coming
     d. an approaching enemy force

Reading Skills and Strategies: Interpreting Word Meanings and Connotations
(10 points; 5 points each)
On the line provided, write the letter of the *best* answer to each of the following items.

_____ 5. When the narrator of "Game" says that Shotwell has made "certain overtures," he uses
     the word *overture* to mean
     a. a proposal or offer
     b. an act of derisive mocking
     c. a musical introduction
     d. a long, knitted cap

_____ 6. When the narrator of "Game" says that he and Shotwell are still on duty "owing to an
     oversight," he uses the word *oversight* to mean
     a. many things to see
     b. supervision
     c. excellent vision
     d. mistake

Literary Element: Imagery *(10 points; 5 points each)*
On the line provided, write the letter of the *best* answer to each of the following items.

_____ **7.** In "For the Union Dead," what does the image of the old South Boston Aquarium
represent?
    a. It is a useless relic of the past.
    b. It is a treasured place of memory.
    c. It is a fantasy that never actually existed.
    d. It is a monument to the American colonial spirit.

_____ **8.** Which of the following sets of images appears throughout the poem?
    a. planes and cars   **c.** fish and bubbles
    b. monuments and guns   **d.** statues and weather vanes

Literary Element: Satire *(5 points)*
On the line provided, write the letter of the *best* answer to the following item.

_____ **9.** What is satirical about "Game" as a title for this story?
    a. The word *game* usually suggests fun, but the events in the story are serious
and deadly.
    b. War is considered to be a game nowadays.
    c. Even though the two characters are suspicious of each other, they are actually
having fun.
    d. Each of the characters plays a different game by himself.

Vocabulary *(20 points; 2 points each)*
Match the definition on the left with the Word to Own on the right. Write the letter of the Word
to Own on the line provided.

_____ **10.** order	**a.** sensors
_____ **11.** trick; deception	**b.** nether
_____ **12.** lower	**c.** console
_____ **13.** satisfied	**d.** precedence
_____ **14.** detecting devices	**e.** exemplary
_____ **15.** approaches; offers	**f.** sated
_____ **16.** at the same time	**g.** acrimoniously
_____ **17.** desklike control panel	**h.** simultaneously
_____ **18.** serving as a model	**i.** overtures
_____ **19.** bitterly; harshly	**j.** ruse

Written Response *(35 points)*

20. Both the Lowell poem and the Barthelme story critique the conditions of life in the United
States during the late twentieth century. On a separate sheet of paper, write a paragraph or
two discussing how Lowell and Barthelme depict the problems of contemporary life. You
should note what each writer specifically criticizes. Support your ideas with at least one
example from each selection.

SELECTION TEST

Speaking of Courage
Tim O'Brien

Comprehension *(35 points; 5 points each)*
On the line provided, write the letter of the *best* answer to each of the following items.

_____ 1. "Speaking of Courage" deals with the subject of
     a. freedom   **c.** greed
     b. self-acceptance   **d.** boredom

_____ 2. Paul's character can *best* be described as
     a. fearful   **c.** reckless
     b. lively   **d.** honest

_____ 3. The chilly interior of the air-conditioned car may represent
     a. the Vietnam War   **c.** Paul's feelings of isolation
     b. recent United States history   **d.** the death of Frenchie Tucker

_____ 4. The descriptions of the stagnant lake and of people going about their business suggest
     a. rejection of politics   **c.** contempt for veterans
     b. fear of the unknown   **d.** indifference to the Vietnam War

_____ 5. Why doesn't Paul talk to anyone about the war?
     a. He's too afraid.
     b. His old friends are gone, and his father won't talk about the subject.
     c. He doesn't want to; he wants to forget about it.
     d. Everyone is too angry about the war to sympathize with him.

_____ 6. The war taught Paul
     a. that people who are brave are stupid
     b. important skills he is using in civilian life
     c. a lot of things he thinks are useless
     d. to never ask questions

_____ 7. What is the significance of the story's taking place on July 4?
     a. It's a day for patriotism, but Paul doesn't feel he's a real patriot.
     b. It's typically the most festive holiday in American small towns.
     c. Paul receives his independence from the tyranny of the town.
     d. The town's lack of patriotic spirit depresses Paul.

Literary Element: Conflict *(20 points; 10 points each)*
On the line provided, write the letter of the *best* answer to each of the following items.

_____ 8. Which of the following statements *best* expresses Paul's internal conflict?
     a. He doesn't want to talk to anyone about the war because they'll find out he wasn't brave.
     b. He worries that when he had a chance to be brave he was a coward.
     c. The war has made him disillusioned with small-town life.
     d. He feels he fought in a war he doesn't support.

_____ **9.** At the end of the story, Paul
   a. has worked out his difficulties by thinking them over while driving around the lake
   b. resolves to try again to talk to his father about his wartime experience
   c. remains unresolved about his feelings, since he can't find anyone to talk to about them
   d. determines to bury his war memories

Vocabulary *(20 points; 2 points each)*
Match the definition on the left with the Word to Own on the right. Write the letter of the Word to Own on the line provided.

_____ **10.** belonging to a city or town   **a.** affluent
_____ **11.** intellectual depth   **b.** tepid
_____ **12.** to become more distant and indistinct   **c.** mesmerizing
_____ **13.** cannons used to fire explosive shells   **d.** drone
_____ **14.** lukewarm   **e.** recede
_____ **15.** monotonous hum   **f.** valor
_____ **16.** perceptible by touch   **g.** municipal
_____ **17.** well-to-do   **h.** mortars
_____ **18.** great courage   **i.** profundity
_____ **19.** hypnotic   **j.** tactile

Written Response *(25 points)*

20. In an attempt to justify continued U.S. involvement in Vietnam, President Richard Nixon said Americans want a peace they can live with, a peace they can be proud of. In what ways do these statements apply to Paul Berlin? On a separate sheet of paper, write a short essay in which you explain the kind of peace Paul needs. Support your ideas with at least two examples from the story.

SELECTION TEST

Monsoon Season
Yusef Komunyakaa

Pupil's Edition page 975

Comprehension *(40 points; 10 points each)*
On the line provided, write the letter of the *best* answer to each of the following items.

_____ 1. The poem "Monsoon Season" is *best* summarized as
   a. the discomfort of a tropical climate
   b. the natural beauty and danger of the jungle
   c. a battle between people and nature
   d. troubled memories of death that the weather evokes

_____ 2. The speaker of the poem tries to count
   a. wet leaves   **c.** raindrops
   b. muddy boots   **d.** grounded choppers

_____ 3. The tone of the poem is *best* described as
   a. fearful   **c.** angry
   b. melancholic   **d.** pastoral

_____ 4. The soldiers seem to be
   a. waiting to be evacuated
   b. making their dinner
   c. sitting around camp during a lull in the war
   d. getting ready to head out on a mission

Literary Element: Imagery *(30 points; 15 points each)*
On the line provided, write the letter of the *best* answer to each of the following items.

_____ 5. Yusef Komunyakaa creates images in "Monsoon Season" that are much like those of a painter because he
   a. creates complexity by layering images
   b. uses violent contrasts of color, texture, and perspective
   c. creates arrangements of shapes that invite the reader into the landscape
   d. employs the techniques of the French Impressionists

_____ 6. The image of the frog and the snake probably represents
   a. the hostility of nature
   b. the behavior of animals during a conflict
   c. the fighting between American and Viet Cong soldiers
   d. the past encountering the present

Written Response *(30 points)*

7. What kind of message do you think "Monsoon Season" delivers? Is it a political message or some other kind of message? On a separate sheet of paper, write one paragraph describing what you think is the message of this poem. Support your ideas with at least two examples from the poem.

SELECTION TEST

The Magic Barrel
Bernard Malamud

Comprehension *(25 points; 5 points each)*
On the line provided, write the letter of the *best* answer to each of the following items.

_____ 1. The social setting of "The Magic Barrel" is
    a. Jewish and suburban
    b. Christian and rural
    c. Jewish and urban
    d. Christian and suburban

_____ 2. The main conflict in the story occurs between
    a. Leo and Lily
    b. Leo and himself
    c. Salzman and himself
    d. Salzman and Stella

_____ 3. The main theme of the story concerns
    a. the observance of old customs in modern times
    b. the rigors of rabbinical studies
    c. marriage and dating rituals
    d. a process of self-discovery

_____ 4. The woman in the photograph seems familiar to Leo because
    a. he met her before
    b. she looks like a movie star
    c. he has the impression that he has met her
    d. she reminds him of his mother

_____ 5. Which of the following statements *best* describes Leo's impression of Salzman?
    a. Salzman is a talented professional.
    b. Salzman is not a trustworthy matchmaker.
    c. Salzman is a studious, careful person.
    d. Salzman is not clever.

Literary Element: Static and Dynamic Characters *(30 points; 15 points each)*
On the line provided, write the letter of the *best* answer to each of the following items.

_____ 6. Salzman is a static character because
    a. he talks a great deal about women who seek husbands
    b. he rarely leaves his chair
    c. his character generally remains the same throughout the story
    d. his professional life hasn't been successful

_____ 7. As a dynamic character, Leo
    a. is socially active throughout the story
    b. undergoes important changes during the story
    c. has no difficulties accomplishing his goals
    d. becomes angry for no reason

Vocabulary *(20 points; 2 points each)*
Match the definition on the left with the Word to Own on the right. Write the letter of the Word to Own on the line provided.

_____ **8.** to restrain; to hold back

_____ **9.** severely criticized

_____ **10.** poor; inadequate

_____ **11.** severe; stern

_____ **12.** customers

_____ **13.** related to weddings or marriage

_____ **14.** clear; obvious

_____ **15.** plots; schemes

_____ **16.** established; customary

_____ **17.** money or goods a bride brings with her in a marriage

a. evident

b. clientele

c. traditional

d. meager

e. ascetic

f. dowry

g. suppress

h. upbraided

i. nuptial

j. machinations

Written Response *(25 points)*

18. On a separate sheet of paper, write one paragraph discussing your reaction to the tradition of matchmaking described in "The Magic Barrel." What are the positive and negative aspects of the process? Support your opinions with at least two examples from the story.

SELECTION TEST

Elegy for Jane   Pupil's Edition page 1002
Night Journey   Pupil's Edition page 1003
Theodore Roethke
The Beautiful Changes   Pupil's Edition page 1006
Boy at the Window   Pupil's Edition page 1007
Richard Wilbur

Comprehension *(40 points; 5 points each)*
On the line provided, write the letter of the *best* answer to each of the following items.

_____ 1. The speaker in "Elegy for Jane" tries to find consolation in
    a. the beauty found in nature   **c.** the presence of the family
    b. great works of literature   **d.** an active social life

_____ 2. In "Elegy for Jane," the speaker compares Jane to
    a. moss under a bed of roses   **c.** a tree branch swaying in the wind
    b. a small stone in a brook   **d.** a bird singing in harmony with nature

_____ 3. The speaker of "Night Journey" cannot sleep because
    a. the speaker's muscles are sore from sitting too long
    b. the speaker is excited to see the countryside
    c. the jerking of the train keeps the speaker awake
    d. the speaker has a lot of personal issues to think about

_____ 4. All of the following in "Night Journey" create the feeling of the train's movement
    except the
    a. appearance of trees   **c.** passengers at rest
    b. beacon's swinging   **d.** iambic trimeter

_____ 5. The speaker of "The Beautiful Changes" mostly describes examples of beauty and
    change
    a. created by human endeavor   **c.** that occur in the spring
    b. found in the natural world   **d.** produced by the speaker

_____ 6. The chameleon and the mantis in "The Beautiful Changes" are described as
    a. endangered species that must be saved
    b. sly predators of smaller creatures
    c. interacting with natural surroundings
    d. resembling beautiful, green leaves

_____ 7. The boy and the snowman in "Boy at the Window" are connected by
    a. the darkness and cold   **c.** their desire to be inside
    b. their fear   **d.** their tears

_____ 8. The speaker in the poem "Boy at the Window"
    a. worries about the snowman   **c.** is moved for the boy
    b. feels outcast from Paradise   **d.** created the snowman

Literary Elements

On the line provided, write the letter of the *best* answer to each of the following items.

Figures of Speech *(20 points; 10 points each)*

_____ 9. Which of the following phrases from "Elegy for Jane" includes a figure of speech?
   a. "I remember the neckcurls limp and damp. . . ."
   b. "And how, once startled into talk . . ."
   c. "The leaves, their whispers turned to kissing . . ."
   d. "I, with no rights in this matter . . ."

_____ 10. "The Beautiful Changes" uses metaphors comparing all of the following **except**
   a. Queen Anne's Lace to waterlilies
   b. a person to a rose
   c. a meadow to a lake
   d. dry grass to a lake

Ambiguity *(10 points)*

_____ 11. One of the ambiguities expressed in the title "The Beautiful Changes" and illustrated in Wilbur's poem is that
   a. beautiful insects are born
   b. beautiful transformations occur in nature
   c. beauty does not exist
   d. beautiful forests are destroyed

Written Response *(30 points)*

12. Roethke and Wilbur use minute details to flesh out the ideas of the four poems you have read. On a separate sheet of paper, state the main idea of one poem by Roethke and one poem by Wilbur and discuss the detailed observations or descriptions used in each poem. Use at least two images from each poem to support your ideas.

SELECTION TEST

Auto Wreck
Karl Shapiro

OPEN
BOOK

Pupil's Edition page 1010

Comprehension *(50 points; 10 points each)*
On the line provided, write the letter of the *best* answer to each of the following items.

_____ **1.** The speaker of "Auto Wreck" feels that
  a. the police officers do little at the scene of an accident
  b. people are not prepared to deal with a death due to an accident
  c. people who speed deserve to die
  d. killing in wartime is justifiable homicide

_____ **2.** The ambulance in the poem resembles all of the following **except**
  a. a life preserver   **c.** a small hospital
  b. an artery   **d.** a bird

_____ **3.** The speaker describes the bystanders as
  a. obstacles to passing traffic   **c.** people recovering from an illness or injury
  b. beating bells   **d.** open wounds festering on the pavement

_____ **4.** An example of a "banal resolution" a bystander at an automobile accident might have is
  a. "There's another one for the grim reaper."
  b. "I'll be sure not to tailgate."
  c. "I better see if my car registration is in order."
  d. "I wish people wouldn't cut me off when they pass me."

_____ **5.** The "richest horror" is
  a. the thought that we will all die   **c.** dying from cancer
  b. dying in an automobile accident   **d.** the bystanders' indifference

Literary Element: Synesthesia *(30 points; 15 points each)*
On the line provided, write the letter of the *best* answer to each of the following items.

_____ **6.** An example of synesthesia in "Auto Wreck" is
  a. "For death in war is done by hands. . . ."
  b. "One with a bucket douches ponds of blood. . . ."
  c. "Pulsing out red light like an artery . . ."
  d. "The traffic moves around with care. . . ."

_____ **7.** Synesthesia can combine the following:
  a. sight, touch, and hearing   **c.** touch, thought, and feeling
  b. sight, thought, and touch   **d.** feeling, thought, and sight

Written Response *(20 points)*

8. In "Auto Wreck," Shapiro illustrates different responses bystanders have to auto accidents. On a separate sheet of paper, describe the different reactions people in the poem have to the automobile accident and discuss the different ways Shapiro describes these reactions. Use at least two references from the poem to support your ideas.

SELECTION TEST

from Black Boy
Richard Wright

Comprehension *(25 points; 5 points each)*
On the line provided, write the letter of the *best* answer to each of the following items.

_____ **1.** In this excerpt from his autobiography, Richard Wright's principal subject is
  a. divorce
  b. racial prejudice
  c. danger
  d. poverty

_____ **2.** In Memphis, Richard's mother locks him out of the house because she wants him to learn
  a. the importance of honesty
  b. to defend himself against bullies
  c. obedience to his elders
  d. good manners

_____ **3.** Richard's mother places him and his brother in an orphanage
  a. in anger
  b. in desperation
  c. by order of the court
  d. at their father's insistence

_____ **4.** The emphasis on food and hunger suggests the young Richard's
  a. emotional deprivation
  b. poor health
  c. high intelligence
  d. rebelliousness

_____ **5.** Rather than stay at the orphanage, Richard
  a. goes with his mother to ask for money from his father
  b. decides to live with his father
  c. lives on the streets
  d. goes to the judge to ask him for help

Reading Skills and Strategies: Interpreting Details *(20 points; 10 points each)*
On the line provided, write the letter of the *best* answer to each of the following items.

_____ **6.** All of the following statements support the general mood of this excerpt **except**
  a. Richard is disappointed by the boat to Memphis
  b. Richard triumphs by beating the gang members with a stick
  c. Richard is horrified that the preacher eats so much fried chicken
  d. Richard is offended when his father offers him a nickel

_____ 7. Based on the details used to describe Richard's father and the woman he lives with, we can infer that Richard
   a. admires his father
   b. wishes the woman were his mother
   c. wants to live with his father and the woman
   d. dislikes his father

Literary Element: Dialogue *(10 points; 5 points each)*
On the line provided, write the letter of the *best* answer to each of the following items.

_____ 8. Which of the following sentences does **not** accurately describe dialogue?
   a. It represents a conversation between two or more people.
   b. It is used in fiction, nonfiction, and other types of writing.
   c. It is only used in drama.
   d. It often reveals thoughts and feelings.

_____ 9. What is the effect of the use of dialogue in this selection?
   a. It reveals how people think and creates pictures of the characters.
   b. It is used very rarely, and so it is surprising when it appears.
   c. It emphasizes regional accents, which makes the characters seem more realistic.
   d. It reminds the reader that the story is a work of fiction.

Vocabulary *(20 points; 2 points each)*
Match the definition on the left with the Word to Own on the right. Write the letter of the Word to Own on the line provided.

_____ 10. fascinated
_____ 11. useless; pointless
_____ 12. irritated; angered
_____ 13. to pass by; slip away
_____ 14. intensely; eagerly
_____ 15. to hide unnoticed
_____ 16. frantic behavior; wildness
_____ 17. drying up; weakening
_____ 18. discouraged
_____ 19. loud noise; uproar

   a. elapse
   b. dispirited
   c. enthralled
   d. ardently
   e. galled
   f. withering
   g. futile
   h. clamor
   i. lurk
   j. frenzy

Written Response *(25 points)*

20. Richard describes a series of difficult situations that he faced as a child. How would you characterize the young Richard? What do you think is the adult writer's attitude toward his childhood? On a separate sheet of paper, write one paragraph addressing these questions. Make at least two references to the selection to support your ideas.

SELECTION TEST

Everything Stuck to Him
Raymond Carver

Pupil's Edition page 1027

Comprehension *(25 points; 5 points each)*
On the line provided, write the letter of the *best* answer to each of the following items.

_____ 1. The person listening to the story of the teenage couple is probably
   a. a complete stranger to the man speaking
   b. the new wife of the husband in the story
   c. the baby in the story—about twenty years later
   d. the teenage wife in the story—about twenty years later

_____ 2. The phrase that *best* describes the teenage couple in the beginning of the tale within the story is
   a. ambitious and optimistic about the future
   b. ambitious yet pessimistic about the future
   c. purposeless yet hopeful that things will change
   d. purposeless and pessimistic about the future

_____ 3. The main conflict between the boy and the girl involves the
   a. question of the boy's commitment to the family
   b. girl's feelings toward her new baby
   c. couple's inability to take care of the baby
   d. daughter's conflicting feelings about the couple's divorce

_____ 4. The young couple assure each other that
   a. their baby cannot possibly be sick
   b. their baby will be brilliant
   c. they will soon leave town
   d. they will not fight again

_____ 5. After he tells the story, the man stands by the window because he
   a. is vividly remembering the past
   b. is disappointed that the story wasn't more exciting
   c. wants to forget the past and focus on the present
   d. wishes the girl would leave

Literary Element: Style *(30 points; 15 points each)*
On the line provided, write the letter of the *best* answer to each of the following items.

_____ 6. Which of the following sentences does **not** describe an element of Carver's style?
   a. He includes lengthy, poetic descriptions.
   b. Most of the characters don't have names.
   c. He seems to have deleted all unnecessary words.
   d. He uses plain language.

_____ **7.** Carver's writing is distinctive for its
    a. use of alliteration
    b. exaggerated speech
    c. deceptive simplicity
    d. long sentences

Vocabulary *(20 points; 4 points each)*
Match the definition on the left with the Word to Own on the right. Write the letter of the Word to Own on the line provided.

_____ **8.** to occur at the same time   **a.** striking

_____ **9.** impressive; attractive   **b.** fitfully

_____ **10.** communication by letters   **c.** overcast

_____ **11.** irregularly; in stops and starts   **d.** coincide

_____ **12.** cloudy; gloomy   **e.** correspondence

Written Response *(25 points)*

13. On a separate sheet of paper, write a paragraph describing what you think might be the present situation of the family in the tale within the story. Are the boy and girl still married? Why or why not? Give at least two examples from the story to support your opinions.

SELECTION TEST

The Fish
Elizabeth Bishop
Remember
Joy Harjo

OPEN
BOOK

Pupil's Edition page 1035

Pupil's Edition page 1040

Comprehension *(50 points; 10 points each)*
On the line provided, write the letter of the *best* answer to each of the following items.

_____ **1.** The fish in Bishop's poem is
   a. dangerous and ugly
   b. young and multicolored
   c. smooth and graceful
   d. aged and battered

_____ **2.** After catching the fish, the speaker
   a. watches it thrash in the boat
   b. is cut by the fish's gills
   c. closely examines it
   d. takes a photo of it

_____ **3.** At the end of Bishop's poem, the speaker's attitude toward the fish can *best* be described as
   a. indifferent   **c.** admiring
   b. disgusted   **d.** disappointed

_____ **4.** What is the refrain in Harjo's poem?
   a. earth   **c.** remember
   b. people   **d.** you

_____ **5.** According to "Remember," every person
   a. must endure a difficult journey through life
   b. is part of the motion and energy of life
   c. should dance to celebrate life's richness
   d. is less important than the moon and stars

Literary Element: Personification *(30 points; 15 points each)*
On the line provided, write the letter of the *best* answer to each of the following items.

_____ **6.** An example of personification in "The Fish" is
   a. a rainbow fills the boat
   b. the fish's skin is like old, peeling wallpaper
   c. the fish's eyes are bigger than the speaker's
   d. the fish is an old warrior with fishhooks for medals

_____ **7.** "Remember" uses personification to
   a. exaggerate the importance of being human
   b. emphasize our connection to the universe
   c. shock the reader
   d. show that people and objects are identical

Written Response *(20 points)*

8. Both "The Fish" and "Remember" describe the relationships between individuals and elements or creatures in the natural world. On a separate sheet of paper, write a paragraph describing relationships between people and other elements or creatures presented in each poem. Do the poets convey a message about what the relationships should be? Give at least one example from each poem to support your interpretations.

SELECTION TEST

The Girl Who Wouldn't Talk
Maxine Hong Kingston   Pupil's Edition page 1044

Comprehension *(25 points; 5 points each)*
On the line provided, write the letter of the *best* answer to each of the following items.

_____ **1.** This story focuses on the subject of
    a. racial injustice   **c.** youths' cruelty
    b. women's rights   **d.** religious persecution

_____ **2.** The narrator stays late after school and
    a. finishes homework
    b. gets in trouble with her teachers
    c. waits for her parents to pick her up
    d. plays on the fire escape

_____ **3.** The narrator knows that the quiet girl can talk because she
    a. reads aloud in class
    b. speaks privately with teachers
    c. whispers during recess
    d. sings to herself

_____ **4.** The narrator's attitude when she begins to antagonize the quiet girl is that the quiet girl
    a. is deliberately trying to make the narrator mad
    b. needs a companion to talk to
    c. is not very intelligent
    d. is weak and needs to be toughened up

_____ **5.** The narrator and the quiet girl
    a. have been fighting with each other for years
    b. share many similar qualities
    c. used to be best friends
    d. eventually resolve their conflict

Reading Skills and Strategies: Drawing Inferences About Characters
(20 points; 10 points each)
On the line provided, write the letter of the *best* answer to each of the following items.

_____ **6.** Based on details in the story, we can reasonably infer that the narrator
    a. becomes ill because she feels guilty
    b. will beg the girl for forgiveness
    c. will buy the girl a gift
    d. will be punished by her parents

_____ **7.** Based on the details in the story, we can draw the inference that the quiet girl will
    a. eventually learn how to speak up
    b. stop spending time with her sister
    c. become domineering and mean
    d. remain quiet

Literary Element: Conflict *(20 points; 10 points each)*
On the line provided, write the letter of the *best* answer to each of the following items.

_____ **8.** Which of the following sentences is **not** an example of conflict?
   a. The narrator and other Chinese American girls struggle to be like the other girls.
   b. The narrator pinches the quiet girl's cheek to make her talk.
   c. The teacher demands that a boy reveal his father's name.
   d. The four girls stay at school after everyone else has left.

_____ **9.** Which of the following statements *best* describes the narrator's internal conflict?
   a. She wants everyone to know she is tough and independent.
   b. She wants to be friendly to the quiet girl, but she can't be.
   c. She wants to be strong and self-possessed, but she sees herself as weak and fragile.
   d. She believes it's her duty to get the quiet girl to talk.

Vocabulary *(10 points; 2 points each)*
Match the definition on the left with the Word to Own on the right. Write the letter of the Word to Own on the line provided.

_____ **10.** usually

_____ **11.** back of the neck

_____ **12.** scornful; mocking

_____ **13.** sides of the forehead

_____ **14.** spent time; hung around

   a. nape
   b. temples
   c. loitered
   d. habitually
   e. sarcastic

Written Response *(25 points)*

15. Why do you think the narrator tries to force the quiet girl to speak? On a separate sheet of paper, write a paragraph explaining your point of view. Use at least two examples from the story to support your ideas.

SELECTION TEST

from Blue Highways
William Least Heat-Moon   **Pupil's Edition page 1055**

Comprehension *(25 points; 5 points each)*
On the line provided, write the letter of the *best* answer to each of the following items.

____ **1.** This selection from *Blue Highways* mainly describes Heat-Moon's experiences while
  a. dining at cafes along highways in the United States
  b. traveling with a dog
  c. searching for cities in Tennessee
  d. meeting interesting people

____ **2.** Heat-Moon claims that the quality of a cafe's food can be judged by
  a. one look at its pies
  b. the number of calendars on the wall
  c. the number of people inside
  d. whether or not second helpings are free

____ **3.** The waitress in the cafe
  a. is rude to Heat-Moon
  b. asks Heat-Moon what the weather's like outside
  c. is curious about Heat-Moon's adventures
  d. talks to Heat-Moon about a trip she's planning

____ **4.** Heat-Moon asks the Wattses
  a. how the town got its name
  b. why so few people live in the area
  c. if he can buy something at their store
  d. how to get to Cookeville

____ **5.** The Wattses can *best* be described as
  a. threatening and suspicious
  b. generous and talkative
  c. apathetic and dull
  d. shy and polite

Reading Skills and Strategies: Analyzing Metaphors *(10 points)*
On the line provided, write the letter of the *best* answer to the following item.

____ **6.** Which of the following is an example of metaphor?
  a. Is life a seven-calendar restaurant?
  b. I'm as energetic as a squirrel.
  c. This story was as perfect as a diamond.
  d. The man's eyes were like polished stones.

Literary Element: Dialect *(10 points; 5 points each)*
On the line provided, write the letter of the *best* answer to each of the following items.

_____ 7. Which of the following sentences explains how Heat-Moon uses dialect?
   a. He mocks the beliefs of people he encounters.
   b. He describes the way people speak in particular areas.
   c. He praises the appearance of everyone he meets.
   d. He exposes the past of every person.

_____ 8. How does the use of dialect contribute to the selection?
   a. It has a strong comical effect.
   b. It makes nonfiction sound like a poem.
   c. It makes the people and the tale seem more realistic.
   d. It reinforces the author's negative perspective.

Vocabulary *(30 points; 3 points each)*
Match the definition on the left with the Word to Own on the right. Write the letter of the Word to Own on the line provided.

_____ **9.** started   **a.** incised
_____ **10.** guarantee   **b.** infallible
_____ **11.** completely soaked   **c.** commenced
_____ **12.** written down   **d.** lore
_____ **13.** sure; never wrong   **e.** saturated
_____ **14.** arranged in order of occurrence   **f.** recollect
_____ **15.** allowing light to pass through   **g.** vouch
_____ **16.** deeply marked   **h.** transcribed
_____ **17.** traditional knowledge or teachings **i.** translucent
_____ **18.** remember   **j.** chronologically

Written Response *(25 points)*

19. On a separate sheet of paper, write a paragraph discussing why you think Heat-Moon chooses to take back roads rather than main highways. Support your ideas with at least two examples from the excerpt.

SELECTION TEST

Son
John Updike

Comprehension *(25 points; 5 points each)*
On the line provided, write the letter of the *best* answer to each of the following items.

_____ **1.** "Son" portrays the relationship(s) between
   a. the narrator and his son
   b. the narrator and his father
   c. a related group of fathers and sons over four generations
   d. a series of husbands and wives over two generations

_____ **2.** The theme of this story can *best* be described as
   a. fathers, mothers, and sons don't get along
   b. sons cannot move away from home soon enough
   c. fathers and sons share similarities and suffer conflicts
   d. fathers and sons should spend a lot of time together

_____ **3.** The first son mentioned in the story is described as
   a. nervous and fragile   **c.** affectionate and jolly
   b. exhausting his mother   **d.** yearning for perfection

_____ **4.** In 1949, the son
   a. dreams of becoming a soccer star
   b. hears his parents arguing
   c. observes his father crying
   d. visits his grandparents

_____ **5.** The narrator's father tells the narrator that
   a. he is proud of his grandchildren
   b. the Christian ministry is a vocation or a calling
   c. the narrator's father should become a musician
   d. his hometown no longer exists

Reading Skills and Strategies: Analyzing Text Structures—Non-chronological Order
(30 points; 15 points each)
On the line provided, write the letter of the *best* answer to each of the following items.

_____ **6.** The story is told in
   a. chronological order
   b. fragments that are set in different time periods
   c. segments, each told by a different character
   d. reverse chronological order, from the present to the past

_____ **7.** One effect of the story's structure is that
   a. between characters, similarities are emphasized
   b. the narrator's confused state of mind is revealed
   c. every family member's story is told
   d. the narrator's family history is described better than his present life

Vocabulary *(20 points; 2 points each)*
Match the definition on the left with the Word to Own on the right. Write the letter of the Word to Own on the line provided.

_____ 8. complete disorder   **a.** antagonists

_____ 9. joking; comical   **b.** siblings

_____ 10. in an affectedly dainty manner   **c.** irksome

_____ 11. school for training ministers, priests, or rabbis   **d.** jocular

_____ 12. equally balanced   **e.** jaunty

_____ 13. adversaries; opponents   **f.** mincingly

_____ 14. confident; carefree   **g.** symmetrical

_____ 15. irritating   **h.** seminary

_____ 16. sisters or brothers   **i.** docile

_____ 17. passive   **j.** anarchy

Written Response *(25 points)*

18. This selection features external conflicts between fathers, sons, and other family members; it also includes fathers' internal conflicts. On a separate sheet of paper, write a paragraph describing one such conflict, explaining how it relates to the story's theme about relationships between fathers and sons. Support your ideas with at least two examples from the story.

SELECTION TEST

Daughter of Invention
Julia Alvarez

Pupil's Edition page 1077

Comprehension *(25 points; 5 points each)*
On the line provided, write the letter of the *best* answer to each of the following items.

_____ 1. Besides the narrator herself, a central character in the story is the
    a. narrator's sister   **c.** narrator's teacher
    b. narrator's mother   **d.** head nun

_____ 2. The family in the story has come to the United States to
    a. expand the father's medical practice
    b. enroll the narrator and her sisters in an American school
    c. live near close relatives
    d. escape the dictator Trujillo

_____ 3. The phrase that *best* describes the adult narrator's feelings about her mother is
    a. bitterness and anger
    b. amusement and affection
    c. indifference and confusion
    d. regret and nostalgia

_____ 4. The narrator thinks her mother's last invention is
    a. suitcase rollers
    b. a ticking key chain
    c. the speech for the teachers
    d. her daughter's poems

_____ 5. Which of the following statements does **not** explain the title's significance?
    a. The mother and daughter are both creative people.
    b. The mother confuses her aphorisms.
    c. The mother's inventiveness helps her daughter in a crisis.
    d. The narrator is the daughter of a famous inventor.

Reading Skills and Strategies: Drawing Inferences About Characters
(20 points; 10 points each)
On the line provided, write the letter of the *best* answer to each of the following items.

_____ 6. Because the narrator's mother stops inventing after reading about the man who creates a suitcase on rollers, we can infer that she
    a. thinks her idea about suitcases is better
    b. is frustrated because he was taken seriously
    c. wants to learn more about wheels for suitcases
    d. is going to find manufacturers for her inventions

_____ 7. We can infer that the narrator's father has a strong reaction to his daughter's speech
because he
   a. admires his wife's influence on his daughter
   b. is proud that the nuns have given his daughter an excellent education
   c. is afraid that his daughter's opinions will get her into serious trouble
   d. believes that the speech should be published in the local newspaper

Literary Element: Conflict *(20 points; 10 points each)*
On the line provided, write the letter of the *best* answer to each of the following items.

_____ 8. The narrator's argument with her father about the speech is an example of
   a. internal dialogue   c. internal conflict
   b. external imagery   d. external conflict

_____ 9. An example of internal conflict is
   a. the father's fear of people in uniforms
   b. the mother's thinking up inventions
   c. the argument over the father being called Trujillo by his daughter
   d. the father's holding to traditional values and the daughter's expressing her own ideas

Vocabulary *(20 points; 2 points each)*
Match the definition on the left with the Word to Own on the right. Write the letter of the Word to Own on the line provided.

_____ 10. wrong terms or names   a. labyrinth
_____ 11. intent on revenge   b. misnomers
_____ 12. place full of intricate passageways; maze   c. ultimatum
_____ 13. separated from the body   d. disclaimer
_____ 14. to make peace   e. disembodied
_____ 15. last offer; final proposition   f. reconcile
_____ 16. showy   g. eulogy
_____ 17. public speech of praise   h. communal
_____ 18. a giving up of a claim or connection   i. florid
_____ 19. belonging to an entire group   j. vengeful

Written Response *(15 points)*
20. In what ways are the narrator and her mother similar? On a separate sheet of paper, write a
paragraph in which you compare the narrator and her mother. Support your ideas with at
least two examples from the story.

SELECTION TEST

The Bells
Young
Anne Sexton

OPEN
BOOK

Pupil's Edition page 1089

Comprehension *(50 points; 10 points each)*
On the line provided, write the letter of the *best* answer to each of the following items.

_____ 1. In "The Bells," the speaker recalls
    a. being scared by lions at the circus
    b. feeling protected by a parent
    c. getting lost in a crowd
    d. eating popcorn at a circus

_____ 2. The circus poster in "The Bells"
    a. shows elephants walking
    b. reminds the speaker of a better time
    c. is about to be replaced
    d. brings back memories

_____ 3. The images in "The Bells" that connect father to child include all of the following **except**
    a. the crowds
    b. the rings
    c. the bells
    d. holding hands

_____ 4. The line "A thousand doors ago" in "Young" could describe any of the following **except** the
    a. places the speaker has lived in or stayed at
    b. intensity of her relationship with her parents
    c. speaker's experiences
    d. passage of time

_____ 5. The child's loneliness in "Young" is reflected in
    a. her talking to the stars
    b. the leaves blowing in the wind
    c. the crickets' ticking
    d. summer evenings

Literary Element: Imagery *(30 points; 15 points each)*
On the line provided, write the letter of the *best* answer to each of the following items.

_____ 6. Which of the following lines from "The Bells" provides the best example of visual imagery?
    a. "and the children have forgotten / if they knew at all . . ."
    b. "This was the sound where it began. . . ."
    c. "Today the circus poster / is scabbing off the concrete wall. . . ."
    d. "the distant thump of the good elephants . . ."

_____ 7. "Young" appeals to all of the senses **except**
    a. touch
    b. smell
    c. hearing
    d. sight

Written Response *(20 points)*

8. Both "The Bells" and "Young" focus on someone in the present remembering the past. On a separate sheet of paper, compare and contrast the speakers' attitudes toward the past. Support your ideas with at least two references from each poem to support your ideas.

SELECTION TEST

from The Way to Rainy Mountain
N. Scott Momaday   **Pupil's Edition page 1093**

Comprehension *(35 points; 5 points each)*
On the line provided, write the letter of the *best* answer to each of the following items.

_____ **1.** According to the origin myth of the Kiowas, the Kiowas entered the world
     a. guided by the sun
     b. through a hollow log
     c. from the top of Rainy Mountain
     d. through the mouth of the Earth Mother

_____ **2.** The main reason that Momaday journeys to Yellowstone and the Black Hills is to
     a. visit his grandmother's grave
     b. understand the same journey his people made to the plains
     c. understand the influence of the Crow culture on the Kiowas
     d. collect myths and songs of the Kiowas

_____ **3.** The legend of the Big Dipper is important to the Kiowas because
     a. the story helped them make a new home
     b. as long as the legend lives, the Kiowas have kinsmen in the sky
     c. their most important gods were gods of the sky
     d. such legends kept Indian children from fearing the dark

_____ **4.** Compared to the other Sun Dances, what was different about the last dance?
     a. Most of the Kiowas were Christians by then.
     b. The dance was held in Montana instead of on Rainy Mountain.
     c. The Kiowas invited some white men to observe the dance.
     d. The Kiowas could not find a buffalo bull for the medicine tree.

_____ **5.** One of Momaday's childhood memories involves
     a. attending the Sun Dance
     b. hearing his mother's stories
     c. the feasts and banquets prepared by the women
     d. the bitterness of the old warriors toward the white man

_____ **6.** The Kiowas learned the culture of the plains from
     a. the Crows
     b. hunting the buffalo
     c. the legends of the Sun God
     d. the Comanches

_____ **7.** Which of the following statements is **not** true about Momaday's grandmother?
     a. She lived in a big, weathered house.
     b. She was present when the Kiowas left the medicine tree.
     c. She knew about things she had seen.
     d. She became a Christian.

Reading Skills and Strategies: Identifying Main Ideas and Supporting Details
(10 points; 5 points each)
On the line provided, write the letter of the *best* answer to each of the following items.

_____ **8.** One of the main ideas in the excerpt from *The Way to Rainy Mountain* is that
  a. the Kiowas befriended the Crows
  b. the Kiowas were a mountain people
  c. the seven sisters became the stars of the Big Dipper
  d. the Kiowas changed as they moved south

_____ **9.** After the soldiers dispersed the Kiowas at the Sun Dance on July 20, 1890, the Kiowas
  a. discovered that many of their own people had been massacred
  b. found that the soldiers had shot all the remaining buffalo
  c. stopped holding the Sun Dance
  d. were put on a reservation near Fort Sill, Oklahoma

Literary Element: Setting *(10 points; 5 points each)*
On the line provided, write the letter of the *best* answer to each of the following items.

_____ **10.** Momaday says that Rainy Mountain
  a. gets rainfall all year
  b. stimulates the imagination
  c. is part of the foothills of the Rocky Mountains
  d. was sacred to the Cherokees

_____ **11.** The setting of Rainy Mountain was important to the Kiowas because they
  a. felt free in the mountains
  b. had plenty of hunting
  c. appreciated the beauty of its forests
  d. determined their worth by how far they could see

Vocabulary *(20 points; 2 points each)*
Match the definition on the left with the Word to Own on the right. Write the letter of the Word to Own on the line provided.

_____ **12.** above all else		**a.** tenuous
_____ **13.** filled with life		**b.** opaque
_____ **14.** to satisfy; to please; to humor		**c.** preeminently
_____ **15.** abundant; rich		**d.** indulge
_____ **16.** hatreds		**e.** infirm
_____ **17.** to scatter		**f.** vital
_____ **18.** not transparent; not letting light pass through		**g.** luxuriant
_____ **19.** carefulness; caution		**h.** enmities
_____ **20.** physically weak		**i.** disperse
_____ **21.** slight; insubstantial; not firm		**j.** wariness

Written Response *(25 points)*

22. Like the Kiowas, Momaday makes a journey. On a separate sheet of paper, trace the Kiowas' journey and describe the purpose of Momaday's journey. Then, explain what became of the Kiowas and Momaday's grandmother, and what Momaday learns about himself. Support your answer with at least two references to the selection.

SELECTION TEST

from In Search of Our Mothers' Gardens
Alice Walker   **Pupil's Edition page 1102**

Comprehension *(25 points; 5 points each)*
On the line provided, write the letter of the *best* answer to each of the following items.

_____ 1. Alice Walker's mother
  a. has expressed her creativity in her domestic work
  b. has won many awards for her flowers
  c. died when Walker was young
  d. is a professional gardener

_____ 2. The quilt depicting the Crucifixion that hangs in the Smithsonian Institution was
  made by
  a. Walker's mother
  b. an anonymous African American woman
  c. Virginia Woolf
  d. one of Walker's neighbors

_____ 3. The author and her mother share a talent for
  a. writing poems
  b. growing flowers
  c. quilt making
  d. storytelling

_____ 4. Which of the following authors is **not** mentioned in this selection?
  a. Virginia Woolf
  b. James Baldwin
  c. Phillis Wheatley
  d. Richard Wright

_____ 5. Walker believes that from her mother and previous generations of African American
  women, she inherited
  a. the knowledge of many different varieties of plants
  b. disdain for domestic chores
  c. respect for strength and love of beauty
  d. appreciation for the importance of relaxation

Reading Skills and Strategies: Identifying the Main Idea *(20 points; 10 points each)*
On the line provided, write the letter of the *best* answer to each of the following items.

_____ 6. The main idea of Walker's essay can *best* be described as
  a. all women are indebted to their creative female relatives and ancestors
  b. people should make certain that children receive a good education
  c. efficient housekeeping is the most important skill in life
  d. all women artists have frustrated mothers

____ 7. Walker supports the main idea of her essay with
   a. several poems
   b. examples and anecdotes
   c. historical statistics
   d. descriptions of paintings made by famous women

Literary Element: Personal Essay *(20 points; 10 points each)*
On the line provided, write the letter of the *best* answer to each of the following items.

____ 8. A personal essay does **not** ordinarily include
   a. autobiographical elements
   b. the author's perspective
   c. prose
   d. an invented plot and imaginary characters

____ 9. This selection is considered a personal essay because
   a. the author reveals intimate details about a person
   b. it is a work of fiction with a subjective focus
   c. it is a short work of nonfiction with a personal slant
   d. the author rambles and has no focus

Vocabulary *(10 points; 2 points each)*
Match the definition on the left with the Word to Own on the right. Write the letter of the Word to Own on the line provided.

____ 10. mental formation of ideas   a. profusely
____ 11. full of energy   b. ingenious
____ 12. clever   c. vibrant
____ 13. material for an artist   d. conception
____ 14. in great quantities   e. medium

Written Response *(25 points)*

15. Why do you think Walker searched for her mother's garden? What did she discover in the process? On a separate sheet of paper, write a paragraph addressing these questions. Support your ideas with at least two examples from the essay.

SELECTION TEST

from **Rules of the Game**
Amy Tan
What For
Garrett Hongo

OPEN
BOOK

Pupil's Edition page 1110

Pupil's Edition page 1122

Comprehension *(25 points; 5 points each)*
On the line provided, write the letter of the *best* answer to each of the following items.

_____ 1. Waverly's family makes many concessions to allow her to practice chess. Which of the following concessions is **not** one that they make?
   a. She gets her own room.
   b. She doesn't have to wash dishes.
   c. She can stay out after dark.
   d. She doesn't have to finish her meals.

_____ 2. Waverly runs away from her mother because
   a. her mother has punished her
   b. her mother pays attention only to Waverly's brothers
   c. she wants to play chess, and her mother won't let her
   d. she is embarrassed that her mother shows her off in public

_____ 3. An unspoken but implied point in "Rules of the Game" is that
   a. there is no such thing as a child prodigy
   b. chess, like many other games and sports, has traditionally been considered a male enterprise
   c. chess is a fast-paced game of bluffing
   d. Waverly is part of a long tradition of famous women chess players

_____ 4. "What For" discusses the speaker's
   a. childhood activities and concerns
   b. adult interests and preoccupations
   c. dreams
   d. many hobbies

_____ 5. As a child, the speaker in "What For"
   a. hoped to become a healer who worked wonders with words
   b. planned to become financially successful for his father's sake
   c. wished he had grown up in another part of the world
   d. made a lei for his father

Reading Skills and Strategies: Identifying Specific Details *(20 points; 10 points each)*
On the line provided, write the letter of the *best* answer to each of the following items.

_____ 6. In "Rules of the Game" the gift that Winston receives for Christmas is a
   a. chess set
   b. model submarine
   c. glass vial of lavender toilet water
   d. coin bank in the shape of the world

_____ 7. In Hongo's poem, the speaker mentions his or her
   a. mother and father
   b. brothers and sisters
   c. father and uncles
   d. grandparents and father

Literary Elements

On the line provided, write the letter of the *best* answer to each of the following items.

Motivation *(10 points)*

_____ 8. Which of the following statements *best* explains one of Waverly's motivations for striving to excel in chess?
   a. Her talent is a source of anxiety.
   b. Her chess tournaments often allow her to skip math classes.
   c. Playing chess is a form of rebellion against authority.
   d. Her ability makes her the most popular child at school.

Refrain *(10 points)*

_____ 9. The refrains in "What For"
   a. suggest a hymn or song, and support the poem's spiritual theme
   b. are a contrast to the poem's theme of chaos and confusion
   c. give the poem a martial tone
   d. expose the speaker's disappointment with his life

Vocabulary *(20 points; 2 points each)*

Match the definition on the left with the Word to Own on the right. Write the letter of the Word to Own on the line provided.

_____ 10. quick answer
_____ 11. highly praised
_____ 12. concealed
_____ 13. extremely gifted person
_____ 14. inherited
_____ 15. bad-smelling
_____ 16. complicated
_____ 17. lurched sideways
_____ 18. consecutive
_____ 19. acts of giving in

a. ancestral
b. touted
c. concessions
d. successive
e. retort
f. malodorous
g. intricate
h. obscured
i. prodigy
j. careened

Written Response *(15 points)*

20. Both "Rules of the Game" and "What For" portray relationships between children and their parents. On a separate sheet of paper, write a paragraph comparing and contrasting the two parent-child relationships. Support your ideas with at least one example from each selection.

SELECTION TEST

New African
Andrea Lee   Pupil's Edition page 1129

Comprehension *(20 points; 4 points each)*
On the line provided, write the letter of the *best* answer to each of the following items.

_____ 1. "New African" focuses primarily on
    a. community spirit
    b. the rules of writing
    c. the civil rights movement
    d. childhood memories

_____ 2. This story takes place
    a. in the 1980s
    b. in the 1960s
    c. in suburban Alabama
    d. during an unusually warm autumn

_____ 3. During the church service, Sarah feels restless because she
    a. is bored and would rather be playing
    b. has not eaten anything all day
    c. plans to be baptized soon and is impatient
    d. quarreled with her brother earlier

_____ 4. Sarah's aunts
    a. are all schoolteachers
    b. want her to be baptized
    c. disagree about whether she should be baptized
    d. never talk to Sarah about religion

_____ 5. The adult Sarah remembers her father as a
    a. stern and disapproving parent
    b. shy and retiring figure
    c. charismatic and affectionate person
    d. brilliant scholar

Reading Skills and Strategies: Intrepreting a Character *(20 points; 10 points each)*
On the line provided, write the letter of the *best* answer to each of the following items.

_____ 6. Reverend Phillips's freely admitting going to jail in Alabama signifies that he
    a. has no pride
    b. wants to embarrass his daughter
    c. is pleased he now lives in Philadelphia
    d. is proud of his role in the civil rights movement

____ **7.** Reverend Phillips's delight in starting debates at the dinner table indicates all of the following **except** that he
   a. enjoys winning an argument
   b. is a bright man
   c. has nothing to talk about at dinner
   d. takes delight in oratory

Literary Element: Internal Conflict *(20 points; 10 points each)*
On the line provided, write the letter of the *best* answer to each of the following items.

____ **8.** Which of the following statements *best* describes an internal conflict that Sarah experiences?
   a. She argues with Aunt Bessie over proper behavior.
   b. She challenges her father's insistence that she should go to church.
   c. She struggles to decide whether to build another treehouse.
   d. She considers whether she should become baptized.

____ **9.** Sarah knows her family would be happy if she were baptized, but
   a. she doesn't feel called on to be baptized
   b. she refuses to do so as revenge
   c. no one verbally encourages her to do so
   d. she thinks that getting better grades in school is more important

Vocabulary *(20 points; 2 points each)*
Match the definition on the left with the Word to Own on the right. Write the letter of the Word to Own on the line provided.

____ **10.** life-threatening; extreme

____ **11.** strongly resisting

____ **12.** all-knowing

____ **13.** wisely cautious

____ **14.** lack of clarity; uncertainty

____ **15.** calm and composed

____ **16.** put on for show

____ **17.** violation of something sacred

____ **18.** vague longing

____ **19.** driving away

a. sacrilege
b. sedate
c. defiantly
d. affected
e. wistfulness
f. ambiguousness
g. mortal
h. discreet
i. dispelling
j. omniscient

Written Response *(20 points)*

20. At the end of "New African," Sarah says that her father gave her a gift of freedom through his silence. What do you think she means by this statement? Why was this freedom important to Sarah? On a separate sheet of paper, write a paragraph answering these questions. Support your ideas with at least two examples from the story.

SELECTION TEST

Autobiographical Notes
James Baldwin   **Pupil's Edition page 1142**

Comprehension *(25 points; 5 points each)*
On the line provided, write the letter of the *best* answer to each of the following items.

_____ 1. In the first part of "Autobiographical Notes," Baldwin describes his
    a. theories regarding the purpose of life
    b. fondness and aptitude for poetry
    c. adventures in the French countryside
    d. early development as a writer

_____ 2. Baldwin states that it is a writer's duty to
    a. write about patriotic or familial subjects
    b. fight against governmental conspiracies
    c. examine attitudes in a deep, thoughtful manner
    d. focus on a single important image in all writings

_____ 3. Baldwin guesses that some of the influences on his writing are
    a. television, detective novels, and sacred music
    b. his father's sermons, the works of Henry James, and sports
    c. the writing of Charles Dickens, the King James Bible, and African American speech
    d. advertising, talk shows, and action movies

_____ 4. Baldwin insists on perpetually criticizing America because he
    a. loves America more than any other country
    b. has been exiled because of his political activism
    c. wants America to be more like France
    d. thinks America needs to be more like Africa

_____ 5. Which of the following words does **not** describe the tone of "Autobiographical Notes"?
    a. reflective   **c.** enraged
    b. direct   **d.** critical

Reading Skills and Strategies: Using Study Strategies *(30 points; 15 points each)*
On the line provided, write the letter of the *best* answer to each of the following items.

_____ 6. One of Baldwin's main ideas is that
    a. he read to his siblings
    b. writers are shaped both by what helps and what hurts them
    c. he had a fellowship when he was twenty-one
    d. two early books he wrote did not get published

_____ 7. To support his point that it is difficult to be an African American writer, Baldwin
says that
    a. traveling is difficult
    b. he is better accepted in Europe than in the United States
    c. society will not let Ralph Ellison write about life's ambiguities
    d. the problems for African Americans are widely written about

Vocabulary *(20 points; 2 points each)*

Match the definition on the left with the Word to Own on the right. Write the letter of the Word to Own on the line provided.

_____ **8.** crushed; destroyed	**a.** censored
_____ **9.** to take over	**b.** explicit
_____ **10.** cheerless	**c.** assess
_____ **11.** riddle	**d.** interloper
_____ **12.** clear, logical, and consistent	**e.** bleak
_____ **13.** cut or changed to remove material deemed objectionable	**f.** pulverized
_____ **14.** clear; definite	**g.** coherent
_____ **15.** intruder	**h.** conundrum
_____ **16.** critical; decisive	**i.** appropriate
_____ **17.** to evaluate; judge the value of	**j.** crucial

Written Response *(25 points)*

18. It has been more than forty years since Baldwin wrote *Notes of a Native Son,* the book in which "Autobiographical Notes" appears. If Baldwin were writing this essay today, how do you think it would be different? How would it be the same? On a separate sheet of paper, write a paragraph that answers these questions. Cite at least two statements from the essay to support your ideas.

SELECTION TEST

Mirror
Mushrooms
Sylvia Plath
The Lifeguard
James Dickey

Pupil's Edition page 1149

Pupil's Edition page 1150

Pupil's Edition page 1156

OPEN
BOOK

Comprehension *(40 points; 5 points each)*
On the line provided, write the letter of the *best* answer to each of the following items.

_____ 1. Which of the following claims does the mirror in Plath's poem "Mirror" make about itself?
a. It is not cruel, only truthful.
b. It can allow people to see what they want to see.
c. It is something that people do not really see.
d. It is lonely and neglected.

_____ 2. When the woman in "Mirror" sees her reflection, she
a. realizes that she must forget the past
b. is reminded of her maternal grandmother
c. decides to polish the mirror's surface
d. becomes agitated and upset

_____ 3. At the end of "Mirror," the woman sees
a. a goldfish in a tank
b. herself aging
c. the person she wanted to become
d. a young girl playing

_____ 4. Which of the following is true of the mushrooms in "Mushrooms"?
a. They need light to flourish.
b. They take time to grow.
c. They are poisonous.
d. They are taking over.

_____ 5. One of the main ideas of "The Mushrooms" is that quiet people
a. eat a great deal
b. have a lot of strength
c. are pushy and demanding
d. do not work very hard

_____ 6. At first the children in "The Lifeguard" believe that
a. they are in trouble with the lifeguard
b. the lifeguard will save the drowning boy
c. the lifeguard makes beautiful dives
d. they should not have been sleeping

_____ 7. "The Lifeguard" swims to the boathouse because
a. he does not want to face the children
b. he thinks the current has drawn the boy toward the boathouse
c. he wants to get some lifesaving equipment
d. he needs to catch his breath

_____ 8. At the end of "The Lifeguard" the speaker
a. returns to the village a hero
b. rescues a boy from drowning
c. finds his hands filled with mud
d. imagines he saved the boy

Literary Elements

On the line provided, write the letter of the *best* answer to each of the following items.

Personification *(20 points; 10 points each)*

____ **9.** Which of the following descriptions from "The Mirror" is an example of personification?
   a. The mirror is silver and exact.
   b. The candles and the moon are liars.
   c. The opposite wall is pink with speckles.
   d. A woman's face replaces the darkness.

____ **10.** The mushrooms in "Mushrooms" are personified in all of the following ways **except** that
   a. they talk quietly
   b. their fists push through needles
   c. they breathe
   d. their toes take hold

Tone *(10 points)*

____ **11.** The tone in "The Lifeguard" may be described as
   a. proud and confident
   b. hopeful and patient
   c. frustrated and agonized
   d. fearful and impatient

Written Response *(30 points)*

12. Plath and Dickey use imagery to appeal to their readers. On a separate sheet of paper, describe the images used in two of the poems and the effect that each image creates. Support your description with at least two examples from each poem.

SELECTION TEST

Straw into Gold
Sandra Cisneros

Comprehension *(25 points; 5 points each)*
On the line provided, write the letter of the *best* answer to each of the following items.

_____ 1. At the beginning of the essay, Cisneros recalls being
    a. instructed by her grandmother in the art of making tortillas
    b. locked in a room and ordered to spin straw into gold
    c. invited to dinner while living in France
    d. asked to make a gourmet meal for a dozen people

_____ 2. Cisneros compares the challenge of making tortillas to
    a. writing a critical essay
    b. living abroad for a year
    c. living in a house with six brothers
    d. writing a poem as a child

_____ 3. When her family moved into a permanent home in Chicago, Cisneros
    a. met people who would become characters in her stories
    b. overcame her shyness and fear of strangers
    c. became homesick for the other places she had lived
    d. acquired her own room where she could write

_____ 4. Which of the following statements is **not** true about Cisneros's life?
    a. She taught herself to garden.
    b. She left home before her older brothers did.
    c. She traveled throughout Europe.
    d. She moved to Texas.

_____ 5. Cisneros's adult impression of herself as a child is that she was
    a. athletic
    b. a serious, competitive student
    c. a rumpled, skinny, awkward girl
    d. a popular, sociable girl

Reading Skills and Strategies: Identifying Main Ideas *(20 points; 10 points each)*
On the line provided, write the letter of the *best* answer to each of the following items.

_____ 6. The main idea of this essay is *best* described as
    a. traveling throughout the world has not changed the author
    b. Texas and Mexico are geographically and culturally similar
    c. the author is a gifted writer to whom everything has come easily
    d. the author's experiences have shaped her personality and her writing

_____ 7. Which one of the following details is **not** essential to a summary of this essay?
    a. Cisneros has spent a lot of time traveling.
    b. Cisneros examines her past to find clues to the writer she became.
    c. Cisneros lived in the pre-Alps.
    d. Cisneros is an accomplished writer.

Literary Element: Allusion *(20 points; 10 points each)*
On the line provided, write the letter of the *best* answer to each of the following items.

____ **8.** An allusion is *best* described as
    a. the comparison of two unlike objects
    b. a reference to another known person or thing in history, literature, art, or some other branch of culture
    c. writing in which characters or events are compared to literary terms
    d. poetic language that contains references to philosophical debates

____ **9.** The famous tale that the title of this essay alludes to is
    a. Cinderella
    b. Rumpelstiltskin
    c. Snow White
    d. The Grasshopper and the Ant

Vocabulary *(20 points; 2 points each)*
Match the definition on the left with the Word to Own on the right. Write the letter of the Word to Own on the line provided.

____ **10.** wandering		**a.** subsisting
____ **11.** take all of one's attention		**b.** edible
____ **12.** impressive; having distinction		**c.** taboo
____ **13.** staying alive		**d.** obsess
____ **14.** capable of being eaten		**e.** prestigious
____ **15.** did well; blossomed		**f.** flourished
____ **16.** without conscious reasoning		**g.** nostalgia
____ **17.** something that is forbidden		**h.** ventured
____ **18.** longing		**i.** nomadic
____ **19.** dared or risked going		**j.** intuitively

Written Response *(15 points)*

20. In "Straw into Gold," Cisneros mentions many things she draws upon as subjects for her writing. What do these things have in common? Why do you think she chooses these things over others? On a separate sheet of paper, write a paragraph describing what Cisneros considers appropriate subjects for her writing. Support your ideas with at least two examples from the essay.

SELECTION TEST

The Latin Deli: An Ars Poetica
Judith Ortiz Cofer   **Pupil's Edition page 1167**
The Satisfaction Coal Company
Rita Dove   **Pupil's Edition page 1171**

Comprehension (*35 points; 7 points each*)
On the line provided, write the letter of the *best* answer to each of the following items.

_____ 1. The central character in the "The Latin Deli" is
    a. the ghost of the speaker's lost love
    b. a woman who runs a store
    c. a poet who writes in Spanish
    d. the speaker's sister

_____ 2. Most of the descriptions in "The Latin Deli" refer to
    a. pharmaceutical items   **c.** food and language
    b. money and work   **d.** toys and gifts

_____ 3. The speaker of "The Satisfaction Coal Company" recounts Thomas cleaning the offices
of a coal company
    a. for fifty years
    b. as a child
    c. every day of the week
    d. during the 1930s

_____ 4. In the first part of "The Satisfaction Coal Company," the man
    a. steps outside on a cold, snowy day
    b. walks past a gorge filled with trees
    c. sees a dog running down the street
    d. converses with his new neighbor

_____ 5. In the last part of "The Satisfaction Coal Company," the speaker suggests that Thomas
remembers his past experiences with
    a. bitterness and regret
    b. joy and laughter
    c. thoughtful nostalgia
    d. casual indifference

Reading Skills and Strategies: Responding to Aesthetic Elements
(*20 points; 10 points each*)
On the line provided, write the letter of the *best* answer to each of the following items.

_____ 6. "The Satisfaction Coal Company" includes all of the following images **except**
    a. an older man freezing on the front porch
    b. coal miners coming out of a mine
    c. a neighbor getting the mail
    d. a train picking up speed

_____ 7. The speaker in "The Satisfaction Coal Company" includes the image of the children cleaning on Saturdays because it
   a. illustrates how everyone had to work during the Depression
   b. shows how depressed Thomas has become
   c. demonstrates the joy Thomas had in his children
   d. reveals how much Thomas needed the children to help him at work

Literary Element: Concrete and Abstract Language *(20 points; 10 points each)*
On the line provided, write the letter of the *best* answer to each of the following items.

_____ 8. Which of the following quotations is the *best* example of concrete language in "The Latin Deli"?
   a. "the green plantains / hanging in stalks like votive offerings"
   b. "they speak to her and each other / of their dreams"
   c. "who spends her days selling canned memories"
   d. "how she smiles understanding"

_____ 9. What is the *best* interpretation of the abstract language in the last three lines of "The Latin Deli"?
   a. Some of the woman's customers forget what they came to buy.
   b. The woman constantly attempts to meet the unspoken needs of her expatriate customers.
   c. People from different countries ask the woman to guess what they want.
   d. The woman needs to stock more important goods in her store.

Written Response *(25 points)*

10. On a separate sheet of paper, write a paragraph comparing and contrasting the woman in "The Latin Deli" with the man in "The Satisfaction Coal Company." Describe the characters' attitudes toward their work and toward memories of past experiences, and explain the social roles they occupy. Support your ideas with at least two examples from each poem.

From "The Latin Deli: An Ars Poetica" by Judith Ortiz Cofer from *The Americas Review*, vol. 19, no. 1. Reprinted by permission of **Arte Público Press-University of Houston, 1991.**

THE AMERICAN LANGUAGE

High Tech's Influence

On the line provided, write the letter of the *best* answer to each of the following items.
(10 points each)

_____ 1. The word *technology* as it is used today refers to
   a. simple practical arts
   b. applied science
   c. pure science
   d. advances in physics

_____ 2. The technology of the early nineteenth century that had the greatest effect on
   language was
   a. fossil fuels
   b. electronics
   c. aeronautics
   d. steam

_____ 3. New railroad words came from
   a. inventions
   b. combinations of existing words
   c. borrowing from other forms of transportation
   d. all of the above

_____ 4. The words *telegraph* and *photograph* derive from
   a. Greek root words
   b. German technological terms
   c. Latin phrases
   d. French idioms

_____ 5. An acronym is
   a. an alphabetical designation of a person
   b. a word formed from the combination of the first letters of the words in a phrase
   c. an abbreviation of a long word
   d. a coined word that means "high technology"

_____ 6. Examples of acronyms include
   a. lingo, jargon, and argot
   b. telly, TV, and television
   c. radar, sonar, and WAC
   d. cabin, steward, and rudder

_____ 7. The twentieth-century invention that has had an effect on American culture similar to
   that of the railroad in the nineteenth century is
   a. the airplane
   b. television
   c. the space shuttle
   d. radio

_____ **8.** Many words used in aeronautics are borrowed from
   a. running
   b. sailing
   c. automotives
   d. communications

_____ **9.** Standard English words whose meanings have been altered by their technical use in the computer industry include
   a. adjectives that are used as nouns
   b. pronouns that refer to computer parts
   c. nouns that have been changed to verbs
   d. adverbs that are no longer in use

_____ **10.** Examples of computer language include
   a. sonar, Mayday, under pressure
   b. CAT scan, red cap, berth
   c. access, crash, boot
   d. sidetrack, laser, bailout

LITERARY ELEMENTS TEST

Satire

On the line provided, write the letter of the *best* answer to each of the following items.
(*10 points each*)

_____ 1. What are the two essential elements of satire?
  a. realism and naturalism
  b. hostility and ignorance
  c. wit and an object of scorn
  d. comedy and tragedy

_____ 2. In "Game," Donald Barthelme is satirizing all of the following **except**
  a. nature
  b. materialism
  c. politics
  d. violence

_____ 3. Which of the following details from "Game" is an example of hyperbole?
  a. The narrator at first struggles to behave normally, but then gives up.
  b. If either man acts oddly, his companion is supposed to shoot him.
  c. Shotwell is studying for a master's degree in business administration.
  d. The two characters are free to eat if they're hungry and sleep if they're tired.

_____ 4. Irony can be broadly defined as the difference between
  a. incongruity and hyperbole
  b. fantasy and criticism
  c. appearance and reality
  d. satire and comedy

_____ 5. Which of the following details from "Game" is the *best* example of incongruity?
  a. Shotwell's attaché case contains jacks and a ball.
  b. The narrator writes descriptions of a baseball bat.
  c. Shotwell probably does not read the narrator's bat description.
  d. The frozen food tastes stale after it is defrosted.

_____ 6. What is the underlying purpose of all satire?
  a. to express and emphasize a moral
  b. to ridicule politicians and businessmen
  c. to make ironic statements about emotions
  d. to explain people's foolish actions

_____ 7. Which of the following details in "Game" is the *best* example of satirical fantasy?
  a. The characters are supposed to insert their keys in locks.
  b. The characters live underground and watch a console.
  c. The narrator sometimes hears Shotwell weep while sleeping.
  d. The air-conditioning system makes noises in the latrine.

_____ **8.** Which of the following words *best* describes incongruity?
    a. intermittent
    b. inefficient
    c. inconsistent
    d. insecure

_____ **9.** Which of the following details in "Game" is the *best* example of irony?
    a. The characters sometimes sing each other lullabies.
    b. The enchiladas are covered with silver paper.
    c. Shotwell makes notes with a ballpoint pen.
    d. The characters were polite to each other at first.

_____ **10.** Which of the following details in "Game" is an example of gallows humor?
    a. the diamond
    b. the book *Introduction to Marketing*
    c. the concrete walls
    d. Shotwell's name

LITERARY PERIOD TEST

Contemporary Literature

Applying Skills

This test asks you to use the language skills and strategies you have learned. Before you begin reading, take a minute to remember what you know about chronological order, conflict, and imagery. Read the excerpt from the novel *Bone*, and then answer the questions that follow.

FROM *Bone*
by Fae Myenne Ng

Everything had an alert quality. Brisk wind, white light. I turned down Sacramento and walked down the hill at a snap-quick pace toward Mah's Baby Store.

Mason was the one who started calling it the Baby Store, and the name just stuck. The old sign with the characters for "Herb Shop" still hangs <u>precariously</u> above the door. I've offered to take it down for Mah, but she's said No every time. Mason thinks she wants to hide.

An old carousel pony with a <u>gouged</u> eye and chipped tail stands in front of the store like a guard looking out onto Grant Avenue. I tapped it as I walked past, my quick good-luck stroke. A string of bells jingled as I pushed through the double doors.

A bitter ginseng odor and a honeysuckle <u>balminess</u> greeted me. Younger, more Americanized mothers complain that the baby clothes have absorbed these old world odors. They must complain about how old the place looks, too, with the custom-made drawers that line the wall from floor to ceiling, the factory lighting. Leon wanted to tear down the wall of <u>mahogany</u> drawers and build a new storage unit. But Mah doesn't want him touching anything in her store, and I was glad, too, because I love the tuck-perfect fit of the drawers, and the *tock!* sound the brass handles make against the hard wood.

Mah was showing off her newest stock of jackets to a woman and her child. I gave a quick nod and went straight to the back, where the boxes were stacked two-high. The fluorescent lights glowed, commercial bright.

The woman tried to bargain the price down but Mah wouldn't budge; she changed the subject. "Your girl is very pretty. How about I don't charge tax?"

Hearing that gave me courage. Mah was in a generous, no-tax mood, and that gave me high hopes for some kind of big discount, too. I knew I'd be tongue-tied soon, so I tried to press my worry down by telling myself what Grandpa Leong used to tell me, that the best way to conquer fear is to act.

Open the mouth and tell.

As soon as the woman and her child walked out the door, I went up to Mah and started out in Chinese, "I want to tell you something."

Mah looked up, wide-eyed, expectant.

I switched to English, "Time was right, so Mason and I just went to City Hall. We got married there."

Mah's expression didn't change.

"In New York," I said.

No answer.

"You know I never liked banquets, all that noise and trouble. And such a waste of so much money."

She still didn't say anything. Suddenly I realized how quiet it was, and that we were completely alone in the store. I heard the hum of the lights.

"Mah?" I said. "Say something."

She didn't even look at me, she just walked away. She went to the back of the store and ripped open a box. I followed and watched her bend the flaps back and pull out armfuls of baby clothes. I waited. She started stacking little mounds. She smoothed out sleeves on top of sleeves, zipped zippers, and cupped the colored hoods, one into another. All around our feet were tangles of white hangers.

"Nina was my witness." My voice was whispery, strange.

Mah grunted, a huumph sound that came out like a curse. My translation was: Disgust, anger. There's power behind her sounds. Over the years I've listened and <u>rendered</u> her Chinese grunts into English words.

She threw the empty box on the floor and gave it a quick kick.

"Just like that.
Did it and didn't tell.
Mother Who Raised You.
Years of work, years of worry.
Didn't! Even! Tell!"

What could I say? Using Chinese was my undoing. She had a world of words that were beyond me.

Mah reached down and picked up a tangle of hangers. She poked them into the baby down coats, baby overalls, baby sleepers. Her wrists whipped back and forth in a way that reminded me of how she used to butcher birds on Salmon Alley. Chickens, pheasants, and pigeons, once a frog. The time with the frog was terrible. Mah skinned it and then stopped. She held the twitching muscle out toward us; she wanted us to see its pink heart. Her voice was spooky, breathless: "Look how the heart keeps beating!" Then the frog sprang out of her hand, still vigorous.

Now I said in English, "It was no big deal."

"It is!"

Mah was using her sewing-factory voice, and I remembered her impatience whenever I tried to talk to her while she was sewing on a deadline.

She rapped a hanger on the counter. "Marriage is for a lifetime, and it should be celebrated! Why sneak around, why act like a thief in the dark?"

I wanted to say: I didn't marry in shame. I didn't marry like you. Your marriages are not my fault. Don't blame me.

Just then the bells jingled and I looked up and saw two sewing ladies coming through the door. I recognized the round hair, the hawk eyes.

"What?" I was too upset to stop. "What?" I demanded again. "You don't like Mason, is that it?"

"Mason," Mah spoke his name soft, "I love."

For love, she used a Chinese word: to embrace, to hug.

I stepped around the boxes, opened my arms and hugged Mah. I held her and took a deep breath and smelled the dried honeysuckle stems, the bitter ginseng root. Above us, the lights beamed bright.

I heard the bells jingle, the latch click, and looked up to see the broad backs of the ladies going out the door toward Grant Avenue. They were going to Portsmouth Square, and I knew they were talking up everything they heard, not stopping when they passed their husbands by the chess tables, not stopping until they found their sewing-lady friends on the benches of the lower level. And that's when they'd tell, tell their long-stitched version of the story, from beginning to end.

Let them make it up, I thought. Let them talk.

Vocabulary: New Words in Context *(10 points; 2 points each)*
Each of the following underlined words has also been underlined in the selection. Re-read those passages and use context clues to help you select an answer. On the line provided, write the letter of the word or phrase that *best* completes each sentence.

_____ **1.** A plate that is placed <u>precariously</u> on a table
   a. looks elegant and stylish
   b. is in danger of falling
   c. does not draw attention

_____ **2.** A <u>gouged</u> piece of wood probably displays
   a. grooves or holes
   b. new decoration
   c. knot holes

_____ **3.** A scent that gives off <u>balminess</u> is
   a. soothing   **b.** unfamiliar   **c.** addictive

_____ **4.** <u>Mahogany</u> is a type of
   a. paper   **b.** pasteboard   **c.** wood

_____ **5.** Words that have been <u>rendered</u> have been
   a. mocked   **b.** confronted   **c.** translated

Vocabulary

Base Words, Roots, and Word Families *(15 points; 3 points each)*

On the line provided, write the letter of the *best* answer to each of the following items.

_____ **6.** The three word parts that a word can be divided into are
   a. roots, inflections, and endings
   b. base words, Greek words, and Latin words
   c. word families, affixes, and gerunds
   d. roots, prefixes, and suffixes

_____ **7.** The word *embrace* is
   a. composed of a root and a prefix
   b. a base word
   c. a technical term
   d. archaic

_____ **8.** *Omniscient* and *omnipresent*
   a. are metaphors
   b. do not contain suffixes
   c. come from the same root
   d. share the same prefix

_____ **9.** Which of the following words contains a suffix?
   a. express
   b. precariously
   c. undo
   d. banquet

_____ **10.** Which of the following words is **not** a base word?
   a. heart
   b. stock
   c. gouged
   d. talk

Elements of Literature   *Formal Assessment* **237**

Comprehension *(20 points; 5 points each)*
On the line provided, write the letter of the *best* answer to each of the following items.

_____ **11.** When the narrator comes into the store
    a. two women come in behind her
    b. she finds that her mother has sold the business
    c. she immediately begins talking to her mother
    d. her mother is doing business with a customer

_____ **12.** In the excerpt, we learn all of the following things about Mah **except** that she
    a. used to butcher birds
    b. eloped when she was her daughter's age
    c. normally does not bargain with customers
    d. has been married more than once

_____ **13.** What seems to reconcile the mother and daughter?
    a. The daughter helps her mother fold baby clothes.
    b. The daughter reminds her mother of past problems.
    c. The mother says she adores Mason.
    d. The mother gives her daughter advice.

_____ **14.** How does the narrator's mood at the end of the selection differ from her mood at its beginning?
    a. She has become preoccupied.   **c.** She seems depressed.
    b. She is more relaxed.   **d.** She regrets her action.

Reading Skills and Strategies: Drawing Inferences *(10 points)*

15. Write a paragraph explaining what you can infer about Mah and her past from what she says and does and from what the narrator says about her in the excerpt from *Bone.* Support your inferences with details from the text.

Literary Elements
  Conflict *(10 points)*

  16. What is the most significant external conflict in this story? On a separate sheet of paper, write the letter of the answer you choose, and briefly defend your choice. Use at least one example from the excerpt to support your ideas.
    a. the narrator deciding whether or not to say that Mah married in shame
    b. the narrator trying to talk to her mother about having gotten married without her mother's knowledge
    c. the customer bargaining with the narrator's mother
    d. the narrator confronting the customers about gossiping

  Imagery *(10 points)*

  17. On a separate sheet of paper, write one paragraph that discusses how the sensory imagery contributes to the story. Support your ideas with at least two examples from the story.

Written Response *(25 points)*

18. The idea of "the created self" is a common theme within contemporary literature. On a separate sheet of paper, write a short essay that relates the theme of the created self to the excerpt from *Bone.* Your answer should make at least one comparison and one contrast between the excerpt from *Bone* and two selections from Collections 18 through 21.

BEGINNINGS

LITERARY PERIOD INTRODUCTION
TEST, page 1

1. c   2. b   3. b   4. c   5. b
6. d   7. d   8. a   9. d   10. c

Collection 1: Visions and Voyages

from *Of Plymouth Plantation*

SELECTION TEST, page 3

Comprehension

1. c   2. b   3. a   4. d   5. c
6. c   7. a

Literary Element

8. a   9. c

Vocabulary

10. c   11. j   12. g   13. a   14. f
15. b   16. i   17. d   18. e   19. h

Written Response

20. Responses will vary. In a model response, students should fulfill the following criteria:
    • demonstrate understanding of the prompt
    • clearly describe the Pilgrims' relationship with the American Indians
    • support their ideas with at least two examples from the selection. For example:
      • Initially, the Pilgrims fear the American Indians will attack them with bow and arrow.
      • The Pilgrims distrust the American Indians, especially after they steal some tools from the Pilgrims.
      • Their relationship improves after they meet Samoset and Squanto, who both speak English. They return the Pilgrims' tools and the Pilgrims make a treaty with them. However, the treaty shows that the Pilgrims still exercise caution.

from *A Narrative of the Captivity*

SELECTION TEST, page 5

Comprehension

1. d   2. a   3. c   4. b   5. c

Reading Skills and Strategies

6. a   7. c

Literary Element

8. c   9. d

Vocabulary

10. c   11. a   12. b   13. a   14. d
15. c   16. b   17. b   18. a   19. d

Written Response

20. Responses will vary. In a model response, students should fulfill the following criteria:
    • demonstrate understanding of the prompt
    • describe how Rowlandson links the events of her captivity to the suffering of people in the Bible
    • support their ideas with at least two examples from the selection. For example:
      • When she is kept apart from Mary, Rowlandson thinks of Jacob losing his sons.
      • When they cross the river, she thinks of the verse in Isaiah in which God says he will not let the river drown his people.

from *The History of the Dividing Line*

SELECTION TEST, page 7

Comprehension

1. b   2. d   3. c   4. d   5. d

Reading Skills and Strategies
6. b

Literary Element
7. b   8. a

Vocabulary
9. e   10. c   11. j   12. a   13. h
14. b   15. d   16. i   17. g   18. f

Written Response
19. Responses will vary, but students should use at least one example from the selection to support their ideas. Sample responses follow.
   a. Byrd writes that the American Indians were no more heathen than the first settlers and that intermarriage would encourage the conversion of the American Indians to Christianity.
   b. Byrd states that the American Indians would have complained less when their land was taken by the English if marriages between the two groups had taken place. He notes that much bloodshed might have been prevented if friendly relations had been established through marriage.
   c. Byrd notes that the French colonists in Canada were more inclined to marry American Indians. He believes that this attitude has strengthened relations between the two groups.
   d. *(Credit may be given for an original response that is supported by evidence from the selection.)*

Collection 2: The Examined Life

Here Follow Some Verses upon the Burning of Our House, July 10, 1666
Huswifery

SELECTION TEST, page 11
Comprehension
1. d   2. c   3. b   4. a   5. a

Reading Skills and Strategies: Analyzing Text Structures—Inversion
6. c   7. b

Reading Skills and Strategies: Analyzing Text Structures—Extended Metaphors
8. c   9. d

from *The Interesting Narrative of the Life of Olaudah Equiano*

SELECTION TEST, page 9
Comprehension
1. c   2. b   3. c   4. a   5. a
6. a   7. b

Literary Element
8. b   9. d

Vocabulary
10. e   11. d   12. g   13. j   14. h
15. a   16. b   17. f   18. i   19. c

Written Response
20. Responses will vary. In a model response, students should fulfill the following criteria:
  • demonstrate understanding of the prompt
  • clearly compare the way Equiano was treated during his enslavement in Africa with the treatment he received on the slave ship
  • support their ideas with at least two references to details in the selection. For example:
    • Equiano states that he would have parted with ten thousand worlds to exchange his place on the ship with that of the lowest slave in Africa.
    • Equiano had never been flogged during his enslavement in Africa, but such treatment was common on the ship.

Literary Element
10. d   11. a

Written Response
12. Responses will vary. In a model response, students should fulfill the following criteria:
  • demonstrate understanding of the prompt
  • clearly describe either Bradstreet's extended metaphor of a house built by God or Taylor's extended metaphors of a spinning wheel, a loom, or clothing
  • explain what the metaphor suggests about the speaker's religious beliefs
  • support their ideas with at least two details from the poem. For example:
    • Bradstreet's metaphor of the house built by God suggests that the speaker believes in a comforting, pleasant spiritual life that resembles a gloriously furnished home.

- In Bradstreet's poem, references to the house as enduring and as lying above suggest that it represents an afterlife that the speaker looks forward to.
- Taylor's metaphor of a spinning wheel conveys the speaker's desire to serve God as completely as possible in every aspect of his or her life.
- Phrases in "Huswifery" such as "And make my Soul thy holy Spool to be" and "Make me thy Loom" suggest that the speaker believes that complete devotion to God's will is the only way to live a faithful life.

from *Sinners in the Hands of an Angry God*

SELECTION TEST, page 13

Comprehension
1. b   **2.** d   **3.** c   **4.** a   **5.** c
6. b   **7.** a

Reading Skills and Strategies
8. c

Literary Element
9. d   **10.** b

Vocabulary
11. c   **12.** i   **13.** f   **14.** a   **15.** g
16. j   **17.** h   **18.** e   **19.** b   **20.** d

Written Response
21. Responses will vary. In a model response, students should fulfill the following criteria:
- demonstrate understanding of the prompt
- clearly describe two major ideas expressed by Edwards in his sermon. For example:
  - God is angry with most human beings for being wicked and for not accepting Christ as their Savior.
  - God has prepared excruciating torments for those who are not "born again" in Christ.
- support their ideas with at least two details in the selection. For example:

- Edwards emphasizes God's wrath, which seems to be directed toward almost all human beings. He illustrates the potency of this anger by comparing it to a pit of flames, a potential flood, and a bow and arrow ready to pierce the flesh.
- Edwards refers to the fiery pit of hell that awaits all "sinners" and vividly describes people hanging over this place of torture.

from *The Autobiography*

SELECTION TEST, page 15

Comprehension
1. d   **2.** a   **3.** c   **4.** b   **5.** c
6. b   **7.** d   **8.** c   **9.** a

Vocabulary
10. i   **11.** c   **12.** g   **13.** d   **14.** j
15. e   **16.** b   **17.** h   **18.** f   **19.** a

Written Response
20. Responses will vary. In a model response, students should fulfill the following criteria:
- demonstrate understanding of the prompt
- explain why they chose one particular virtue as the most difficult for Franklin to master
- support their ideas with at least two details in the selection. For example:
  - Franklin's tendency to speak with anyone at length supports the choice that silence is the virtue most difficult for him to maintain. He seems to enjoy speaking with a variety of people, such as Dr. Brown and the woman who gives him lodging in Burlington.
  - Franklin's apparent pride indicates that attaining humility may be difficult for him. Franklin displays pride in his accomplishments and takes care to show himself in the best light throughout the selection. For example, he notes his courage when he saves the drunken passenger who fell overboard and his generosity in giving away rolls.

Collection 3: The American Dream

Speech to the Virginia Convention

SELECTION TEST, page 17

Comprehension
1. a   **2.** d   **3.** c   **4.** c

Reading Skills and Strategies
5. b   **6.** d

Literary Element
7. d   8. a   9. a

Vocabulary
10. a   11. f   12. j   13. b   14. g
15. i   16. e   17. h   18. d   19. c

Written Response
20. Responses will vary. In a model response, students should fulfill the following criteria:
   • demonstrate understanding of the prompt
   • write a paragraph describing Henry's main point, two of his supporting ideas, and the different possible reactions of the delegates
   • support their ideas with details from the selection. For example:
     • Henry's main point is to persuade the delegates to fight the British, rather than to continue pursuing a peaceful means of resolution.
     • Henry supports his point of view by noting past failed attempts at peaceful reconciliation with the British.
     • He emphasizes that this is the time to act and that waiting will only make the situation more difficult to combat.
     • Delegates' possible reactions may include agreeing or disagreeing with Henry's viewpoint or even being neutral.

from *The Crisis, No. 1*

SELECTION TEST, page 19

Comprehension
1. c   2. c   3. d   4. c   5. d

Reading Skills and Strategies
6. c   7. d

Literary Element
8. a   9. c

Vocabulary
10. d   11. i   12. f   13. b   14. j
15. g   16. a   17. h   18. e   19. c

Written Response
20. Responses will vary. In a model response, students should fulfill the following criteria:
   • demonstrate understanding of the prompt
   • respond to the quotation by explaining how it reflects a theme in the selection. For example:

• Paine is appealing to the colonies to cease thinking of themselves as separate entities and instead to think of themselves as a united force fighting for a common cause.
• explain what Paine means by "lay your shoulders to the wheel." For example:
  • The phrase means the colonists should work together arduously and in unity to gain independence.
• explain to what the "object" refers. For example:
  • The "object" to which Paine refers is freedom or independence from Britain.

from *The Autobiography: The Declaration of Independence*

SELECTION TEST, page 21

Comprehension
1. d   2. a   3. c   4. b   5. c

Reading Skills and Strategies
6. b   7. c

Literary Element
8. b   9. d

Vocabulary
10. a   11. e   12. j   13. f   14. h
15. c   16. d   17. i   18. b   19. g

Written Response
20. Responses will vary. In a model response, students should fulfill the following criteria:
   • demonstrate understanding of the prompt
   • explain what they think Adams admired in Jefferson's style and describe two ways that the Declaration displays the hallmarks of good writing. For example:
     • Jefferson carefully develops each of his main ideas.
     • Jefferson uses different stylistic devices, such as parallelism.
     • Jefferson uses both emotional and intellectual appeals to persuade his readers.

THE AMERICAN LANGUAGE TEST, page 23

1. d   2. c   3. d   4. a   5. a
6. b   7. c   8. d   9. c   10. a

LITERARY ELEMENTS TEST, page 25

The Plain Style and The Conceit

The Plain Style

1. a   **2.** b   **3.** c   **4.** d   **5.** c

The Conceit

6. b   **7.** a

LITERARY PERIOD TEST, page 27

Vocabulary Skills

1. a   **2.** c   **3.** b   **4.** c

Vocabulary: When a Dictionary Can Help

5. b   **6.** a   **7.** d   **8.** b

Comprehension

9. b   **10.** c   **11.** d   **12.** b   **13.** b

Reading Skills and Strategies: Identifying Tone

14. The only supportable answer is that the tone is subjective. Examples of phrases and explanations about the phrases will vary. Sample responses follow.

- "It is not composed, as in Europe, of great lords who possess everything, and of a herd of people who have nothing."
  The word *herd* indicates a negative attitude toward this separation of wealth.
- ". . . he views not the hostile castle and the haughty mansion . . ."
  Both *hostile* and *haughty* cast this vision of a landscape in a negative light.
- "all clad in neat homespun"
  The word *neat* produces a positive image of the farmers and wives that may not be literally accurate.

Reading Skills and Strategies: Identifying the Main Idea

15. Responses will vary, but students should use at least one example from the selection to support their ideas. The only supportable answer is **a.** A sample response follows.

- **a.** Crèvecoeur criticizes the inequality of the European social structure. He mentions that the rich and poor are not "so far removed from each other as they are in Europe." He cites the "pleasing uniformity" of the housing and the lack of "titles" in North America. Finally, he says that this equality will be lasting.

Literary Element

16. Responses will vary. In a model response, students should fulfill the following criteria:

- demonstrate an understanding of the prompt
- compare the plain style with the style of Crèvecoeur's letter.
- support their ideas with at least two references to details in the essay indicating a departure from the plain style. For example:
- use of metaphor in "embryos of all the arts . . ."
- use of metaphor in "silken bands of mild government . . ."
- use of personification in "hostile castle and the haughty mansion . . ."
- use of imagery in "clay-built hut and miserable cabin, where . . ."
- use of imagery in "a congregation of respectable farmers and their wives, all clad in neat homespun, well mounted, or riding their own humble wagons."
- use of metonymy in "no European foot . . ."

American Romanticism

LITERARY PERIOD INTRODUCTION TEST, page 30

1. a   **2.** c   **3.** b   **4.** a   **5.** d
6. c   **7.** d   **8.** b   **9.** a   **10.** a

Collection 4: The Transforming Imagination

Rip Van Winkle

SELECTION TEST, page 32

Comprehension

1. d   **2.** d   **3.** b   **4.** b

Reading Skills and Strategies

5. c   **6.** d

Literary Element

7. c   **8.** a

Vocabulary

9. e   10. c (or f)   11. f (or c)   12. a
13. i   14. j   15. d   16. h
17. b   18. g

Written Response

19. Responses will vary. In a model response, students should fulfill the following criteria:
    - demonstrate understanding of the prompt
    - clearly describe what Rip escapes and explain why the wish fulfillment theme is either appealing or unappealing
    - support their ideas with at least two incidents from the selection. For example:
        - His scolding wife dies while he is away.
        - He has avoided the responsibilities of being a father, since his children have grown up.
        - He has been relieved of financial burdens.
        - He has escaped years of the tyranny of British rule.

Thanatopsis

SELECTION TEST, page 34

Comprehension

1. b   2. a   3. c   4. a   5. c

Reading Skills and Strategies

6. d

Written Response

7. Responses will vary. In a model response, students should fulfill the following criteria:
    - demonstrate understanding of the prompt
    - clearly describe Bryant's views on the nature of individual lives and analyze his use of language inversion, sound effects, and rhythm to communicate those views
    - support their ideas with at least two examples from the poem. For example:
        - The poem suggests that everyone experiences both happiness and sadness. The poem's speaker refers to both "gayer hours" and "darker musings."
        - The speaker emphasizes the transient, fleeting quality of human lives. He or she states "each one as before will chase / His favorite phantom" in life, stressing the futility and impermanence of worldly pursuits.
        - Bryant inverts syntax to make the individual seem less important than other things; he uses sound effects like "poured" to unify the poem; and he varies rhythm so that different ideas and images are emphasized.

The Tide Rises, the Tide Falls
The Cross of Snow

SELECTION TEST, page 35

Comprehension

1. b   2. a   3. b   4. c   5. c
6. c   7. d

Literary Element

8. b   9. b

Written Response

10. Responses will vary, but students should use at least two examples from the selections to support their ideas. The best answers are **a** and **c**. A sample response to each choice follows.
    a. In "The Tide Rises, the Tide Falls," the speaker balances life and death, the permanence of nature and the transitoriness of human existence, renewed life and death. In "The Cross of Snow," the speaker's fond memories are described along with his sorrow.
    b. In "The Tide Rises, the Tide Falls," the speaker expresses his feelings about mortality. In "The Cross of Snow," the speaker describes his reaction to the death of a woman he loved.
    c. In "The Tide Rises, the Tide Falls," the speaker mentions darkness and the disappearing footprints, which suggest a mood of loneliness and isolation. In "The Cross of Snow," the speaker dwells on the sadness of losing a loved one.
    d. *(Partial credit can be given if students point out that the speaker in each of the poems appears to draw a lesson from nature.)*
11. Responses will vary. In a model response, students should fulfill the following criteria.
    - demonstrate understanding of the prompt
    - identify Longfellow's view of life as either optimistic or pessimistic, and select at least two references from the poems to support their ideas. For example:
        - The fact that "The Cross of Snow" is a love poem shows that Longfellow is optimistic.
        - Longfellow's optimism is expressed in his loving descriptions of his wife, such as "legend of a life more benedight."
        - Longfellow's pessimism is evident in "The Tide Rises, the Tide Falls" when he suggests that people have little control over their destinies.
        - Humans may go about their business, unconcerned about the tide; however, death is inevitable, as suggested in the refrain "The tide rises, the tide falls."

from *Snow-Bound: A Winter Idyll*

SELECTION TEST, page 37

Comprehension
1. b **2.** d **3.** a **4.** d **5.** b

Reading Skills and Strategies
6. a

Written Response
7. Responses will vary. In a model response, students should fulfill the following criteria:
   - demonstrate understanding of the prompt
   - present clear descriptions of the transformations. For example:
     - The outdoor landscape is transformed by both the snow and the moonlight.
     - The indoor environment is transformed by the fire and the sense of coziness and warmth.
   - provide clear explanations of Whittier's use of imagery. For example:
     - Exotic images, including "strange domes and towers" and "Transfigured in the silver flood," convey a sense of amazement at the outdoor landscape's transformation.
     - Phrases such as "Burst, flowerlike, into rosy bloom" describe the transformation of the home after the building of a fire.

The Chambered Nautilus *Old Ironsides*

SELECTION TEST, page 38

Comprehension
1. a **2.** c **3.** d **4.** a **5.** b
6. a

Literary Element
7. b **8.** a

Written Response
9. Responses will vary, but students should use at least one example from the selection to support their ideas. The best answers are **b** and **c**. A sample response to each choice follows.
   a. *(Partial credit can be given if students point out that in "Old Ironsides" the speaker attempts to persuade the reader to help save the old ship.)*

b. The subject of "Old Ironsides" is the USS *Constitution*. The subject of "The Chambered Nautilus" is a chambered shell, which the speaker refers to as a ship.

c. In "Old Ironsides," the speaker expresses a respect for the past glories of the U.S. naval fleet. In "The Chambered Nautilus," the speaker expresses the opinion that experience helps people to move on to better things.

d. *(Partial credit can be given if students point out that the speaker in "The Chambered Nautilus" refers to her or his spiritual outlook.)*

10. Responses will vary. In a model response, students should fulfill the following criteria:
    - demonstrate understanding of the prompt
    - identify characteristics of American Romanticism found in Holmes's poems
    - make at least two references to details from poems to support their ideas. For example:
      - In "The Chambered Nautilus," the focus is on the beauty and truth found in nature.
      - "Old Ironsides" emphasizes the value of the past over the benefits of progress.

THE AMERICAN LANGUAGE TEST, page 40

1. b **2.** c **3.** a **4.** d **5.** b
6. c **7.** b **8.** b **9.** c **10.** a

LITERARY ELEMENTS TEST, page 42

The Sonnet
1. c **2.** c **3.** a **4.** b **5.** d
6. b **7.** c **8.** d **9.** c **10.** b

LITERARY PERIOD TEST, page 44

Vocabulary Skills
1. F **2.** F **3.** T **4.** T

Vocabulary: Using Context Clues
5. a **6.** c **7.** a **8.** d

Comprehension
9. b **10.** d **11.** c **12.** d **13.** d

Reading Skills and Strategies
14. Responses will vary, but students should use at least one example from the selection to support their ideas. The only supportable answer is **d**. A sample response follows.

d. The speaker begins by inviting the "stranger" to escape the "sorrows, crimes, and cares" of the world by entering the wood. He describes the soothing effect of the wood with such words as "calm," "balm," "contentment," "tranquility," and "love."

15. Responses will vary. In a model response, students should fulfill the following criteria:
    - demonstrate understanding of the prompt
    - state whether they agree or disagree with the statement given
    - support their position with details from the poem. For example:
      - If they agree:
        - Bryant calls the shade a "kindred" calm.
        - He says that pain comes from the "haunts of men."
        - He says the wind will "come to thee, / Like one that loves thee."
        - He ends by saying that the wind will give its embrace.
      - If they disagree:

- Bryant compares the wind to someone who loves the speaker. Bryant's comparison of nature to humanity indicates that the love between people is important, and perhaps more significant a consolation than is nature. If he believed otherwise, he might have made different comparisons.
- Bryant writes that the rivulet laughs. Laughter is a human action that uplifts those who suffer.

Literary Element

16. Responses will vary. A sample response follows.

Detail	Positive Association in Poem	Possible Negative Association
shade	"calm"	shadowy, unknown, threatening
"throngs of insects"	"dance"	annoyance, biting, stinging
roots of uprooted trees	"breathe fixed tranquility"	threatening fingers, destruction, death
wind	"cool," "in play," "light embrace"	power, storm

The American Renaissance: A Literary Coming of Age

LITERARY PERIOD INTRODUCTION TEST, page 47

1. a	**2.** c	**3.** d	**4.** a	**5.** b
6. c	**7.** d	**8.** b	**9.** a	**10.** a

Collection 5: The Life Worth Living

from *Nature*

SELECTION TEST, page 49

Comprehension

1. b	**2.** d	**3.** d	**4.** a	**5.** c

Literary Element

6. b   **7.** c

Vocabulary

8. e	**9.** c	**10.** g	**11.** d	**12.** h
13. j	**14.** b	**15.** i	**16.** a	**17.** f

Written Response

18. Responses will vary. In a model response, students should fulfill the following criteria:
    - demonstrate understanding of the prompt

- explain how the quotation represents Emerson's ideas about society and nature. For example:
  - Emerson is saying that solitude—being away from people—is something to be desired.
  - It is not only society that keeps a person from experiencing solitude, however. Even when a person is physically isolated from others, if nature is remote, he or she will not experience the benefits of solitude.

from *Self-Reliance*

SELECTION TEST, page 51

Comprehension

1. a   **2.** d   **3.** b   **4.** d

Reading Skills and Strategies
5. b   6. c

Literary Element
7. d   8. c

Vocabulary
9. e   10. d   11. g   12. b   13. a
14. i   15. h   16. c   17. j   18. f

Written Response
19. Responses will vary. In a model response, students should fulfill the following criteria:
   - demonstrate understanding of the prompt
   - state the theme of Emerson's essay. For example:
     - Individuals should trust themselves and nurture their special gifts, and should not concern themselves with society's insistence on conformity and consistency.
   - state whether or not the quotation contradicts Emerson's theme
   - support their ideas with at least two examples from the selection. For example:
     - Students arguing that the quotation contradicts Emerson's theme may cite the following examples: that belonging to society leads to conformity and consistency; that toil can make a person great.
     - Students arguing that the quotation does not contradict the theme may cite the following examples: that everyone must accept himself or herself; that everyone must accept his or her destiny.

from *Walden, or Life in the Woods*

SELECTION TEST, page 53
Comprehension
1. a   2. b   3. c   4. d   5. a

Reading Skills and Strategies: Drawing Inferences—Generalizations
6. c   7. a

Reading Skills and Strategies: Unlocking Meaning in Metaphors
8. c

Literary Element
9. d

Vocabulary
10. d   11. e   12. j   13. i   14. f
15. b   16. a   17. c   18. g   19. h

Written Response
20. Responses will vary. In a model response, students should fulfill the following criteria:
   - demonstrate understanding of the prompt
   - explain the meaning of the quotation. For example:
     - Thoreau did not wish to spend his life engaged in what he considered useless pursuits required by society, and he felt that most people fritter away their lives with meaningless activities.
   - support their ideas with three examples of what Thoreau considered to be "not life." For example:
     - luxury; needless expense; needless complexity; eating too many meals or types of food; a life of conformity; lack of planning; lack of a worthy aim; commerce (business, industry); being around crowds of people; exporting ice; talking by telegraph; traveling thirty miles an hour

from *Resistance to Civil Government*

SELECTION TEST, page 55
Comprehension
1. b   2. d   3. a   4. c   5. b

Reading Skills and Strategies
6. d

Literary Element
7. c   8. c

Vocabulary
9. i   10. h   11. b   12. c   13. j
14. e   15. f   16. g   17. d   18. a

Written Response
19. Responses will vary. In a model response, students should fulfill the following criteria:
   - demonstrate understanding of the prompt
   - describe Thoreau's purpose. For example:
     - Thoreau wrote this essay to persuade readers to accept his point of view about government and civil disobedience.
   - summarize four other major points of the essay. For example:

- Thoreau states that the government is apt to be "perverted" by the interests of a few and thus apt to act immorally. The fact that the current government supported slavery and was at war with Mexico to extend slavery was further proof of that corruption.
  - He states that a person's conscience should take precedence over the law or the government.
  - He says that a person is not morally obligated to devote himself or herself to eradicating wrongs but *is* obligated not to support wrongdoing.
  - He criticizes the hypocrisy of those who say they are against slavery and the war in Mexico, yet give their allegiance to the government and pay their taxes. He says that if all who claim to abhor slavery would refuse to pay their taxes and would be locked in jail, slavery would be abolished.
- He describes his night in jail, beginning with the "foolishness" of his jailers, who did not understand that he considered himself free (free to disobey the government, he seems to be implying).
- He makes other observations about his jail experience, including how he saw his town and its people differently when he came out the next day. He faults the townspeople for choosing lives of subservient conformity.

Collection 6: The Realms of Darkness

The Fall of the House of Usher

SELECTION TEST, page 57

Comprehension

1. b   2. a   3. b   4. d   5. b
6. a

Reading Skills and Strategies

7. N   8. P   9. N   10. P   11. N

Literary Element: Atmosphere

12. a   13. b

Literary Element: Poe's Symbols

14. c

Vocabulary

15. d   16. a   17. h   18. g   19. b
20. j   21. e   22. c   23. i   24. f

Written Response

25. Responses will vary. In a model response, students should fulfill the following criteria:
    - demonstrate understanding of the prompt
    - suggest at least two reasons why the narrator stays on at the house
    - support their ideas with at least two details from the story. For example:
      - The narrator may stay on because of concern for Roderick. The narrator has come to help his friend; he decides to stay even when he can't cheer up Roderick.
      - The narrator is fascinated by the events at the house of Usher. He describes them in great detail; he is curious about the mysterious Madeline.

- The narrator himself is going insane. His own senses begin to become abnormally acute; he, too, wonders whether Madeline has been buried alive.

The Raven

SELECTION TEST, page 59

Comprehension

1. c   2. d   3. d   4. b   5. a
6. a   7. c

Reading Skills and Strategies

8. c   9. a

Literary Element

10. a   11. c

Written Response

12. Responses will vary. In a model response, students should fulfill the following criteria:
    - demonstrate understanding of the prompt
    - describe both external and internal causes for the narrator's suffering
    - support their ideas with at least two details from the poem. For example:
      - The narrator is already suffering before the bird arrives. (internal)
      - The narrator is mourning a personal loss. (external)
      - The narrator asks questions that he knows will be answered with "Nevermore." (internal)
      - The bird's persistence contributes to the narrator's despair. (external)

The Minister's Black Veil

SELECTION TEST, page 61

Comprehension
1. b   2. a   3. d   4. c   5. c
6. c

Reading Skills and Strategies: Drawing Inferences
7. a

Reading Skills and Strategies: Understanding Archaisms
8. a

Literary Element
9. b   10. d

Vocabulary
11. b   12. a   13. h   14. i   15. g
16. d   17. j   18. e   19. c   20. f

Written Response
21. Responses will vary. In a model response, students should fulfill the following criteria:
    - demonstrate understanding of the prompt
    - suggest at least two ways the main character's calling affects the story
    - support their ideas with at least two references to details in the selection. For example:
      - A minister might be the type of person least suspected of inner secrets.
      - A minister might be inclined toward introspection and therefore realize his condition more readily than someone with another vocation.
      - As a spiritual leader, a minister's actions might carry more authority; he knows that if he takes this role seriously it will have an effect on his parishioners.

The Quarter-Deck

SELECTION TEST, page 63

Comprehension
1. b   2. a   3. b   4. d   5. a
6. a

Reading Skills and Strategies
7. c   8. d

Literary Element
9. a   10. d

Vocabulary
11. rejoinder   12. inscrutable
13. tacit   14. volition
15. imprecations

Written Response
16. Responses will vary. In a model response, students should fulfill the following criteria:
    - demonstrate understanding of the prompt
    - clearly describe three of Ahab's personal characteristics that contribute to his ability to elicit devotion and loyalty. For example:
      - perseverance, as demonstrated by his pursuit of the whale
      - persuasive speaking, as demonstrated when he rallies support to hunt Moby-Dick
      - a clear goal, as demonstrated by his desire to kill Moby-Dick
      - an ability to convince others that what is good for him is also good for them, as demonstrated by the quarter-deck speech
    - identify which of these qualities are characteristics of a leader who deserves devotion and loyalty.

from *Moby-Dick*

SELECTION TEST, page 65

Comprehension
1. b   2. b   3. a   4. b   5. b
6. d   7. d

Reading Skills and Strategies
8. a   9. b

Vocabulary
10. b   11. c   12. d   13. a   14. e

Written Response
15. Responses will vary. In a model response, students should fulfill the following criteria:
    - demonstrate understanding of the prompt
    - suggest at least two ways in which Ahab acquires power
    - discuss whether this power is supported by or in conflict with seeing the truth
    - support their ideas with at least two references to evidence in the selection. For example:
      - The pursuit takes over Ahab's mind, giving him a powerful focus but leaving him unable to see reality reasonably.
      - Ahab's single-mindedness, although actually a sign of a deranged mind, gives him the aura of purpose and self-confidence.

- Ahab is powerful partly because of his position as captain, yet he would not have been named captain of this expedition had he not hidden his true purpose in sailing.
- Ahab ignores the practical concerns of the voyage, such as making money.

LITERARY ELEMENTS TEST, page 67

Poe's Symbols

1. a **2.** d **3.** a **4.** d **5.** b
6. c **7.** a **8.** d **9.** a **10.** c

LITERARY PERIOD TEST, page 69

Vocabulary Skills

1. a **2.** b **3.** c **4.** a **5.** c

Vocabulary: Etymologies

English Word	Latin Words of Origin	Meaning from List Below
6. supererogatory	*super* = above, *rogare* = to ask	**a.** doing "above" what is asked
7. malicious	*malus* = bad	**c.** marked by the desire to cause harm
8. discourse	*dis* = apart, *currere* = to run	**d.** speaking on various subjects by "running" from one to the next
9. indispensable	*in* = not, dis = apart, *pensare* = to weigh	**b.** marked by such "weight" that it cannot be set aside

Comprehension

10. c **11.** d **12.** d **13.** a **14.** b

Reading Skills and Strategies

15. Responses will vary, but students should use at least two examples from the letter to support their ideas. The only supportable answer is **c.** A sample response follows.
  c. His honesty is evident in the following comments.
  - He talks about his problems: not being able to leave, his troubles with writing.

- He apologizes for talking about himself, but explains and expects Hawthorne to understand.

16. A sample response follows.
  a. He does not want to write just for money, yet he cannot write what will not sell.
  b. He is determined to finish writing his book, but does not know exactly how he will be able to finish.
  c. Not even the very best writing will bring in enough money to support him.

Literary Element

17. Responses will vary. In a model response, students should fulfill the following criteria:
  - demonstrate understanding of the prompt
  - state their agreement or disagreement with the statement given
  - support their ideas with at least two examples from the letter. For example:
    - the ideas are not powerful because
      - Melville assumes a familiarity with his work and his life that readers may not be able to reconstruct. ("As the fishermen say, 'he's in his flurry' when I left him some three weeks ago.")
      - Melville mixes his "general" statements with mundane concerns of farming and his busy life (". . . but see my hand! four blisters on this palm . . .").
    - the ideas are powerful because
      - the reader is able to see a real human being and is therefore more interested in his ideas (". . . in the evening I feel completely done up . . .").
      - he writes not only with intellect but also with emotion; the reader is able to determine not only what Melville thinks but also how he feels ("If ever, my dear Hawthorne, in the eternal times that are to come, you and I shall . . .").

A New American Poetry: Whitman and Dickinson

LITERARY PERIOD INTRODUCTION
TEST, page 72

1. a **2.** a **3.** b **4.** d **5.** c
6. d **7.** b **8.** b **9.** c **10.** a

Collection 7: The Large Hearts of Heroes

I Hear America Singing from *Song of Myself 10, 33, and 52*
A Sight in Camp in the Daybreak Gray and Dim

SELECTION TEST, page 74

Comprehension

1. a   2. d   3. c   4. b   5. d
6. a

Reading Skills and Strategies: Summarizing a Text

7. d

Reading Skills and Strategies: Comparing Themes Across Texts

8. b

Literary Elements

9. a   10. a   11. d   12. b

Written Response

13. Responses will vary. In a model response, students should fulfill the following criteria:
    - demonstrate understanding of the prompt
    - demonstrate an understanding that imaginative empathy involves feeling what is not actually experienced
    - support their ideas with references to at least two poems. For example:
      - In "Song of Myself," Number 33, the images of the women and babies are surprising.
      - In "Song of Myself," Number 52, the hawk's action provides immediacy, for it is described as if it is happening at the moment of writing (use of present tense).
      - In "Song of Myself," Number 10, the reader is addressed directly, implying that the poet and the reader know each other.
      - In "Song of Myself," Number 33, the description of the runaway slave includes images of physical sensation ("twinges," "sting," "cover'd with sweat") that the slave would feel and that the reader is asked to feel with him.

Collection 8: Tell It Slant

Poetry of Emily Dickinson

SELECTION TEST, page 76

Comprehension

1. b   2. b   3. a   4. b   5. b
6. a   7. c   8. c   9. d

Reading Skills and Strategies

10. c   11. d

Literary Element

12. d   13. a   14. d

Written Response

15. Responses will vary. In a model response, students should fulfill the following criteria:
    - demonstrate understanding of the prompt
    - demonstrate an understanding that an author may describe different aspects of a single concept in different poems
    - find differences in the way love is treated and use references to the text to support the existence of different aspects of love. For example:
      - In "Heart! We will forget him!" there is uncertainty about whether the loved one can be forgotten; in "Fall," there is uncertainty about when the love will be fulfilled.
      - In "Heart!" the speaker wants the heart's compliance in forgetting a loved one; in "Fall," the speaker wants knowledge of the length of separation.
      - In "Heart!" the loved one has left forever; in "Fall," he is expected to return.

THE AMERICAN LANGUAGE TEST, page 78

1. b   2. c   3. a   4. d   5. b
6. a   7. d   8. b   9. c   10. b

LITERARY ELEMENTS TEST, page 80

Free Verse and Slant Rhyme

1. a   2. b   3. c   4. a   5. c
6. b   7. c   8. b   9. b   10. d

Vocabulary Skills

1. b 2. b 3. c 4. c 5. a

Comprehension

6. a 7. c 8. d 9. c 10. b

Reading Skills and Strategies

11. Responses will vary, but students should use at least two examples from the poem to support their ideas. The only supportable answers are **b** and **d**.
    Sample responses follow.
    a. *(This is not a supportable response.)*
    b. "Signor" could refer to any superior figure or deity to which the speaker of the poem is "obedient." "Obedience" may apply to following a particular religious doctrine.
    c. *(This is not a supportable response.)*
    d. "Signor" could refer to the father of the speaker. The child is obedient to a parent, just as the sea is obedient to the moon. The parent leading the child by the hand corresponds to the moon pulling the tides of the sea.
12. Responses will vary. In a model response, students should fulfill the following criteria:
    • demonstrate understanding of the prompt
    • state their agreement or disagreement with the statement given (agreement with the statement is more easily supported than disagreement)

• support their ideas with at least two examples from the poems. For example:
• the statement is supported because
  • Whitman talks about the "ship aboard the ship" and "Ship of the body, soul," both of which imply direction coming from within.
  • Dickinson writes of a "Signor" who gives direction. This is a source outside of or distant from the body, just as the moon is distant from the sea. The poem makes the point that control can be exacting even though it is exercised from a distance.
• the statement is not supported because
  • Whitman could be referring to an external source that directs the body and the soul just as the ocean-bell sends a warning.
  • Dickinson could be writing of a "master" within us—distant only because it is hidden.

Literary Element

13. Responses will vary. A sample response follows.

Element of Free Verse	Example
imagery	"the freighted ship tacking speeds away under her gray sails"
repetition	"voyaging, voyaging, voyaging"
alliteration	"O you give good notice"
figure of speech	"ship of the soul"

The Rise Of Realism: The Civil War and Postwar Period

LITERARY PERIOD INTRODUCTION TEST, page 86

1. a 2. b 3. d 4. a 5. d
6. b 7. c 8. a 9. b 10. c

Collection 9: Shackles

from *The Narrative of the Life of Frederick Douglass*

SELECTION TEST, page 88

Comprehension

1. c 2. a 3. c 4. d 5. d
6. b 7. a

Literary Element

8. c 9. b

Vocabulary

10. A 11. S 12. A 13. A 14. S
15. S 16. A 17. S 18. A 19. S

Written Response

20. Responses will vary. In a model response, students should fulfill the following criteria:

- demonstrate understanding of the prompt
- clearly describe the way Douglass is mistreated and his response to this abuse
- use at least three examples from the selection to support their descriptions. For example:
  - Douglass is beaten when he is too ill to work. He responds by going to Master Thomas for help.
  - When Covey chases Douglass upon his return, Douglass hides in a cornfield.
  - When Covey attempts to tie Douglass with a rope, Douglass fights back.
- analyze how Douglass responds to abuse by overcoming fear and becoming defiant and self-empowered
  - Despite being sick and seriously injured from the beating, Douglass has the inner strength and determination to walk seven miles through woods and briars to seek help.
  - Douglass learns to fight back to save himself from further mistreatment and to regain his dignity.

12. acute
13. appreciable
14. reveling
15. gaudy
16. judicious
17. fastidious
18. poignant
19. laborious
20. preposterous

Written Response
21. Responses will vary. In a model response, students should fulfill the following criteria:
- demonstrate understanding of the prompt
- clearly explain why they think Mrs. Sommers spends the fifteen dollars in the way she does rather than in the way she had originally planned. For example:
  - She had seen better days and wants to revisit them.
  - She is overcome by an impulse, and once she purchases the silk stockings, the dam of prudence bursts.
  - She wants to escape, if only temporarily, from her everyday existence of scrimping and doing without.
  - She wants to wear beautiful clothes and enjoy herself.
- provide two examples from the story that support their explanations. For example:
  - Once she buys the silk stockings, she has to have a new pair of boots and gloves.
  - She indulges in pleasures she once enjoyed, such as dining in a nice restaurant, going to the theater, and buying magazines.

A Pair of Silk Stockings

SELECTION TEST, page 90
Comprehension

1. c	**2.** a	**3.** d	**4.** a	**5.** b
6. c	**7.** c	**8.** b	**9.** b	**10.** d

Vocabulary
11. veritable *or* gaudy

Collection 10: From Innocence to Experience

from *Life on the Mississippi*

SELECTION TEST, page 92
Comprehension

1. b	**2.** c	**3.** a	**4.** a	**5.** c

Reading Skills and Strategies

6. b	**7.** d	**8.** a

Literary Element

9. a	**10.** b

Vocabulary

11. c	**12.** i	**13.** a	**14.** g	**15.** b
16. j	**17.** e	**18.** h	**19.** f	**20.** d

Written Response
21. Responses will vary. In a model response, students should fulfill the following criteria:
- demonstrate understanding of the prompt
- clearly describe how Twain feels after becoming a riverboat pilot. For example:
  - He is satisfied with his achievement.
  - He is disappointed.
  - He is ambivalent about finally reaching his goal.
- support their ideas with at least two examples from the selection. For example:
  - Twain is satisfied because he has become so familiar with the river that he enjoys reading it like a book, and he considers this knowledge valuable.

- He is disappointed, because the river's beauty and romance are gone for him. The river's features are now simply useful, and he compares his feelings to those of a doctor who no longer appreciates a beautiful patient.
- He is ambivalent, because he is pleased with his mastery and finds it useful, but the romance of the river is gone forever for him.

An Occurrence at Owl Creek Bridge

SELECTION TEST, page 94

Comprehension
1. c   2. a   3. d   4. a   5. a
6. b   7. d

Literary Element
8. b   9. c

Vocabulary
10. f   11. j   12. a   13. c   14. g
15. b   16. i   17. e   18. d   19. h

Written Response
20. Responses will vary. In a model response, students should fulfill the following criteria:
- demonstrate understanding of the prompt
- clearly show how Bierce hints that Farquhar's escape is a fantasy
- support their ideas with at least two examples from the story. For example:
  - When Farquhar comes to the surface of the stream after his fall, his physical senses are preternaturally keen and alert, and he sees things that are not possible to see
  - The forest seems wild and endless to Farquhar, and he thinks there is something uncanny in that revelation.
  - Farquhar sees golden stars in strange constellations that seem to have a secret and malign significance.

A Mystery of Heroism

SELECTION TEST, page 96

Comprehension
1. d   2. c   3. c   4. b   5. a
6. d   7. b

Literary Element
8. d   9. a

Vocabulary
10. f   11. h   12. a   13. j   14. e
15. b   16. d   17. i   18. c   19. g

Written Response
20. Responses will vary. In a model response, students should fulfill the following criteria:
- demonstrate understanding of the prompt
- clearly explain whether they think Collins's act is heroic, foolish, or a combination of both
- support their ideas with at least three examples from the story. For example:
  - Collins acts foolishly because he acts in response to the goading of his comrades, knowing that he may die trying to get the water. The well and the buildings close to it are being heavily shelled. The meadow in front of the well is besieged with crossfire.
  - Collins acts heroically when he takes the other men's canteens to fill, when he returns to give the dying lieutenant water, and when he gives his comrades hope as they cheer for him.
  - Collins acts foolishly at times and heroically at other times. He is foolish in giving into the soldiers' goading and in continuing his trip under heavy shelling. However, he is heroic when he returns to the lieutenant and gives him water.

To Build a Fire

SELECTION TEST, page 98

Comprehensions
1. d   2. b   3. a   4. c   5. a

Reading Skills and Strategies
6. a   7. d

Literary Element
8. d   9. b

Vocabulary
10. d   11. g   12. e   13. c   14. h
15. j   16. a   17. i   18. f   19. b

Written Response
20. Responses will vary, but students should use at least two examples from the story to support their ideas. The best answer is **b**. A sample response to each choice follows.

a. The man underestimates the cold because this is his first winter in the Yukon, and to him the extreme cold means only that he will be uncomfortable. He does not consider that people can survive within only a narrow range of temperature.

b. The man has no control over the temperature, his body's reactions to the cold, or unforeseen events like falling into the water.

c. The dog is better suited to the Yukon because its instinct causes it to fear the cold, it senses danger, and it wants the man to go into camp or seek shelter and build a fire.

d. Traveling with a companion may not have helped because of the extreme temperatures, the threat of hidden springs beneath the snow, and the possibility that a companion's hands and feet may have been just as frozen as the man's.

THE AMERICAN LANGUAGE TEST, page 100

1. b   **2.** d   **3.** a   **4.** b   **5.** c
6. d   **7.** a   **8.** d   **9.** c   **10.** a

LITERARY ELEMENTS TEST, page 102

Douglass's Metaphors
1. a   **2.** c   **3.** d   **4.** b   **5.** d
6. c   **7.** b   **8.** c   **9.** d   **10.** c

LITERARY PERIOD TEST, page 104

Vocabulary Skills
1. b   **2.** b   **3.** a   **4.** c   **5.** c

Vocabulary: Affixes
6. d   **7.** e   **8.** a   **9.** c   **10.** b

Comprehension
11. c   **12.** b   **13.** b   **14.** d   **15.** a

Reading Skills and Strategies: Analyzing Text Structures
16. Responses will vary. A sample response follows.

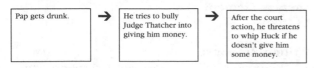

Pap gets drunk. → He tries to bully Judge Thatcher into giving him money. → After the court action, he threatens to whip Huck if he doesn't give him some money.

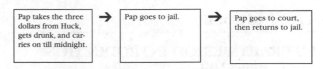

Pap takes the three dollars from Huck, gets drunk, and carries on till midnight. → Pap goes to jail. → Pap goes to court, then returns to jail.

Reading Skills and Strategies: Identifying Comic Devices
17. Responses will vary. In a model response, students should fulfill the following criteria:
- demonstrate understanding of the prompt
- identify comic devices each narrator uses and clearly explain how these devices create humor
- use at least two examples from each selection to support their descriptions. For example:
  - In the selection *Life on the Mississippi,* Twain's narrator uses comic metaphors to poke fun at himself when Mr. Bixby leaves the boat in his charge and then suddenly reappears. The narrator compares the passengers to rats and talks about the steamboat as though it were a person. Both devices play up the narrator's belief that his situation is serious; Bixby's calm manner and explanation of the situation contrasts with the narrator's anxiety and interpretation of events. Through metaphor and contrast, humor is created.
  - In the selection from *Adventures of Huckleberry Finn,* Huck uses understatement when he explains the judge's reaction to Pap's rejection of reformation. The understatement highlights the irony of the judge having believed that he could reform Pap.

Literary Element: Point of View
18. Responses will vary, but students should use at least one example from the selection to support their ideas. A sample response to each choice follows.

a. Huck talks about a potentially painful subject—his father's getting drunk—but describes it in such hilarious terms that it is amusing rather than sad.

b. Huck's initial reaction to Pap and his vivid description of Pap's appearance automatically align the reader with Huck's point of view.

c. Some of the events Huck recounts—Pap's verbal abuse of Huck, his constant demands for money, and his drunkenness—would be too difficult for some readers to accept if they were told in a straightforward fashion.

d. Twain has always been known for his humor. For instance, Huck's account of the judge's dinner with Pap is much funnier than an objective account would have been.

The Moderns

**LITERARY PERIOD INTRODUCTION
TEST, page 109**

1. a   2. b   3. c   4. d   5. c
6. d   7. b   8. b   9. a   10. c

Collection 11: Loss and Redemption

A Wagner Matinée

SELECTION TEST, page 111

Comprehension

1. d   2. b   3. a   4. b   5. c
6. b   7. a

Literary Element

8. c   9. b

Vocabulary

10. g   11. b   12. d   13. j   14. f
15. c   16. i   17. e   18. a   19. h

Written Response

20. Responses will vary. In a model response, students should fulfill the following criteria:
    - demonstrate understanding of the prompt
    - describe what Clark perceives is Georgiana's reaction to the concert
    - support their ideas with at least two references to details in the story. For example:
        - She clutches Clark's coat sleeve when the horns play; he assumes this is because she has been deprived of music for thirty years.
        - Her quiet weeping indicates to Clark that her love for music has never died.

His Father's Earth

SELECTION TEST, page 113

Comprehension

1. c   2. a   3. c   4. a   5. b
6. a   7. b

Literary Element

8. d   9. b

Vocabulary

10. g *or* h   11. c   12. i   13. a
14. e   15. j   16. f   17. d
18. h *or* g   19. b

Written Response

20. Responses will vary. In a model response, students should fulfill the following criteria:
    - demonstrate understanding of the prompt
    - clearly describe how the story is linked to the idea of home
    - support their ideas with at least two references to details in the story. For example:
        - the boy's excitement about returning home
        - the portrait of the father as nurturing and welcoming
        - the description of birdsong, which makes home seem nearly as exciting as the circus
        - the fact that the story begins and ends at home

Design
Nothing Gold Can Stay
Once by the Pacific
Neither Out Far Nor In Deep
Birches
The Death of the Hired Man

SELECTION TEST, page 115

Comprehension

1. b   2. d   3. a   4. c   5. b

Reading Skills and Strategies: Understanding Blank Verse

6. a   7. b   8. c

Reading Skills and Strategies: Drawing Inferences About Characters

9. d   10. c

Literary Element

11. b

Written Response

12. Responses will vary. In a model response, students should fulfill the following criteria:

- demonstrate understanding of the prompt
- explain whether they view Frost's poems as being pessimistic or realistic
- support their ideas with at least two references to details in the poems. For example:
  - the pessimistic, angry view of destructive humanity in "Once by the Pacific"
  - the pessimistic view in "Design," with evil lurking even in the most seemingly innocent things
  - the realistic view in "Nothing Gold Can Stay," which portrays beauty as rare and transient, but affirms and celebrates its existence
  - the realistic view in "Birches," in which the boy (and the speaker) can take time out from chores and responsibilities to experience the joy of playing

---

Bells for John Whiteside's Daughter
Shine, Perishing Republic

Collection 12: The Dream and the Reality

Winter Dreams

SELECTION TEST, page 119

Comprehension

1. a   2. d   3. c   4. a   5. b

Reading Skills and Strategies: Drawing Inferences About Character

6. c   7. a

Reading Skills and Strategies: Understanding Paradoxes

8. c   9. a

Literary Element

10. b   11. c

Vocabulary

12. f or i   13. h   14. b   15. i or f
16. j   17. c   18. d   19. a
20. e   21. g

Written Response

22. Responses will vary. In a model response, students should fulfill the following criteria:
  - demonstrate understanding of the prompt

SELECTION TEST, page 117

Comprehension

1. b   2. d   3. a   4. c   5. c
6. d   7. c

Literary Element

8. a   9. c

Written Response

10. Responses will vary. In a model response, students should fulfill the following criteria:
  - demonstrate understanding of the prompt
  - clearly contrast Ransom's sad, fond, and accepting tone with Jeffers's bitter, cynical tone
  - support their ideas with at least one reference to a specific image in each poem. For example:
    - Ransom's cheerful memory of the little girl scaring the geese and of her moving swiftly and gracefully
    - Jeffers's entirely negative remarks about American cities, industries, and dead ideals, and his images of a natural world destroyed by human corruption

---

- complete the statement. For example:
  - At the end of the story, tears stream down Dexter's face because he is mourning the loss of a dream or ideal.
- support their ideas with at least two ideas or examples from the story. For example:
  - When Devlin tells Dexter that Judy used to be pretty, Dexter's ideal of Judy as a striking, irresistible beauty is destroyed.
  - When Dexter tries to conjure up the feelings he once had for Judy, he fails. Not only has he lost the glorious image of his ideal, but also he has lost touch with his former feelings.
  - Dexter has left behind the world of his youth, where his dreams once flourished.

The Leader of the People

SELECTION TEST, page 121

Comprehension

1. a   2. b   3. d   4. b   5. a

Reading Skills and Strategies

6. d   7. c

Literary Element

8. b   9. c

Vocabulary

10. e   11. c   12. j   13. g   14. a
15. f   16. b   17. d   18. h   19. i

Written Response

20. Responses will vary. In a model response, students should fulfill the following criteria:
   - demonstrate understanding of the prompt
   - describe two conflicts in the story. For example:
     - external conflicts between Jody's mother and father over Grandfather's repetitious stories
     - the external conflict between Jody and his father about what Jody is allowed to do
     - the internal conflict Grandfather has between his glorified version of history and historical reality
   - describe the personalities of the characters involved. For example:
     - Jody's mother is thoughtful.
     - Jody is considerate.
     - Jody's father is hard-working and abrupt.
     - Jody's grandfather places a lot of emphasis on the past.
   - explain whether they think the conflicts are resolved, and use at least two examples from the story to support their opinions. For example:
     - Jody's mother and father don't actually settle their conflict; however, when Carl apologizes to Grandfather in shame, the conflict is over.
     - The conflict between Jody and his father is not over, but it may have been lessened when Jody went to get the stick to kill the mice.
     - Grandfather realizes that westering is over and that most people do not want to hear about it.

The Secret Life of Walter Mitty

SELECTION TEST, page 123

Comprehension

1. d   2. b   3. a   4. b   5. a

Reading Skills and Strategies

6. c   7. b

Literary Element

8. b   9. b

Vocabulary

10. f   11. e   12. j *or* b   13. b *or* j
14. i   15. h   16. a   17. g
18. d   19. c

Written Response

20. Responses will vary. In a model response, students should fulfill the following criteria:
   - demonstrate understanding of the prompt
   - explain whether they think Mitty is trying to escape from reality and, if so, what that reality is
   - support their ideas with at least two examples from the story. For example:
     - Mitty is trying to escape from his passivity in the face of constant directives from his wife: buy puppy biscuits, wear overshoes, drive more slowly.
     - Mitty is trying to escape from the boredom of his daily life. He daydreams about more exciting and glamorous existences, such as being a courageous pilot.

A Worn Path

SELECTION TEST, page 125

Comprehension

1. b   2. a   3. c   4. a   5. d
6. a   7. d

Literary Element

8. d   9. b

Vocabulary

10. d   11. i   12. a   13. c   14. h
15. b   16. e   17. j   18. f   19. g

Written Response

20. Responses will vary. In a model response, students should fulfill the following criteria:
   - demonstrate understanding of the prompt
   - describe Phoenix's character. For example:
     - Phoenix is a devoted grandmother and a persistent person.
   - support their ideas with at least two examples from the story. For example:
     - Although she is weary from the long journey, she continues along the path to the doctor to get medicine for her grandson.
     - Phoenix's eyes are bothering her, but she has made the journey so many times that her feet know the way.
     - Although the hunter tells her to go home, she remains devoted to her goal.

- She overcomes a number of obstacles in order to reach the doctor. These obstacles include a barbed-wire fence, a maze of cornstalks, and a thorn bush.

Collection 13: No Time for Heroes

Richard Cory
Miniver Cheevy

SELECTION TEST, page 127

Comprehension

1. c   2. d   3. a   4. a   5. b
6. c   7. d   8. a

Written Response

9. Responses will vary. In a model response, students should fulfill the following criteria:
   - demonstrate understanding of the prompt
   - clearly describe what the characters yearn for in both poems
   - support their ideas with at least one example from each poem. For example:
     - The townspeople yearn for the riches that Cory possesses.
     - Cory's suicide is evidence of his yearning for contentment that lies beyond his grasp.
     - Miniver Cheevy yearns for the glory of past ages and places, such as King Arthur's court.

Soldier's Home

SELECTION TEST, page 129

Comprehension

1. c   2. c   3. b   4. d   5. a
6. c   7. a

Reading Skills and Strategies

8. b   9. c

Vocabulary

10. j   11. a   12. b   13. e   14. f
15. i   16. h   17. c   18. d   19. g

Written Response

20. Responses will vary. In a model response, students should fulfill the following criteria:
    - demonstrate understanding of the prompt
    - explain that Krebs thinks he is lying because he does not reveal all that he has experienced in war or what he is feeling about hometown life
    - support their ideas with at least two references to details in the story. For example:
    - Krebs's withholding of details about his horrendous experiences in the war
    - Krebs's inability to communicate how alienated he feels from ordinary life
      - Krebs's secretive comparisons between the women in his hometown and the women he met in Europe

The Love Song of J. Alfred Prufrock

SELECTION TEST, page 131

Comprehension

1. b   2. a   3. c

Reading Skills and Strategies: Identifying Main Ideas and Supporting Details

4. b

Reading Skills and Strategies: Understanding Rhythm, Rhyme, Metaphors, and Allusions

5. d

Literary Element

6. d

Written Response

7. Responses will vary. In a model response, students should fulfill the following criteria:
   - demonstrate understanding of the prompt
   - clearly identify a passage or image from the poem that communicates a feeling of despair
   - give at least one reason why the passage or image impresses them. For example:
     - The passage about measuring life with coffee spoons creates an image of people who don't have the courage to undertake risky actions.
     - The image of living in a world of illusions (an underground sea chamber) only to be rudely awakened (drowned) conveys a feeling that contemporary life is deadening and threatening.
     - The image of cheap hotels and sawdust restaurants creates a gloomy, bleak landscape.

The Life You Save May Be Your Own

SELECTION TEST, page 132

Comprehension

1. c   2. a   3. a   4. d   5. b

Reading Skills and Strategies

6. d   7. b

Literary Element: Foreshadowing

8. b   9. b

Literary Element: the Four "Modes" of Fiction

10. a

Vocabulary

11. h   12. g   13. c   14. a   15. j
16. b   17. i   18. d   19. e   20. f

Written Response

21. Responses will vary. In a model response, students should fulfill the following criteria:
    - demonstrate understanding of the prompt
    - explain their ideas about what the storm symbolizes. For example:
    - support their ideas with at least two examples from the story. For example:
       - warning to Shiftlet that God disapproves of his nefarious ways
       - comment on the egregious transactions between human beings demonstrated in the story
       - punishment for Shiftlet's abandonment of young Lucynell

Collection 14: Shadows of the Past

Richard Bone
"Butch" Weldy
Fiddler Jones
Petit, the Poet
Mrs. George Reece

SELECTION TEST, page 134

Comprehension

1. d   2. a   3. b   4. b   5. c
6. c   7. d   8. b   9. a   10. a
11. d   12. a   13. c   14. d   15. b

Written Response

16. Responses will vary. In a model response, students should fulfill the following criteria:
    - demonstrate understanding of the prompt
    - describe how the theme of how characters react to their pasts applies to three characters in the poems
    - support their ideas with at least one example from each poem. For example:
       - Richard Bone regrets chiseling false epitaphs and not living life more honestly.
       - "Butch" Weldy is upset at being blown from the tank and not receiving compensation from Rhodes or Rhodes's son.
       - Fiddler Jones is happy to have been called to dances and picnics to fiddle.
    - Petit feels driven by the urge to write poetry, at the expense of sharing in the life of the village.
    - Mrs. George Reece regrets her husband's being unjustly sent to prison, but triumphs in having raised her children well despite adversity.

Recuerdo

SELECTION TEST, page 136

Comprehension

1. a   2. a   3. c   4. d   5. a

Reading Skills and Strategies

6. b   7. d

Written Response

8. Responses will vary. In a model response, students should fulfill the following criteria:
    - demonstrate an understanding of the prompt
    - discuss what elements evoke a happy memory for the speaker
    - support their ideas with at least two references to the poem. For example:
       - Repetition of the first line creates a lilting, carefree mood.
       - Rhymed couplets set a lively tone.

- The fire, the fruit, the dawn—all of these images bring back the memory of happy days.
- The speaker ends the poem with the generosity of the two lovers and with the woman's gratitude.

The Jilting of Granny Weatherall

SELECTION TEST, page 137

Comprehension
1. a **2.** c **3.** b **4.** c **5.** c

Reading Skills and Strategies
6. c **7.** b

Literary Element
8. d **9.** b

Vocabulary
10. j **11.** d **12.** a **13.** e **14.** h
15. c **16.** i **17.** g **18.** f **19.** b

Written Response
20. Responses will vary. In a model response, students should fulfill the following criteria:
- demonstrate understanding of the prompt
- explain that Granny Weatherall may want God to give her a sign of assurance or affirmation
- note that the sign is not given
- explain that Granny Weatherall draws a comparison between God's unresponsiveness and George's jilting of her

A Rose for Emily

SELECTION TEST, page 139

Comprehension
1. b **2.** d **3.** d **4.** a **5.** b

Reading Skills and Strategies
6. a **7.** d

Literary Element
8. d **9.** d

Vocabulary
10. d **11.** e **12.** h **13.** f **14.** j
15. a **16.** b **17.** i **18.** c **19.** g

Written Response
20. Responses will vary. In a model response, students should fulfill the following criteria:
- demonstrate an understanding of the prompt
- describe how Emily has been affected by her father and by her family's sense of its position in society
- support their ideas with at least two examples from the story. For example:
  - Her father had driven away the men who might have been interested in her, so she has been lonely and emotionally repressed. She may be angry at the way he brought her up and chased off any suitors. She may want to keep in any way she can any man who pays attention to her.
  - In the tradition of her family, Emily may think of herself as an aristocrat. Sartoris trumps up a story that her father loaned money to the town, and she willingly believes it. This illusion about her father gives her a sense of superiority, and she is resolute about not having to pay taxes after her father dies. She can manipulate people around her, such as the druggist, who sells her poison without securing from her the reason she is buying it. Through her aristocratic demeanor, she is able to keep people at a distance. For example, the Board of Aldermen does not confront Emily about the smell around her house. This ability to bluff and to distance people allows her to get away with murder.

Collection 15: I, Too, Sing America

Go Down, Death
America

SELECTION TEST, page 141

Comprehension
1. a **2.** b **3.** d **4.** c **5.** b
6. d **7.** a **8.** c **9.** a

Literary Element: Personification
10. c **11.** b

Literary Element: Free Verse and the Orator's Style
12. c **13.** d

Written Response

14. Responses will vary, but students should use at least one example from the poem to support their ideas. The only supportable answers are **a, b,** and **c.** A sample response to each choice follows.

   a. In lines 1–3, the speaker describes injustices that America has perpetrated and their effect on him.

   b. The speaker says that time will see America sink into the sand like a treasure.

   c. The speaker remarks on America's grand size and energy.

   d. *(This is not a supportable response.)*

Tableau
Incident

SELECTION TEST, page 143

Comprehension

1. d	**2.** b	**3.** b	**4.** c	**5.** b
6. a	**7.** d	**8.** c	**9.** a	**10.** b

Written Response

11. Responses will vary, but students should use at least one example from the poem to support their ideas. The only supportable answers are **a, b,** and **d.** A sample response to each choice follows.

   a. *(Partial credit can be given.)* The Baltimore boy's racial insult was very cruel.

   b. The Baltimore boy's cruel word and gesture surprised and deeply hurt the speaker as a child. The memory of the incident stands out because of the pain and confusion it caused the speaker.

   c. *(This is not a supportable response.)*

   d. *(Accept any response that is supported by the selection.)*

12. Responses will vary. In a model response, students should fulfill the following criteria:
   - demonstrate understanding of the prompt
   - compare and contrast the interactions between people of different races in the two poems
   - support their ideas with at least two references to examples from each of the poems. For example:
     - Both poems refer to racial tension. In "Tableau," onlookers express disapproval of a friendship between an African American boy and a white boy. In "Incident," one boy's racism incites him to insult the other.

   - A contrast exists between the interactions portrayed in each poem. The interaction between the two boys in "Incident" causes pain, whereas the interaction between the boys in "Tableau" is friendly.

---

from *Dust Tracks on a Road*

SELECTION TEST, page 145

Comprehension

1. c	**2.** a	**3.** c	**4.** b	**5.** c

Reading Skills and Strategies

6. c   **7.** d

Vocabulary

8. j	**9.** h	**10.** g	**11.** a	**12.** c
13. f	**14.** e	**15.** b	**16.** d	**17.** i

Written Response

18. Responses will vary. In a model response, students should fulfill the following criteria:
   - demonstrate understanding of the prompt
   - describe the literary characters that attract Hurston. Students do not need to mention the names of the characters. They should, however, describe their personalities. For instance, the characters she enjoys are action oriented, clever, adventurous, brave, and decisive, and the characters that do not attract her are the sweet and gentle girls.
   - support their ideas with at least two references to details in the selection. For example:
     - Thor speeds across the sky in his chariot.
     - Odin plucks out his eye without flinching.
     - Hercules chooses Duty over Pleasure.
     - David is an exciting Old Testament character.

The Weary Blues
Harlem

SELECTION TEST, page 147

Comprehension

1. a	**2.** c	**3.** a	**4.** c	**5.** d
6. c				

Literary Element: Rhythm

7. b   **8.** b

Literary Element: Tone

9. c   **10.** a

Written Response

11. Responses will vary. In a model response, students should fulfill the following criteria:
    - demonstrate understanding of the prompt
    - clearly describe at least one example of the hardships faced by African Americans that the speaker in "Harlem" expresses. For example:
      - the inability to find employment because of racist hiring practices
      - the problem of inflation
      - past encounters with injustice in the form of lies, kicks, and false reassurances
    - clearly describe the musician's experience in "The Weary Blues," which includes feelings of sadness, loneliness, and the desire to escape his troubles
    - compare and/or contrast the plight of Harlem residents with the musician's situation. For example:
      - Comparisons may be drawn between the singer's expression of sadness and the hardships suffered by Harlem residents, who live in a racist society.
      - Contrasts may be made between the personal feeling expressed by the lone singer in "The Weary Blues" and the collective suffering of Harlem residents expressed by the speaker in "Harlem."

Collection 16: Make It New!

The River-Merchant's Wife: A Letter

SELECTION TEST, page 149

Comprehension
1. a   **2.** c   **3.** b   **4.** a

Reading Skills and Strategies
5. b   **6.** c

Literary Element
7. a   **8.** b

Written Response
9. Responses will vary. In a model response, students should fulfill the following criteria:
   - demonstrate understanding of the prompt
   - describe the mood of the poem and explain how two images help create that mood. For example:
     - The mood is somber and sad.
     - Images, such as moss growing thick by the gate and two butterflies turning yellow with August, convey a sense of passing time and sadness over the distance between the speaker and her husband.

The Red Wheelbarrow
The Great Figure
Spring and All

SELECTION TEST, page 150

Comprehension
1. a   **2.** b   **3.** a   **4.** c   **5.** b
6. c   **7.** c   **8.** a   **9.** b   **10.** a
11. c   **12.** d   **13.** b   **14.** d   **15.** b

Written Response
16. Responses will vary. In a model response, students should fulfill the following criteria:
    - demonstrate understanding of the prompt
    - describe how the two poems by Williams foster an element of surprise
    - support their ideas with references to at least one example in each poem. For example:
      - "The Red Wheelbarrow" creates a sense of expectation in its first line. The reader expects that the rest of the poem will describe something extraordinary or dramatic, but instead it describes an ordinary scene.
      - The title of "The Great Figure" leads the reader to believe that the poem might be about a famous person or monument. Instead, it describes a common occurrence in cities.
      - The first stanza of "Spring and All" creates a sense of gloom by focusing on the hospital, disease, the cold, mud, weeds, and the color brown. However, the poem ends on a positive note, for out of death comes life.

Anecdote of the Jar
Disillusionment of Ten O'clock

SELECTION TEST, page 152

Comprehension

1. b   2. b   3. d   4. d   5. d

Reading Skills and Strategies

6. c   7. b

Written Response

8. Responses will vary. In a model response, students should fulfill the following criteria:
   - demonstrate understanding of the prompt
   - discuss Stevens's use of metaphors and symbols. For example:
     - In "Anecdote of the Jar," the jar symbolizes the way the imagination or art shapes whatever it touches. The wilderness symbolizes that which can be tamed or shaped.
     - The title "Disillusionment at Ten O'clock" is a reference to or symbol of man's unimaginative dreams. "Ten O'clock" is a "normal" bedtime.
     - White night-gowns stand for unimaginative lives or lack of imagination.
     - The gowns of bright colors with contrasting colored rings seem to be a metaphor for an active imagination or an imaginative life. The lacy socks and the beaded belts continue the metaphor of the imagination or creative spirit.

Poetry

SELECTION TEST, page 153

Comprehension

1. c   2. a   3. d   4. b   5. b

Written Response

6. Responses will vary, but students should use at least one example from the poem to support their ideas. The only supportable answers are **b**, **c**, and **d**. A sample response to each choice follows.
   - **a.** (This is not a supportable response.)
   - **b.** The speaker argues that some poems focus on material that is both important and genuine, while other poems are merely trivial and pretentious. The speaker dislikes the latter type of poetry.
   - **c.** The speaker refers to the importance of imagination in poetry in lines 22 and 24. The

last stanza emphasizes how the material of poetry should be true, frank, and real.
   - **d.** (Accept any response that is supported by the selection.)

Chicago
what if a much of a which of a wind
somehere i have never travelled, gladly beyond

SELECTION TEST, page 154

Comprehension

1. b   2. c   3. a   4. b   5. c
6. a   7. c

Literary Element

8. a   9. d

Written Response

10. Responses will vary. In a model response, students should fulfill the following criteria:
    - demonstrate understanding of the prompt
    - compare the three poems, listing at least two ways that they are similar. For example:
      - All poems make use of imagery. Chicago laughs like a fighter. One of Cummings's poems vividly describes a nuclear holocaust, while the other compares the speaker to a flower.
      - All poems are free verse.

THE AMERICAN LANGUAGE TEST, page 156

1. c   2. d   3. b   4. b   5. a
6. d   7. c   8. b   9. d   10. c

LITERARY ELEMENTS TEST, page 158

Free Verse and the Orator's Style, The Four "Modes" of Fiction, and The Objective Correlative

Free Verse and the Orator's Style

1. a   2. b

The Four Four "Modes" of Fiction

3. b   4. c   5. d   6. c

The Objective Correlative

7. d   8. c   9. c   10. c

LITERARY PERIOD TEST, page 160

Vocabulary Skills

1. c   **2.** a   **3.** b   **4.** d   **5.** a

Vocabulary: Semantic Feature Analysis

6. a   **7.** c   **8.** d   **9.** b

Comprehension

10. b   **11.** d   **12.** d   **13.** a   **14.** b

Reading Skills and Strategies: Identifying Main Ideas and Supporting Details

15. Responses will vary, but students should use at least one example from the selection to support their ideas. The only supportable answers are **a** and **d**. Sample responses follow.

   a. Makings of the sun are designated as "waste and welter," and the "ripe shrub." The shrub is a thing of the natural world; "waste and welter" could describe the chaotic nature of the natural world. The poet's poems have a "character" of the "planet" to which they belong; this character is (or could be) in the poet's imagination.

   b. *(This is not a supportable response.)*

   c. *(This is not a supportable response.)*

   d. The poems did not have to last but did have to have the "lineament" or "character" of the "planet" of which they are a part. This planet is "on the table," which could mean "on the page" and therefore a reflection of the poet's mind.

Reading Skills and Strategies: Identifying Images

Responses will vary. A sample response follows.

16. **Image:** swamp mist **Sense:** sight
   Image: clay after rain **Sense:** smell
   Image: hands touching each other **Sense:** touch
   Interpretation: These images create a sense of earthiness, beauty, and wonder. The images convey the idea that daybreak in Alabama would be a positive event.

Literary Element

17. Responses will vary. In a model response, students should fulfill the following criteria:
   • demonstrate understanding of the prompt
   • state the tone they think is indicated in each of the poems
   • support their ideas with at least two examples from each of the poems. For example:
      • "Daybreak in Alabama" has an optimistic tone.
         • The poet uses expressions such as "purtiest songs," "kind fingers," and "natural as dew." These expressions indicate a positive tone.
      • "The Planet on the Table" has a reflective tone.
         • The poet uses direct statements that convey little emotion.
         • He uses the following opposition, a rhetorical device typical of reflective discourse: "It was not important that they survive. What mattered was . . ."
         • The words are carefully selected, a fact that indicates reflection.

American Drama

LITERARY PERIOD INTRODUCTION TEST, page 164

1. c   **2.** a   **3.** a   **4.** b   **5.** c
6. b   **7.** c   **8.** d   **9.** b   **10.** c

Collection 17: The Breaking of Charity

The Crucible, Act One

SELECTION TEST, page 166

1. d   **2.** c   **3.** c   **4.** d   **5.** b
6. c   **7.** b   **8.** d

Reading Skills and Strategies

9. b   **10.** a   **11.** d

Literary Element

12. c   **13.** d   **14.** c

Written Response

15. Responses will vary. In a model response, students should fulfill the following criteria:
    - demonstrate understanding of the prompt
    - clearly explain why Tituba, Abigail, and Betty say they saw people accompanying the Devil.
      - All three people are afraid of being punished for dancing and conjuring in the forest. If the accusers lay the blame elsewhere, they will not be punished.
    - describe what circumstances motivate them to name specific individuals
    - support their reasons with at least two references to Act One. For example:
      - Abigail has already blamed Tituba for making her do strange things. Tituba realizes that the people in the room believe Abigail. Tituba hears Parris say that she ought to be whipped to death and Putnam say that she should be hanged. When Hale encourages her to free herself of the Devil and Parris asks her to name names, she complies out of fear of punishment.
      - Abigail claims she saw certain women with the Devil after Hale asks Tituba for help; she realizes that she, too, can escape punishment and that she can be praised for accusing people of associating with the Devil. She names Good and Osburn knowing that Mrs. Putnam is already prejudiced against them and that she will gain Mrs. Putnam's support.
      - Betty claims she saw three people with the Devil after Abigail offers names, for she, too, sees that she will not be punished and will receive praise and protection for naming names.

The Crucible, Act Two

SELECTION TEST, page 168

Comprehension

1. b   2. d   3. b   4. c   5. a
6. c   7. d   8. b   9. a   10. b
11. b

Reading Skills and Strategies
12. d   13. c

Literary Element
14. c   15. d

Written Response

16. Responses will vary. In a model response, students should fulfill the following criteria:

- demonstrate understanding of the prompt
- clearly describe three examples of irony from Act Two and explain why they are ironic. For example:
  - Mary Warren's gift of a doll to Elizabeth Proctor seems to be sincerely given, but the court takes it as a sign of Elizabeth's witchcraft.
  - The one commandment that John Proctor cannot remember is the one that forbids adultery. He has just claimed that he has forgotten his involvement with Abigail Williams.
  - Elizabeth mentions Ezekiel Cheever as an ally to prove Abigail Williams a liar, but it is Cheever who comes to arrest Elizabeth.
  - Reverend Hale remarks that such a charitable person as Rebecca Nurse would not be charged with witchcraft, yet she is accused of murdering Ann Putnam's babies.

The Crucible, Act Three

SELECTION TEST, page 170

Comprehension

1. a   2. b   3. c   4. d   5. c
6. b   7. d   8. a   9. c   10. b
11. c

Reading Skills and Strategies
12. a   13. d

Literary Element
14. b   15. d

Written Response

16. Responses will vary. In a model response, students should fulfill the following criteria:
    - demonstrate understanding of the prompt
    - choose three of the characters listed
    - clearly describe what each of the three characters do to influence the court proceedings
    - clearly explain what risks each character takes and what happens to them as a result
    - support their ideas with at least three references to Act Three. For example:
      - John Proctor admits to his affair with Abigail Williams to prove that she is not a reliable witness. He exposes his transgressions and risks condemnation by his fellow Puritans. Abigail's fury is provoked and he is sent to jail.

- Francis Nurse gathers the signatures of ninety-one members of the church who hold land, testifying to the good character of Rebecca Nurse, Elizabeth Proctor, and Martha Corey. He believes he only risks the rejection of the testament and so reassures the signers that nothing will happen to them. The court decides to summon them, and Nurse is distressed to have falsely reassured them.
- Giles Corey presents a deposition against Thomas Putnam. He risks the rejection of the deposition, but feels he has a good case. Because he does not reveal his source, the deposition is rejected and he is arrested.
- Mary Warren testifies that the girls have been lying, herself included. She risks the disapproval of the people of Salem and Abigail's fury. She recants her confession and rejoins the girls in their pretense.
- The Reverend John Hale encourages Danforth to read the depositions and to listen to Proctor's, Nurse's, Giles's, and Mary Warren's testimony. He risks the displeasure of an extremely powerful man, which could have political, economic, and social consequences. He maintains his integrity by quitting the court and denouncing the proceedings.

- support their ideas with at least three references to the play. For example:
  - John Proctor must decide whether to live or to hang. If he chooses life, he must lie and must sign a false public confession. If he hangs, he will hang as an honest man.
  - If he lives, Proctor will enjoy a renewed relationship with his wife, who confesses that she has doubted herself, been cold, and pushed him into an adulterous relationship. She expresses her love for him and her belief that he is a good man, and says that she does not want him to die. However, signing a false confession will also add to the public condemnation of the convicted people who will not confess to a lie. Proctor's private self would like to live. His public self, however, craves honor for himself, for his family, and for the condemned, who are also innocent. He says that if the lie is made public he will not be able to teach his children to walk upright and that he will have betrayed his friends. His public self is, however, also his complicated private self, for Proctor is a man who strives to do what is right, good, and honorable.
  - Proctor chooses personal and public honor by hanging with the others who have been falsely accused of witchcraft.

The Crucible, Act Four

SELECTION TEST, page 172

Comprehension

1. b	2. b	3. c	4. a	5. d
6. c	7. b	8. c	9. a	10. c
11. d				

Reading Skills and Strategies

12. d   13. c

Literary Element

14. a   15. b

Written Response

16. Responses will vary. In a model response, students should fulfill the following criteria:
- demonstrate understanding of the prompt
- clearly describe the conflict John Proctor faces
- clearly describe the factors that help him come to a decision
- clearly explain the decision he makes

THE AMERICAN LANGUAGE TEST, page 174

1. b	2. c	3. a	4. b	5. c
6. d	7. a	8. b	9. a	10. b

LITERARY ELEMENTS TEST, page 176

Drama

1. c	2. d	3. c	4. a	5. b
6. a	7. c	8. d	9. c	10. d

LITERARY PERIOD TEST, page 178

Vocabulary Skills

1. c	2. a	3. b	4. c	5. b

Vocabulary: Doing Analogies

6. b	7. a	8. c	9. d

Comprehension

10. c	11. b	12. d	13. a	14. b

Literary Element: Conflict

15. *(Responses will vary. A sample response follows.)*

Pairing	Conflict	Support from the Selection
Amanda/Laura	Amanda expects Laura to have the same skill at attracting males that Amanda once had.	**Amanda.** What? No one—not one? You must be joking.
Laura/Tom	Laura wants to let her mother enjoy her dreams; Tom wants to stop them.	**Tom.** I know what's coming! **Laura.** Yes. But let her tell it.
Tom/Amanda	Tom wants to be treated like a grown man, but his mother still treats him like a boy.	**Amanda.** So chew your food and give your salivary glands a chance to function! **Tom.** I haven't enjoyed one bite of this dinner.

Literary Element: Motivation

16. Responses will vary. A sample response follows.
  a. Laura is eager to please and to keep others from worry and bother.
  b. Laura is willing to let others enjoy themselves even when their talk is tedious or boring.
  c. Laura wants to prepare her mother. Laura knows no callers will visit.

Reading Skills and Strategies

17. Responses will vary. In a model response, students should fulfill the following criteria:
  • demonstrate understanding of the prompt
  • explain how Amanda's actions and the responses of Tom and Laura reveal her character. For example:
    • Amanda's actions
      • She goes to the kitchen "airily" and comes back with dessert. This indicates that she enjoys entertaining other people.
      • She "flounces girlishly." This indicates that she still likes to think of herself as the girl who had so many gentleman callers.
    • Tom and Laura's reactions to Amanda
      • Tom walks away from Amanda when she talks to him. This indicates that she is not as compelling as she suggests she is.
      • Tom throws down the paper when Amanda asks who is coming to call. This suggests that Amanda cannot be persuaded to give up her obsession.
      • Laura's rising from the table suggests that she knows that her mother is a person who needs to be humored.

Contemporary Literature

LITERARY PERIOD INTRODUCTION
TEST, page 184
  1. b **2.** a **3.** d **4.** b **5.** c
  6. b **7.** c **8.** b **9.** d **10.** a

Collection 18: The Wages of War

from *Night*

SELECTION TEST, page 186
Comprehension
  1. c **2.** b **3.** c **4.** a **5.** b
  6. d **7.** c **8.** a

Literary Element: Atmosphere
  9. c **10.** b **11.** a

Vocabulary
  12. e **13.** a **14.** b **15.** c **16.** d

Written Response
17. Responses will vary. In a model response, students should fulfill the following criteria:
  • demonstrate understanding of the prompt
  • describe the prisoners' unusual behaviors and thoughts. For example:
    • The prisoners forget to say the Kaddish for Akiba. If they were not in the concentration camp, they would have remembered to say the prayers.
    • Wiesel imagines that Rabbi Eliahou's son runs ahead when Eliahou begins to falter. He runs as though to free himself of a hindrance to survival. Normally, he would have stopped to help.

- explain why these behaviors and thoughts occur. For example:
  - The men are accustomed to seeing death. Their senses are numbed to it.
  - The men are trying desperately to survive. They will disregard friends and family in the fight to stay alive.

The Death of the Ball Turret Gunner
Noiseless Flash

SELECTION TEST, page 188

Comprehension

1. c   2. b   3. d   4. a   5. c

Reading Skills and Strategies

6. c   7. b

Literary Element

8. d   9. b

Vocabulary

10. c   11. e   12. h   13. a   14. j
15. d   16. f   17. g   18. b   19. i

Written Response

20. Responses will vary. In a model response, students should fulfill the following criteria:
  - demonstrate understanding of the prompt
  - explain how *Hiroshima* fits into the nonfiction category. For example:
    - The book is based on fact and filled with statistics and the details of the lives of six people. Hersey maintains objectivity, allowing readers to draw their own conclusions. However, he also provides a glimpse of his personal viewpoint in the details he chooses.
  - explain how *Hiroshima* fits into the category of fiction. For example:
    - Hersey creates vivid character portrayals and builds suspense.
  - support their opinions with at least two examples from "A Noiseless Flash." For example:
    - An example of the author's objectivity is his statement that 100,000 lost their lives.

- Hersey builds suspense when he describes Mr. Tanimoto moving furniture. By interposing information about Mr. Matsui, the wealthy man who allows Mr. Tanimoto to store his furniture with him, and his friend Matsuo, who helps move the furniture, Hersey delays telling the reader about what happens to Mr. Tanimoto.
- By using a combination of nonfiction and fiction techniques, Hersey brings his catastrophic situation to life for readers far more effectively than would a collection of statistics and generalized statements.

For the Union Dead
Game

SELECTION TEST, page 190

Comprehension

1. d   2. c   3. b   4. c

Reading Skills and Strategies: Interpreting Word Meanings and Connotations

5. a   6. d

Literary Element: Imagery

7. b   8. c

Literary Element: Satire

9. a

Vocabulary

10. d   11. j   12. b   13. f   14. a
15. i   16. h   17. c   18. e   19. g

Written Response

20. Responses will vary. In a model response, students should fulfill the following criteria:
  - demonstrate understanding of the prompt
  - clearly discuss Lowell's and Barthelme's views on contemporary life, providing at least one example from each selection to support their ideas. For example:
    - Lowell's poem suggests that historical monuments are not instructive to a culture that is more interested in the future than in the past. Progress, paradoxically, may end up destroying the world.
    - In "Game," the stressful confinement of the men responsible for operating control panels during a nuclear war leads to their childish, paranoid behavior. Barthelme's story exposes the absurdity of life in the nuclear age.

Speaking of Courage

SELECTION TEST, page 192

Comprehension

1. b   2. d   3. c   4. d   5. b
6. c   7. a

Literary Element

8. b   9. c

Vocabulary

10. g   11. i   12. e   13. h   14. b
15. d   16. j   17. a   18. f   19. c

Written Response

20. Responses will vary. In a model response, students should fulfill the following criteria:
   - demonstrate understanding of the prompt
   - apply Nixon's comment about peace to Paul's situation
   - expand on the type of peace Paul needs
   - cite examples from the story to support generalizations about Paul's search for peace. For example:
      - Nixon apparently hoped for a victorious end to the war, while Paul is searching for an inner peace.
      - Paul's needs for peace include the courage to face not only himself but also the uncaring world to which he has returned.
      - In his search for peace, Paul's father's car represents a safe, isolated environment in which to try to work out his troubles.
      - Later in the story, Paul seems better able to cope with the outside world when he stops at the drive-in restaurant and opens his window to order something to eat.

- Finally, at the end of the story, he even gets out of the car to observe the town's fireworks, which he is able to enjoy a little bit. He seems to be trying to rejoin civilian society.

Monsoon Season

SELECTION TEST, page 194

Comprehension

1. d   2. c   3. b   4. c

Literary Element

5. a   6. c

Written Response

7. Responses will vary. In a model response, students should fulfill the following criteria:
   - demonstrate understanding of the prompt
   - describe what they think is the message of the poem
   - support their ideas with at least two examples from the poem. For example:
      - The poem's message seems to be that the horror of war permeates everything a soldier perceives, such as the landscape and the weather. No definite or direct political statements about the Vietnam War are made in the poem. Instead, the language and a series of suggestive images are used to evoke a feeling of being a soldier during the Vietnam War. The monsoon evokes for the speaker the images of the many soldiers who died in the fighting. Even the speaker's poncho feels to him like a body bag and not a piece of protective clothing for a living being.

Collection 19: Discoveries and Awakenings

The Magic Barrel

SELECTION TEST, page 195

Comprehension

1. c   2. b   3. d   4. c   5. b

Literary Element

6. c   7. b

Vocabulary

8. g   9. h   10. d   11. e   12. b
13. i   14. a   15. j   16. c   17. f

Written Response

18. Responses will vary. In a model response, students should fulfill the following criteria:
   - demonstrate understanding of the prompt

- discuss their reaction to the tradition of matchmaking as it is described in the selection
- describe the positive and negative aspects of matchmaking
- support their ideas with at least two examples from the story. For example:
  - The negative aspect of the matchmaking tradition described in "The Magic Barrel" seems to be that it is primarily a financial transaction. Several times, Salzman tries to interest Leo in a marriageable woman by pointing out how much money either she has or her father is willing to give the future husband. Salzman focuses on money and on social status; in contrast, Leo is thinking about love.
  - The positive aspect of the tradition of matchmaking is that it can decrease the time it takes to find a suitable spouse. It allows a family to select someone who is economically, socially, and emotionally suitable for a family member.

Elegy for Jane
Night Journey
The Beautiful Changes
Boy at the Window

SELECTION TEST, page 197

Comprehension

1. a	**2.** d	**3.** b	**4.** c	**5.** b
6. d	**7.** d	**8.** c		

Literary Element: Figures of Speech
9. c   10. b

Library Element: Ambiguity
11. b

Written Response
12. Responses will vary. In a model response, students should fulfill the following criteria:
- demonstrate understanding of the prompt
- state the main idea used in one poem by Roethke and in one poem by Wilbur. For example:
  - In "Elegy for Jane," the speaker mourns the death of a lively student.

- In "Night Journey," the speaker expresses wonder and excitement at the countryside that passes outside the train window.
- In "The Beautiful Changes," the speaker states both that beauty does change and that the beautiful has the power to transform the thoughts of the people who observe it.
- In "Boy at the Window," the speaker expresses the boy's concern for the snowman outside and personifies the snowman's concern for the boy inside.
- discuss the detailed observations or descriptions used by Roethke and Wilbur, and support their ideas with at least two images from each poem. For example:
  - In "Elegy for Jane," the speaker compares Jane to a fish, a wren, a sparrow, a fern, and a pigeon. These comparisons make Jane seem lively, precious, natural, and at ease in the world.
  - In "Night Journey," the speaker describes the trees, the lake, the light, the mountains, and the empty areas that the train passes. They establish the beauty of the countryside and the speaker's fascination with it.
  - In "The Beautiful Changes," the speaker compares a meadow to a lake and notes the image of a loved one holding a rose. These details reflect how nature can create awareness and how people can look at one thing in nature a second time and see even more than they did the first time.
  - In "Boy at the Window," the gnashings and moans of the wind, the pale face of the snowman, and the icy tear create a feeling of coldness, sadness, worry, and isolation.

Auto Wreck

SELECTION TEST, page 199

Comprehension

1. b	**2.** a	**3.** c	**4.** b	**5.** a

Literary Element
6. c   7. a

Written Response
8. Responses will vary. In a model response, students should fulfill the following criteria:
- demonstrate understanding of the prompt
- describe the different reactions of people to an automobile accident.
- discuss the ways Shapiro describes the reactions of the bystanders. For example:

- People are shocked. Shapiro includes descriptions of the bystanders walking as though they were crazy, and contrasts their inability to comprehend the disaster with the police officers' ability to think clearly and to provide a useful service such as cleaning up the area or taking notes on the event.
- People are uncomfortable with death. Shapiro includes descriptions of people cracking grim jokes and implies that they are wondering about their own deaths when they ask themselves who escapes from death.

from *Black Boy*

SELECTION TEST, page 200

Comprehension
1. d 2. b 3. b 4. a 5. a

Reading Skills and Strategies
6. b 7. d

Literary Element
8. c 9. a

Vocabulary
10. c 11. g 12. e 13. a 14. d
15. i 16. j 17. f 18. b 19. h

Written Response
20. Responses will vary. In a model response, students should fulfill the following criteria:
   - demonstrate understanding of the prompt
   - characterize the young Richard and describe the adult writer's attitude toward his childhood
   - support their ideas with at least two references in the selection. For example:
   - Richard seems to have been a sensitive and resourceful child. He is hurt and frightened when he realizes that his mother will not let him into the house until he faces the neighborhood gang, but he fights the boys and wins. The young Richard can also be characterized as perceptive. He is able to perceive the thoughtlessness of adults like the preacher, Miss Simon, and his father, and he resents their patronizing attitude. Richard displays a stubborn pride when he refuses to ask his father for money even though he is extremely hungry.

- The adult author writes about his childhood experiences with some detachment. He describes many harrowing experiences without self-pity. He seems to recognize the distance between his difficult childhood and his adult life as a successful author and between himself and his father when he concludes the selection; he states that the city gave him opportunity and knowledge despite the hardships he experienced there.

Everything Stuck to Him

SELECTION TEST, page 202

Comprehension
1. c 2. a 3. a 4. d 5. a

Literary Element
6. a 7. c

Vocabulary
8. d 9. a 10. e 11. b 12. c

Written Response
13. Responses will vary. In a model response, students should fulfill the following criteria:
   - demonstrate understanding of the prompt
   - describe the present situation of the family and note that the situation between the girl and boy described in the tale within the story has changed
   - support their ideas with at least two examples from the story. For example:
   - The young woman's request to hear a story about when she was a child suggests that the man telling the story is her father. It is also likely that the young couple in the story the man tells are her parents. Since the daughter is visiting her father in Milan and her mother's presence isn't mentioned, the couple in the story are presumably no longer married. Further, the idea that the young couple's relationship has changed is supported by the man's statement that situations change without people wanting them to change.

The Fish
Remember

SELECTION TEST, page 204

Comprehension

1. d   **2.** c   **3.** c   **4.** c   **5.** b

Literary Element

6. d   **7.** b

Written Response

8. Responses will vary. In a model response, students should fulfill the following criteria:
   - demonstrate understanding of the prompt
   - describe relationships between people and other elements or creatures expressed in each poem
   - support their interpretations with at least one example from each poem. For example:
   - Bishop's poem emphasizes the importance of recognizing other creatures as independent beings, rather than regarding them solely as a source of gratification. After carefully examining the fish, the speaker grows to admire it, recognizes its uniqueness, and decides to let it go rather than keep it for food or as a trophy.
   - In "Remember," Harjo states the need for human beings to remember that they are connected to all other elements of the universe. Throughout the poem, she personifies natural elements such as trees, stars, and animals, emphasizing their similarity to human beings.

The Girl Who Wouldn't Talk

SELECTION TEST, page 206

Comprehension

1. c   **2.** d   **3.** a   **4.** d   **5.** b

Reading Skills and Strategies

6. a   **7.** d

Literary Element

8. d   **9.** c

Vocabulary

10. d   **11.** a   **12.** e   **13.** b   **14.** c

Written Response

15. Responses will vary. In a model response, students should fulfill the following criteria:

- demonstrate understanding of the prompt
- clearly explain why they think the narrator tries to force the quiet girl to speak
- support their ideas with at least two examples from the story. For example:
- The narrator cannot stand what she sees as her own shortcomings reflected in the quiet girl. Both girls are similar in that they refrain from trying to hit the ball in baseball, and are chosen last for team sports. The narrator, in frustration with herself, hates the quiet girl's fragility, and strikes out at the quiet girl for what she perceives as a weakness that can easily be overcome. The narrator tries to change the quiet girl by forcing her to speak up and defend herself. In the end, after pinching her, pulling her hair, and taunting her, the narrator tries to bribe her. The narrator has been defeated by what she thought was a pathetic weakling.

from *Blue Highways*

SELECTION TEST, page 208

Comprehension

1. d   **2.** b   **3.** c   **4.** a   **5.** b

Reading Skills and Strategies

6. a

Literary Element

7. b   **8.** c

Vocabulary

9. c   **10.** g   **11.** e   **12.** h   **13.** b
14. j   **15.** i   **16.** a   **17.** d   **18.** f

Written Response

19. Responses will vary. In a model response, students should fulfill the following criteria:
    - demonstrate understanding of the prompt
    - discuss why they think Heat-Moon chooses to take back roads rather than main highways
    - support their ideas with at least two examples from the selection. For example:
    - Heat-Moon seems to be searching for people and experiences that can be found only off the main highways. His desire to visit places with interesting names suggests his unusual aim to follow where his curiosity leads him.

- He seems to find contentment in his travels. He tells the waitress he is searching for harmony, and his experience with the Wattses seems to show that this kind of communion with people is the harmony he is seeking.

- His experience with the Wattses illustrates the goal of his travels—to wander through back roads of the country, looking for places and people of interest and perhaps getting to know them.

Collection 20: From Generation to Generation

Son

SELECTION TEST, page 210

Comprehension

1. c   2. c   3. d   4. b   5. b

Reading Skills and Strategies

6. b   7. a

Vocabulary

8. j   9. d   10. f   11. h   12. g
13. a   14. e   15. c   16. b   17. i

Written Response

18. Responses will vary. In a model response, students should fulfill the following criteria:
    - demonstrate understanding of the prompt
    - describe a conflict from the story and explain how it relates to the story's theme about relationships between fathers and sons
    - support their ideas with at least two examples from the story. For example:
      - The narrator's conflict with and over his son when he is trying to punish him illustrates the story's theme that while fathers and sons have conflicts, they also share a loving relationship. The narrator momentarily allows his son to go unpunished after his son suddenly smiles at him. The father doesn't fully understand the meaning of the boy's smile, but in that moment their bond is stronger than anything else. For this reason the narrator temporarily feels incapable of taking action against his son.
      - The narrator's son constantly criticizes his parents, but they love him in spite of the critcism.

Daughter of Invention

SELECTION TEST, page 212

Comprehension

1. b   2. d   3. b   4. c   5. d

Reading Skills and Strategies

6. b   7. c

Literary Element

8. d   9. a

Vocabulary

10. b   11. j   12. a   13. e   14. f
15. c   16. i   17. g   18. d   19. h

Written Response

20. Responses will vary. In a model response, students should fulfill the following criteria:
    - demonstrate understanding of the prompt
    - compare the narrator and her mother
    - support their ideas with at least two examples from the story. For example:
      - They both enjoy the freedom the United States offers.
      - They both are quick to learn the language of their new country.
      - Both of them like to invent new things. Cukita enjoys creative writing, and her mother strives to create handy, new devices.

The Bells
Young

SELECTION TEST, page 214

Comprehension

1. b   2. d   3. a   4. b   5. a

Literary Element

6. c   7. b

Written Response

8. Responses will vary. In a model response, students should fulfill the following criteria:
    - demonstrate understanding of the prompt
    - compare and contrast the attitudes of the speakers in the poems toward the past.

- support their ideas with at least two examples from each poem. For example:
  - In both poems, the speaker remembers the importance of communicating with someone else. In "The Bells," the speaker describes having the danger of the rings explained after asking about them. The speaker also remembers laughing together with the father. In "Young," the speaker talks to the stars and imagines that God knew her situation.
  - In "The Bells," the speaker remembers a father's love. The speaker describes sitting on the father's shoulders and holding hands with him. In "Young," the speaker says she was lonely and describes her parents only in relation to their respective windows.

from *The Way to Rainy Mountain*

SELECTION TEST, page 215

Comprehension

1. b   2. b   3. b   4. d   5. c
6. a   7. a

Reading Skills and Strategies

8. d   9. c

Literary Element

10. b   11. d

Vocabulary

12. c   13. f   14. d   15. g   16. h
17. i   18. b   19. j   20. e   21. a

Written Response

22. Responses will vary. In a model response, students should fulfill the following criteria:
   - demonstrate understanding of the prompt
   - trace the Kiowas' journey
     - The Kiowas move from Yellowstone to the Black Hills to the Plains to Oklahoma
   - clearly describe the purpose of Momaday's journey
     - Momaday wanted to trace the journey that the Kiowas took when they moved from western Montana to Oklahoma.
     - Momaday wanted to see the places his grandmother had known about but had not been to herself.

- explain what became of the Kiowas and his grandmother
- explain what Momaday learns
- support their answer with at least two references from the selection. For example:
  - The Kiowas changed as they moved south. They acquired the Crows' culture and religion. Instead of being slaves to survival, they became fighters. However, they had an encounter with soldiers at Fort Sill, and the destruction of the buffalo forced the Kiowas to abandon an important religious rite.
  - Momaday's grandmother witnessed the deicide. She became a Christian in later years. Momaday remembers that she continued to celebrate life by feasting and by entertaining relatives and older visitors.
  - Momaday writes that he comes to feel how small his life is.

from *In Search of Our Mothers' Gardens*

SELECTION TEST, page 217

Comprehension

1. a   2. b   3. d   4. b   5. c

Reading Skills and Strategies

6. a   7. b

Literary Element

8. d   9. c

Vocabulary

10. d   11. c   12. b   13. e   14. a

Written Response

15. Responses will vary. In a model response, students should fulfill the following criteria:
   - demonstrate understanding of the prompt
   - explain why they think Walker searched for her mother's garden and what they think she discovered in the process
   - support their ideas with at least two examples from the essay. For example:
     - Walker is searching for the source of her own creative spark. She discovers that her mother, like herself, was also a storyteller.
     - She finds that art is not merely a product of high culture, but also the creations of people who are not typically considered to be artists—people like her mother, who created beautiful flower gardens, and the anonymous woman who sewed the quilt of the Crucifixion.

from *Rules of the Game*
What For

SELECTION TEST, page 219

Comprehension
1. c   **2.** d   **3.** b   **4.** a   **5.** a

Reading Skills and Strategies
6. b   **7.** d

Literary Element: Motivation
8. c

Literary Element: Refrain
9. a

Vocabulary
10. e   **11.** b   **12.** h   **13.** i   **14.** a
15. f   **16.** g   **17.** j   **18.** d   **19.** c

Written Response
20. Responses will vary. In a model response, students should fulfill the following criteria:

- demonstrate understanding of the prompt
- compare and contrast parent-child relationships in "Rules of the Game" and "What For"
- support their ideas with at least one example from each selection. For example:
  - Both children have somewhat distant relationships with their parents, who are preoccupied with the demands of the outside world; Waverly's mother insists that her daughter be successful, and the father in Hongo's poem is exhausted by heavy physical labor.
  - The narrator of "Rules of the Game," however, seems to have an antagonistic relationship with her mother—as seen when the narrator fights with her proud mother about showing her off; in contrast, the speaker in "What For" reveres his father. He is very attentive to his father's suffering and needs, and would like to relieve his father of stress and pain.

Collection 21: The Created Self

New African

SELECTION TEST, page 221

Comprehension
1. d   **2.** b   **3.** a   **4.** b   **5.** c

Reading Skills and Strategies
6. d   **7.** c

Literary Element
8. d   **9.** a

Vocabulary
10. g   **11.** c   **12.** j   **13.** h   **14.** f
15. b   **16.** d   **17.** a   **18.** e   **19.** i

Written Response
20. Responses will vary. In a model response, students should fulfill the following criteria:
- demonstrate understanding of the prompt
- explain Sarah's statement that her father's silence gave her freedom
- explain why Sarah values freedom
- support their ideas with at least two examples from the story. For example:
  - Sarah loves freedom because she values her independence. She demonstrates this love of liberty when she refuses to be pushed into being baptized.
  - By his silence, Sarah's father gives her the freedom to choose what is right for her, regardless of what he might want. Sarah understands that this silence is intentional, not accidental. It gives her the confidence and space to make her own decisions.

Autobiographical Notes

SELECTION TEST, page 223

Comprehension
1. d   **2.** c   **3.** c   **4.** a   **5.** c

Reading Skills and Strategies
6. b   **7.** d

Vocabulary
8. f   **9.** i   **10.** e   **11.** h   **12.** g
13. a   **14.** b   **15.** d   **16.** j   **17.** c

Written Response

18. Responses will vary. In a model response, students should fulfill the following criteria:
    - demonstrate understanding of the prompt
    - explain what they think would be different or the same if Baldwin were writing the essay today
    - support their ideas with at least two examples from the selection. For example:
      - Because he remarks that prose by most African American writers at that time is weak and rough, he would probably be impressed by the accomplishments of African American writers since his time.
      - Baldwin would no longer refer to racism in the U.S. as "the Negro problem" because the word *Negro* is now rarely used. However, he would probably still argue that the racial situation in the U.S. is very troubling and complex, not only for African Americans, but also for others.
      - Baldwin's thoughts on the task of being a writer would perhaps be the same, since writers continue to face the same challenges.

Mirror
Mushrooms
The Lifeguard

SELECTION TEST, page 225

Comprehension

1. a	**2.** d	**3.** b	**4.** d	**5.** b
6. b	**7.** a	**8.** c		

Literary Element: Personification
   9. b   **10.** a

Literary Element: Tone
   11. c

Written Response

12. Responses will vary. In a model response, students should fulfill the following criteria:
    - demonstrate understanding of the prompt
    - describe images used in two of the poems and the effect each image creates
    - support their ideas with at least two examples from each poem. For example:
      - In "Mirror," the speaker describes images of a drowned young girl and an old woman who acts like a hungry fish. The images create a sense of horror and depression.

- In "Mushrooms," the speaker describes mushrooms pushing to the surface, hammering and ramming with their caps. The image creates the impression of an army, determined and forceful in its advance.
- In "The Lifeguard," the speaker describes groping at blackness and washing off black mud. The darkness of the images reflects the speaker's failure. The center of the lake becomes the center of the moon, and this image reflects the speaker's desire to have saved the child. The images help emphasize the depth of the lifeguard's despair.

Straw into Gold

SELECTION TEST, page 227

Comprehension

1. c	**2.** a	**3.** a	**4.** a	**5.** c

Reading Skills and Strategies
   6. d   **7.** c

Literary Element
   8. b   **9.** b

Vocabulary

10. i	**11.** d	**12.** e	**13.** a	**14.** b
15. f	**16.** j	**17.** c	**18.** g	**19.** h

Written Response

20. Responses will vary. In a model response, students should fulfill the following criteria:
    - demonstrate understanding of the prompt
    - describe what Cisneros draws upon as subjects for her writing
    - explain what these things have in common and why Cisneros chooses these things over others
    - support their ideas with at least two examples from the selection. For example:
      - Cisneros draws on her family, her Mexican American heritage, and the neighborhood of her adolescent years as subjects for her writing.
      - She writes about her personal experiences, to which only she can give a unique voice. Using her gift for writing to articulate her life experience conveys a perspective and voice that is solely hers.
      - She writes about people and circumstances that have influenced her life since childhood. For example, her mother, her family's poverty, and the crowds of boys

who were her brothers' friends all have influenced her life.

The Latin Deli: An Ars Poetica
The Satisfaction Coal Company

SELECTION TEST, page 229

Comprehension
1. b **2.** c **3.** d **4.** a **5.** c

Reading Skills and Strategies
6. b **7.** c

Literary Element
8. a **9.** b

Written Response
10. Responses will vary. In a model response, students should fulfill the following criteria:
    - demonstrate understanding of the prompt
    - compare and contrast the woman in "The Latin Deli" with the man in "The Satisfaction Coal Company"
    - describe the characters' attitudes toward their work and toward memories of past experience
    - explain the social role each occupies
    - support their ideas with at least two examples from the selection. For example:
      - The woman in "The Latin Deli" functions as a touchstone for Latino immigrants, reminding them of their heritage and comforting them with familiarity. She seems patient and works hard, but the reader never gets to see into her heart and mind as the reader does with the man in "The Satisfaction Coal Company."
      - In Dove's poem, the man has a nostalgic attitude toward his old job and a time when he felt useful and productive, and life seemed more lively.
      - Unlike the woman in Cofer's poem, the man in "The Satisfaction Coal Company" is no longer a significant person in others' lives.

THE AMERICAN LANGUAGE TEST, page 231
1. b **2.** d **3.** d **4.** a **5.** b
6. c **7.** a **8.** b **9.** c **10.** c

LITERARY ELEMENTS TEST, page 233

Satire
1. c **2.** a **3.** b **4.** c **5.** a
6. a **7.** b **8.** c **9.** a **10.** d

LITERARY PERIOD TEST, page 235

Vocabulary Skills
1. b **2.** a **3.** a **4.** c **5.** c

Vocabulary: Base Words, Roots, and Word Families
6. d **7.** a **8.** c **9.** b **10.** c

Comprehension
11. d **12.** b **13.** c **14.** b

Reading Skills and Strategies: Drawing Inferences
15. Responses will vary. A sample response follows.
    Mah believes that marriage is important, and she states that it should be celebrated. She would have liked to have celebrated her daughter's marriage in a wedding ceremony. She shows the narrator her disappointment that the marriage took place at City Hall when she kicks the box and protests that the narrator didn't even tell her of the upcoming marriage. Mah approves of the marriage, however, for she tells the narrator that she loves Mason. The narrator seems happy with her own marriage, for she tells her mother about it and wants her mother to like Mason. According to the narrator, Mah's own marriages seemed to have been full of problems. The narrator wants to say that her mother married in shame. Perhaps her husbands were not worthy of her, or perhaps she had to marry because of financial problems in her family. Mah's unfortunate marriages may make Mah concerned for her own daughter's happiness, may make her appreciate Mason, and may lead her to want to celebrate, through a ceremony, her daughter's happiness with Mason.

Literary Element
16. Responses will vary, but students should use at least one example from the excerpt to support their ideas. The only supportable answer is **b.** A sample response follows.
    a. (This is an internal conflict and one she resolves quickly.)

b. Responses should mention that this is the most significant external conflict, because the narrator risks being misunderstood by Mah and, consequently, being rejected by her. The tension the narrator feels in having to tell Mah is revealed when she fears being tongue-tied and remembers Grandpa Leong's encouraging her to conquer her fears by taking action.

c. *(This is not a signficant external conflict because it does not concern the two main characters.)*

d. *(Such a conflict does not occur in the story.)*

17. Responses will vary. In a model response, students should fulfill the following criteria:
    - demonstrate an understanding of the prompt
    - discuss how the sensory imagery of the excerpt contributes to the story
    - support their ideas with at least two references to the selection. For example:
      - Sensory images such as the odor of ginseng and honeysuckle, the sound of the brass handles against the mahogany, the sound of the mixture of Chinese and English, and the shop full of baby clothes all contribute to bringing the shop alive.
      - The narrator vividly remembers her mother holding out a frog's heart for her children to see. This memory gives the reader a strong sense of a mother who wanted to share with her children her knowledge about the realities of life, no matter how disturbing they may be.
      - All these images quickly and vividly describe the setting and the characters.

Written Response

18. Responses will vary. In a model response, students should fulfill the following criteria:
    - demonstrate understanding of the prompt
    - discuss how the selection relates to the theme of the created self
    - make at least one comparison and one contrast between the excerpt and two selections from Collections 18 through 21. For example:
      - The process of self-creation in the excerpt from *Bone* involves communication and confrontation. When the excerpt begins, the narrator has already defied her mother by getting married without telling her. In order to affirm her right to make decisions about her life, the narrator must tell her mother the upsetting news. By the end of the excerpt, the conflict has been resolved and the narrator seems relieved.
      - The selection from *Bone* is similar to "New African" in the sense that the process of self-creation in both works involves both internal and external conflicts. Both protagonists risk provoking the disapproval of a parent and of their community through their actions. However, these conflicts are a necessary part of establishing their independent identities.
      - The narrator of the excerpt from *Bone* has already created herself by doing what she thinks is best, which means going against what her mother wants. She wants her mother to accept her newly created self. In contrast, in his *Autobiographical Notes,* Baldwin describes the process of his creation. He addresses a much larger audience to get people to understand how difficult it is for African Americans to create and to express themselves in society today.